I0085714

The Lewes House Collection of Ancient Gems

[now at the Museum of Fine Arts, Boston]

J.D. Beazley
Student of Christ Church
1920

Edited by

John Boardman

BAR International Series 1074
2002

Published in 2016 by
BAR Publishing, Oxford

BAR International Series 1074

Studies in Classical Archaeology II
The Lewes House Collection of Ancient Gems [now at the Museum of Fine Arts, Boston]
by J.D. Beazley, Student of Christ Church, 1920. Edited by John Boardman

ISBN 978 1 84171 453 0

© Beazley Archive and Museum of Fine Arts, Boston and the Publisher 2002

The authors' moral rights under the 1988 UK Copyright,
Designs and Patents Act are hereby expressly asserted.

All rights reserved. No part of this work may be copied, reproduced, stored,
sold, distributed, scanned, saved in any form of digital format or transmitted
in any form digitally, without the written permission of the Publisher.

BAR Publishing is the trading name of British Archaeological Reports (Oxford) Ltd.
British Archaeological Reports was first incorporated in 1974 to publish the BAR
Series, International and British. In 1992 Hadrian Books Ltd became part of the BAR
group. This volume was originally published by Archaeopress in conjunction with
British Archaeological Reports (Oxford) Ltd / Hadrian Books Ltd, the Series principal
publisher, in 2002. This present volume is published by BAR Publishing, 2016.

Printed in England

BAR
PUBLISHING

BAR titles are available from:

BAR Publishing
122 Banbury Rd, Oxford, OX2 7BP, UK
EMAIL   info@barpublishing.com
PHONE   +44 (0)1865 310431
FAX   +44 (0)1865 316916
www.barpublishing.com

to
Andrew Gow

Frontispiece: Gem no. **50**, Head of man,
signed by Dexamenos. Mottled jasper. Height 21mm.

The Lewes House Collection of Ancient Gems

Published with a grant from The Jowett Copyright Trustees
of Balliol College, University of Oxford.

J.D. Beazley was an undergraduate at Balliol
between 1904 and 1908.

Editorial Preface

Oxford University Press published Beazley's *The Lewes House Collection of Ancient Gems* in 1920. Only 400 copies were printed and few more than 300 sold. It is therefore a rare book. But it is also a landmark, since it was the first publication of engraved gems in what might be called the modern manner; indeed in many respects it remains a model few have even approached since. It is re-published here, with Beazley's descriptions and commentary, with updated references (see below), and with enlarged photographs of impressions to demonstrate their quality: they were reproduced at natural size in the 1920 edition. Mary B. Comstock has compiled the lists of additional references which appear at the end of this book, and Cornelius C. Vermeule has added an appreciation of Warren as collector. Others in Boston who have aided the project in various ways are: Brenda Breed, Maria Daniels, Greg Heins, Alan E. Kaiser, Nathan Otterson, Courtney Sarro, Florence Wolsky; and in Oxford, the staff of the Beazley Archive. Donna Kurtz, the Archivist, kindly encouraged the preparation of the book for the new series of *Studies in Classical Archaeology*, published by the Beazley Archive and BAR. The photographs of impressions are by the Oxford Institute of Archaeology photographer, Robert L. Wilkins; the photographs of the original pseudo-scarab backs on the last plate (by Greg Heins) are Courtesy, Museum of Fine Arts, Boston.

Beazley acknowledges in his preface his debt to Adolf Furtwängler's great work of 1900 which comprehensively and authoritatively set in order the history of gem engraving in the Greek and Roman world. It was lavishly illustrated with good reproductions at life size. This, and his catalogue of the Berlin collection, set the standards for the start of the 20th century. Thanks to his work engraved gems were recognized as being more than decorative jewellery to which only the vaguest of dates could be assigned and whose role in antiquity was relatively trivial, despite being a favourite quarry for collectors and an inspiration to Renaissance and later artists. They were seen to be deserving of individual study in great detail for both their technique and subjects, and capable of being ordered and understood in terms of workshops and artists, capable even of elucidating social and sphragistic practices in the classical world. Many were the work of consummate artists, some of whom signed their work, and unlike so many monuments of antiquity they were generally complete, though seldom in their former settings, they were in perfect condition, and were original works, not copies.

The craft of gem engraving had never really lapsed since antiquity and it enjoyed a new lease of life with other Neo-classical arts of the 18th and 19th centuries. Gems were collected by travellers on the Grand Tour as original souvenirs of antiquity, capable of instructing about portraiture and myth probably more effectively than coins and sculpture, which were the other major sources for collectors. As such they made a considerable contribution to the understanding and reception of classical art in modern Europe. There was accordingly a brisk trade in them and in collections of impressions made from them. Private collections, which were to become the core of many national collections, proliferated. When E.P. Warren started collecting the available specimens were far fewer, yet he succeeded in bringing together what was probably the richest of them all, in terms of sheer quality.

Beazley had already made his name as a connoisseur of Greek vase painting, successfully defining and identifying the hands of the many artists, good to bad, of the Athenian studios of the 6th to 4th centuries BC. This was to be his life work. But he had already shown an interest in gem engraving, possibly encouraged by his friendship with Warren, who also had a fine collection of Greek vases. At the time he was working on the Warren gems at Lewes House Beazley was also cataloguing for auction (Sotheby 4-5, July, 1921) the Story-Maskelyne collection of gems. Nevil Story-Maskelyne had been Professor of Mineralogy at Oxford (1856-95), a notable connoisseur of gems and especially of their materials, who had catalogued the great Marlborough Collection in 1886. Beazley, in taking on this work, seems also to have inherited, if this is the right term, much of Story-Maskelyne's working material - a very large collection of impressions from various sources, as well as a remarkable (and still, I think, unique) collection of electrotypes, made from the best of the wax impressions. He thus had an incomparable reference collection in Oxford, to which he added, and he had also been able to see many collections worldwide in the course of travels which were mainly devoted to studying vases. His collection of impressions is now in the Beazley Archive at Oxford, much augmented from various sources.

Beazley treated the gems, rings and cameos listed in this volume as monuments deserving as much attention in description of detail, even to the forms of letters in inscriptions, as any other major work of art. He kept a notebook of meticulous drawings of details of the backs of the scarabs, which he did not illustrate, but described, and had casts made of many, which have been photographed for this edition. And he added as much commentary in depth about the subject matter, mythological, biological and historical, as each suggested. The result of this approach has been that other scholars have been, though not all or always, as diligent in publication, to the point that gem studies now stand in as high esteem as any other in classical art history.

He was working on this material over eighty years ago, yet, as with much of Beazley's work - notably his publication of the Boston vases - it is not outdated, except in terms of reference to other objects or knowledge of pieces which have only become known in recent years. The references and comment we have added will make the work more easily used in a modern library but do not essentially 'improve' what Beazley wrote. It has been especially instructive to realize just how much, or little, was available for comparative study in collections and publications eighty years ago. Since there is so much more now, Beazley's non-gem comparanda are indeed outdated, and are not replaced here since they tell clearly enough what was then available for study, and to update and enlarge them would amount to a complete re-writing of the text, and obscure Beazley. So we have kept the spellings and terms (like 'Petrograd') which were current in 1920, and although this gives the book something of the style of a 'period piece', it remains of an academic quality which is hard to match today.

> ...I remember a Don at Oxford learned in Greek gems telling me how all the other Dons would be interested in curious knowledge and facts about any gem, but its beauty always, or nearly always escaped them...

This must be Beazley; from a letter of March 1920 by the calligrapher/designer Francis Crease to Evelyn Waugh, then an undergraduate at Oxford (E. Waugh, *A Little Learning* (1964/1983) 154).

John Boardman

The Collector and Collection

Some of the best works of Greek, Etruscan, and Roman art in the collection of Edward Perry Warren were not initially sold to the Museum of Fine Arts, Boston, or the Metropolitan Museum of Art in New York. The intaglios, rings, and cameos, studied by John Beazley and published by Oxford as *The Lewes House Gems*, were among Warren's most treasured personal possessions. The book ensured that the world of gem scholars and collectors would appreciate this aspect of Warren's life. After the darkness of the First World War, it must have been sheer delight for Beazley to work on them in Oxford and at Lewes House, Warren's village seat near the warm Sussex coast, in the congenial atmosphere of Anglo-American intellectual life. Bernard Ashmole, a wounded M.C. from the Somme and one day to be Beazley's successor at Oxford, spoke of such pleasures as he studied Warren's coins and sculptures for articles in the 1920s and 1930s.

In his virtual lifetime of collecting, Warren's connoisseur's eye sought and was captivated by only the best. As the third decade of the twentieth century came upon him, Warren was prepared to spend the last eight years of his life in finding the perfect homes for his most treasured antiquities.

From 1911 to 1915 Warren had set aside a group of superlative objects (including a barrel of banded agate attributed here by Beazley to Dexamenos) as a donation for Bowdoin College in Brunswick, Maine. On the Maine coast near Bath, Brunswick was the Warren family's ancestral seat in America and the home of the S.D. Warren Paper Company, the source of the family's wealth.

He offered the 'Lewes House Gems' to the Museum of Fine Arts, Boston (which his father and older brother, both named Samuel D. Warren, had each served as President) in order to keep the collection together and in the area where his family lived. Warren had acquired his gems from every source imaginable since the 1890's. He bought at the most fashionable sales (Tyszkiewicz), from the most distinguished antiquarian-dealers (Rhousopoulos), from his old Harvard Professors (Charles Eliot Norton), from runners in Paris and Athens (a Greek from the Peloponnese, a Carian from Caria), and even near the classical sites (Castrogiovanni, Enna in Sicily).

Earlier, in 1899, E.P. Warren had made it possible for the Boston Museum to purchase a group of thirty-four gems, including sixteen that had once belonged to the collection of George, third Duke of Marlborough. Among the sixteen was the celebrated 'Marlborough Gem', the cameo showing the mystic wedding of Eros and Psyche, by Tryphon. The fame of this gem, its importance and the influence it was known to have had on Neo-classical art, helped to persuade the Trustees that the Museum should buy the collection, affording the Museum a fine foundation for a gem collection that was later to be crowned by the acquisition of the Lewes House gems.

Convincing the Trustees again to buy such small and esoteric works of ancient art was no easy task, since at that time the Museum was more interested in purchasing art in other areas, such as English furniture and American silver. The price was very favourable, but the Trustees were reluctant to act. They were swayed by one of their number, Edward Waldo Forbes,

Harvard Class of 1895, who had also been a pupil of Professor Norton. Forbes, a descendant of Ralph Waldo Emerson and Director of the Fogg Museum at Harvard, was also a major donor of ancient art to the Museum of Fine Arts. As the accession numbers show, the process of acquiring the gems occurred over seven years: 1921, 1923 (a small number), and 1927, the year before Warren's untimely death during elective surgery. The Museum of Fine Arts authorities soon and ever after realized that they had bought wisely and well, of the very best.

All the family, friends, and disciples who knew Edward Perry 'Ned' Warren are gone, and thus the collector's unusual qualities can only be remembered by those who were young as Ned grew old. Among these were the relatives who felt Ned's actions may have caused the death of his brother Sam. Sam's daughters were particularly bitter. When I first came to the Museum of Fine Arts as a young Curator of Classical Art, and my wife, Emily, came as Professor at Wellesley College, where ladies of the family had studied, we met Warrens at social functions and at older friends' homes. Mrs Fiske Warren, Ned's sister-in-law, still poured tea in her town-house on Marlborough Street, underneath the great portrait of herself and her daughter, Mrs Rachel Barton, by John Singer Sargent.

In 1958, thirtieth anniversary of the deaths of Edward Perry Warren and his lifelong collaborator John Marshall, I dedicated a memorial essay to Warren about one of his last gifts to the Classical Department and sent copies to the nieces. One elderly Boston Brahmin called me to say, "I don't ever want to hear of that man again". Others volunteered similar responses. Then attitudes gradually changed. Our Department's phone rang with the unforgettable accents of two cousins. "May we call on you and could you show us things that Ned collected?" They appeared, were escorted around the galleries and the Departmental library, went away obviously mellowed and impressed, and called again, separately. Back they came with Greek gold medallions showing Artemis and other goddesses as tondo busts, with Etruscan scarabs in gorgeous Castellani mountings, and Greek coins set (without damage to them) as brooches or bracelets. All these items had been gifts from Ned to their mother and aunts, Ned's sisters-in-law. They even agreed to bequeath or donate them to the Museum of Fine Arts, but I could never bring them to do so in Ned's memory.

It is now more than seventy years since Ned's death, and it is hard to evaluate his impact on the taste of his age. Two recent books have treated the family as a whole and Ned's Grecian life-style at Lewes House and beyond (Martin Green, *The Mount Vernon Street Warrens: A Boston Story,* 1989; David Sox, *Bachelors of Art: Edward Perry Warren and the Lewes House Brotherhood,* 1991). Family was important because it gave Edward Perry Warren his connections, his education, and the wherewithal to live the life of a wealthy Oxford don in Sussex. His band of friends may make for barbed prose and raised eyebrows of a trivial, passing sort, but they played a major part in his collecting activities, his network of messengers ('runners'), and even his work in cleaning and conserving delicate jewellery, bronze sculptures, terracotta figures, and coins, not to forget Gearing's cleaning of the so-called Boston Throne in a shed at Lewes.

What can best be said about Edward Perry Warren is what was said on architect Sir Christopher Wren's epitaph in St Paul's Cathedral. To look around for Ned's monuments one travels not just to Boston or Bowdoin College or Leipzig University or the Ashmolean Museum at Oxford, but to the Metropolitan Museum in New York (bronzes and silver), the Cleveland Museum of Art (tondo by Filippino Lippi), the Courtauld Institute, London (Cranach's Judgement of Paris), and the Harvard University Art Museum, Cambridge (head of a Pergamene giant, *inter alia*). Rodin's *Kiss* is a major ornament of the Tate Gallery, from which Lord Duveen of Millbank took his title. Thanks to the patience of Warren's executor Asa Thomas and the work of the National Art Collections Fund, contributions were gathered throughout the Anglo-American world to give that great example of early modern sculpture a home along the banks of the Thames.

Were it not for Edward Perry Warren's excellence of taste and the quality of his collecting, the Museum of Fine Arts, Boston, might not have owned, in addition to the Lewes House gems, such treasures as the 'Bartlett Head' of Aphrodite and the head of the maiden from Chios, both probably from the circle of the workshop of Praxiteles, and the many small bronzes in the collection, including the early archaic 'Mantiklos' Apollo, with its dedicatory inscription, an illustration of Warren's unerring ability to choose significant objects. Among the great vases that the Museum owes to Warren are the masterpiece and name vase of the Pan Painter as well as the Makron skyphos with scenes from the life of Helen of Troy. The spectacular gold jewellery selected by Warren for the Museum includes the two remarkable pins decorated with bees, lions, leaves and sphinxes, and the earring on which Nike drives a chariot drawn by two galloping horses.

There was yet another, endearing, side to Ned's life and personality. He loved animals and birds, as did John Marshall. A raven hopped around on their shoulders when they were working, and the staff from Lewes House whom I met in the town in the early 1950s spoke kindly of the Scottish deer hounds and the farm animals in the park, the house, and the stables. The legacy of canine love (Ned called John 'puppy') passed on to Sylvia Warren, whom Emily and I knew in the 1960s and later. Ned's niece had a big Palladian country house along the Charles River between Needham and Dover. She too raised deer hounds and, in another dimension, Norwich terriers. For her pleasure and to supplement the incomes of her estate agent and his helpers, Sylvia Warren, the liveliest of Brahmin spinsters, took in boarders, the four-footed variety. Our three dalmatians spent up to three months or more a year with 'Aunt Sylvia'. In bursts of sentiment Emily and I would send postcards to Diocletian, (Constan)Tina, and their son Maximianus. When we returned from Greece and Asia Minor to reclaim our canines, the cards were carefully posted up in their kennels. Legend has it Sylvia would read the postcards to the dogs when they arrived. All of this may seem irrelevant to the *Collector's Collection*, but it was the closest we could come in 1963 to life among the Warrens in 1923 or 1913 or 1903.

Cornelius C. Vermeule

This Edition

In this volume we have reproduced Beazley's text, adding in the appropriate places the remarks which he placed as Addenda on his pages 115-117. His own copies of the book, now in the possession of John Boardman and the Beazley Archive in Oxford, contained a number of marginal comments which have only been added to the text here where they have something to offer other than fresh references to objects cited. Within his descriptions some new references have also been introduced, since they may help the modern reader. This has been done for references to other gems, where the reader might wish to identify the individual piece mentioned. For his other comparanda we have added little, mainly *ABV* or *ARV* references to vases, or to *LIMC*, not touching references to coins or other objects. It seemed necessary to retain some indication of what was available to a scholar such as Beazley working over eighty years ago, and there are many more recent sources for further research into specific subjects which were not available to him. His text is in itself a document in the history of classical scholarship, not just a research study to be updated.

Everything in square brackets is non-Beazley. We have tacitly corrected any numerical or orthographical errors in Beazley's text. We have also added measurements for each stone. After the Plates in this book appear the post-Beazley references to later publications and comments on each piece, collected by Mary B. Comstock in Boston. At the end of each entry in the main text has been added here and there, in square brackets, a brief comment so that the reader can place them in context, and sometimes a brief remark enlarging on Beazley's commentary. These depend on the fuller bibliographies at the end of the book, which will engage the specialist. This is not an attempt at re-publication.

Beazley included three cylinder seals (nos. 6-8), omitted here as inappropriate in an otherwise mainly Mediterranean collection. He had two plates (Plates A, B) of comparanda, which are also omitted, but not his Figs. 1-3 which have a more personal appeal since he served as model for the demonstration of how an eastern leather headdress was worn. For these see gem no. 98. His eight plates showed each gem at life size in photographs of plaster impressions, with two plates of enlargements of a selection of 21 pieces (Plates 9, 10). Beazley had casts of the backs of the scarabs in the collection; these are now in Oxford and photographs of them have been included, grouped on the last two plates together with new photographs of three pseudo-scarab backs.

In this edition all pieces are shown in photographs of plaster impressions, reproduced at 4:1. The cameos too are shown in cast, not original; casts can often reveal modelling that the colour contrast conceals. It is easy for readers to become so used to such enlargements that they forget how small the originals are, but the larger images are necessary to do justice to the workmanship, and at this size they can be properly judged as major works of art despite their absolute size.

Most of Beazley's marginalia in his copies of the catalogue seem to have been added in the few years after the publication, and, after his work on the Story-Maskelyne collection, he did not revert to the subject in publication except in passing, using the evidence of gems in equal measure to that from other sources. Many of the marginalia in his copy were prompted by Andrew Gow from Cambridge, and Beazley acknowledges in his Preface how much Gow helped him. Gow was certainly the anonymous reviewer of this book in *Classical Review* 34 (1920) 116-117: he makes a point of mentioning the artist Simone Martini, who had a special role in the Gow-Beazley relationship since they had jointly bought a picture they had attributed to him in early days. The review also associates for the first time in print the name of the connoisseur Giovanni Morelli with Beazley's method of attribution of Greek vases. It was much the same principle that led him to the attributions he makes in this book, looking for characteristic treatments that might betray a master's hand. There is more on this association and technique in J. Boardman, *A History of Greek Vases* (2001) Chapter 2, and on Beazley and Warren in *idem* "The Lewes House Gems: Beazley and Warren" in *Classicism* 217-221.

Gow's command of the wilder shores of knowledge (for any classicist) was especially useful to Beazley. A tantalizing letter from him (dated 26.2.55), which Beazley kept in his copy of the book, refers to the name of the artist of gem no. 28, which was probably found in Egypt late in the last century and was made about 500 BC: a name recorded only on this ancient gem, in no ancient text (for a gem engraver), and on which we cannot further comment:

My dear Jack,
In case you want to know about three emeralds about the size of a thumbnail engraved about 500 B.C. by Epimenes, the greatest artist of the world, with a horse's head, lion's head, and two men fighting, see A. Lake, *African Adventures* pp. 55-89. They were engraved in Crete, belonged to Vasco da Gama, were repeatedly stolen, and were finally restored in sensational circumstances by the author to a Portuguese who was taking them to Portugal. The author is a professional big-game hunter whose exploits in that field, though somewhat highly coloured, I should judge to be substantially factual. This story sounds like lurid fiction, but the name of Epimenes is not likely to be a household word among big-game hunters.

John Boardman

Author's Preface

My principal debts are on the one hand to Mr. E.P. Warren, for setting me the pleasant task of cataloguing his choice and splendid collection of ancient gems, and for placing his time, his scholarship, and his experience at my disposal; and on the other to the late Professor Furtwängler, whose great history will be found quoted on every page. Mr. Andrew Gow encouraged me, collaborated in part of the work, read the proofs, and made many useful suggestions. The late Dr. L.W. King wrote, and Dr. Stephen Langdon revised, the account of two Oriental stones with which I was not competent to deal [nos. 6 and 7, omitted in this edition]. Mr. Arthur Smith enabled me, at the earliest possible moment, to study the collection of gems at the British Museum, and assisted me in several other ways. Sir Arthur Evans allowed me to consult him on several questions, Mr. G.F. Hill on certain numismatical points, Professor Percy Gardner on another, the late Professor Haverfield on one or two Roman matters, Mr. J.A. Howe on a geological one, and my colleague, Mr. G.T. Hutchinson, on horses and deer.

Permission to publish illustrative pieces was kindly granted by Mr. Arthur Smith, by Mr. C.F. Bell of the Ashmolean, by Dr. L.D. Caskey of the Museum at Boston, and by Miss Richter of the Metropolitan Museum in New York: by Lady Cook, by Lord Southesk, and by Sir Arthur Evans. Mr. De Ridder not only gave me leave to publish a stone in the Louvre, but sent me his own imprints of two gems in the De Clercq Collection. [These, in *LHG* plates A and B, are omitted in this edition.] Mr. A.P. Ready furnished me with imprints of the Lewes House gems, and of British Museum gems while the originals were inaccessible. My wife has done me many services.

To all these helpers I offer my sincere thanks.

The gems are arranged according to period, and, within the period, chronologically as far as possible. In the free Greek period it has been convenient to keep the animals together, and in the Greco-Roman the portraits. Some of the finest gems have been reproduced twice: in their real size; and with a magnification of two diameters [all are enlarged in this edition].

Some of the terms employed in describing beetles are taken from the frontispiece of Petrie's *Scarabs and Cylinders*.

I. Intaglios

Cretan and Mycenean

1. [27.655]

Bought in Athens, 1898, and said to have come from Mycenae.

Lenticular. Translucent sard. [24 x 24 x 10 mm]

Ground line. Two lions biting a stag in the throat. All three animals are standing on their hind legs. The heads of the lions frontal and their forelegs stretched straight down. The stag's head is pressed right back, and its tongue lolls out of its mouth: its forelegs are very long.

A bull with its head pressed back like our stag's occurs on a lenticular red jasper from Rethymnos in the Evans collection [Kenna, *Cretan Seals* no. 317]: the period is Late Minoan I-II.

[Boardman, *GGFR* pl. 179.]

2. [27.656]

Bought in 1900 from Professor C.E. Norton.

Lenticular. Sard. [24 x 24 x 10 mm]

A lion attacking a bull. The lion's head is concealed by the bull's; such a design, as where two bodies are conjoined in one head (F., pl. 3, 23 [*CMS* I, no. 46]) a motive which, according to Evans, is found in Late

Minoan I and is characteristic of Late Minoan II and III.

[Boardman, *GGFR* pl. 180.]

3. [23.576]

Sent from Athens, 1904.

Lenticular. Murky sard. [32 x 32 x 16 mm]

A lioness standing on a bull and tearing at its foreleg. The lioness is maned (see no. 58): her head is frontal and the face very narrow.

Somewhat similar stones in Athens, 3137 (F., III, 51, fig. 31) and 2573 [*CMS* I, nos. 36, 116]. For the antipodal position, compare the lenticular onyx from the Vaphio tomb (F., pl. 3, 32 [*CMS* I, no. 239]).

[Boardman, *GGFR* pl. 182.]

4. [27.658]

From Mycenae. Bought in Paris. Formerly in the Evans collection. Evans, *JHS* 21, 156 (enlarged drawing); Von Fritze, *JdI* 18, 60, fig. 5, after Evans.
Rock-crystal ring with engraving on the convex elliptical bezel. [27 x 16 mm]

Two ground lines. On either side of a tree, a bull couched with head turned back: behind each, another tree.

An example of a not uncommon motive, two animals grouped symmetrically about a tree or pillar: so on two gold rings from Mycenae in Athens (F., III, 42 and pl. 3, 25 [*CMS* I, nos. 58, 87]) and another from Enkomi in the British Museum (*BM Finger Rings* pl. 1, no. 7): see Evans, *loc. cit.*, and Jolles, *JdI* 19, 34. A Greek example of the motive on a stone in the Arndt collection, published by Bulle in *Zeitschrift des Münchner Altertumsvereins* 1903-4 (*Antike geschnittene Steine* plate, no. 12).

[Boardman, *GGFR* pl. 181.]

5. [27.657]

From Crete. Bought in Paris, 1911. Formerly in the Evans collection. Previously in the possession of the schoolmaster at Chersonesos in Crete.

Thin equiconvex cylinder, flattened at the ends [as *AGDS* II, no. 33]: a shape first found, according to Evans, in Middle Minoan III (*c.* 1850-1600 BC). Streaked chalcedony. [21 x 17 mm]

A cow suckling and licking her calf.

A common subject on Mycenean gems: examples in Athens (F., pl. 3. 10, from Mycenae [*CMS* I no. 20]), in Berlin (*Berlin* no. 24, pl. 1), in Munich [*CMS* XI, no. 188], in Boston [98.713 and 01.7548, *CMS* XIII, nos. 30, 29], in New York, in the British Museum (*JHS* 17, pl. 3, 9 [*CMS* VII, no. 160]), and from Crete (*Collection d'un archéologue explorateur* pl. 2, 13).

[Boardman, *GGFR* pl. 133.]

6, 7, 8 *vacant*
(Mesopotamian and Persian)

Phoenician and Greco-Phoenician

9. [27.762]

From the Bruschi collection at Corneto. *Annali* 1885, pl. G-H, 22; F., pl. 61, 12.

Scarab in golden band-setting, with globulated wires along the sides of the beetle. Sard. [17 x 12 x 9 mm]

The beetle summary. Slightly ridged. No winglets. Along the lower edge of the thorax, two lines. A line between the elytra.

Line border. A king, bearded and hook-nosed, holding a lion by the mane and brandishing a mace: he wears a helmet and a long gown. In front of him, a naked man, bald and snub-nosed, crawls away up a hill. Above, a flying bird of prey: behind, a cartouche with irregular markings. The hill is cross-hatched. Apparently a contamination of two motives, the slaughter of a lion and the slaughter of an enemy: see F., III, 109.

Similar cartouches on other Phoenician scarabs (F., pls. 7, 56 [*Tharros* pl. 63d] and 15, 8; Babelon, *Collection Pauvert de la Chapelle* pl. 4, 25). That the object is a cartouche and not, as Furtwängler calls it, a shield, is shown by the sard scarab formerly in the Morrison collection (*Morrison Catalogue* pl. 1, 34) where it is inscribed with mock hieroglyphics.

Perhaps early sixth century.

[The series to which this and nos. 10 - 13 *bis* belong is generally now known as Classical Phoenician. They were made during the Persian period (late sixth to fourth centuries BC) and are particularly common on western sites - Carthage, Tharros in Sardinia and in Spain, notably Ibiza. But they are also met in the east and it likely that they were made primarily in the east. The range of subjects embraces the Phoenician/ egyptianizing, Levantine/Syrian, and Greek. This example is unlikely to be earlier than the late sixth century. The king brandishes an axe with a curved blade, not a mace; the object behind is neither a shield nor a cartouche, but a squatting ape; there are odd patterns on the king's dress (floral, animal?).]

10. [27.763]

From the Bruschi collection at Corneto. F., pl. 64, 4.

Scarab. Translucent sard. [13 x 10 mm]

The beetle rough. Carinated: falling away at the rump. No winglets or vertical border. The elytra not separated.

Hatched border. Bes, clad in a lionskin, running with a wild goat in either hand.

The same subject on a scarab of similar style (imprint in Cades among the 'Persian subjects'), and on a green jasper scarab in the British Museum (*BM Gems* no. 276).

Mid sixth century.

[Boardman, *Archaic* 36, no. 64, querying the identity of Bes, who looks quite different in the Classical Phoenician series, though often with animals. Probably Greek.]

11. [27.659]

From Iviza (Vives, *La necrópoli de Ibiza* 71, no. 354). Formerly in the Kennedy collection (sale catalogue, March 1918, no. 213, 1). Vives, pl. 25, 10. Perez-Cabrero, *Ibiza arqueológica* 28, no. 8.

Scarab. Green jasper. [16 x 12 x 9 mm]

The beetle careful. No winglets or vertical border: the plinth large. The stone is scooped away on either side of the rump, as in nos. 12 and 13, and in two scarabs now in the collection of Miss Lamb [Boardman, *Ibiza* nos. 98, 163].

A hatched border along the lower edge of the thorax. Between the elytra a line: two short lines start from this line near the top and form a triangle with the border of the thorax.

Hatched border. A winged and bearded monster, composed of lion's body and legs and human body and arms: the hands raised in adoration. The wings very slightly recurved, as in the Phoenician scarab in London, F., pl. 64, 3 [*BM Gems* no. 277]: an ancient Phoenician rendering (see Poulsen, *Der Orient und die frühgriechische Kunst* 15 and *passim*). The long hair is filleted and gathered up behind: the lower edge pelleted, the rest hatched.

The same position of the hands on another scarab from Iviza, now in Miss Lamb's collection [Boardman, *Ibiza* no. 93]: the posture of the worshipper [*ibid.*, no. 4] is transferred to the deity.

Early fifth century.

Addendum: Mr. A.S.F. Gow points out that the monster need not be a deity but may be in the nature of a cherub or the like.

[See on no. 9. The winged man-lion is inspired by comparable monsters of the Persian period, but makes the eastern and Egyptian gesture of adoration.]

12. [27.764]

From Iviza (Vives, *La necrópoli de Ibiza* 75, no. 10). Formerly in the Kennedy collection (sale catalogue no. 212, 1). Vives, pl. 25, 21. Perez-Cabrero, *Ibiza arqueológica* 28, no. 5.

Scarab. Green jasper. [14 x 10 x 6 mm]

The beetle as in nos. 11 and 13, except that the border below the thorax consists of two lines.

Hatched border. Head of a youth wearing a crested helmet which is compounded of a silen's head, in front, and a lion's head behind. The hair falls in a thick mat behind, with rows, separated by grooves, of short striations. The silen has horse's ears and his beard is hatched: his head is of the usual Greco-Phoenician type.

A late Etruscan stone (F., pl. 18, 45 [Zazoff, no. 535]) is engraved with a youthful head wearing a cap compounded of a silen's head and a lion's. Helmets and caps of similar make are found, no doubt under Carthaginian influence, on late Italiote and on Greco-Roman stones (F., pl. 29, 75 and 77; *Berlin* pl. 57, 7809 and 7810). A helmet with the upper part in the form of a silen's face is worn by a warrior on a late Etruscan bronze cista in the British Museum (746: Murray, *Handbook of Archaeology* 136; this detail indistinct in the reproduction). The helmet on an archaic Greek scarab in the British Museum (F., pl. 6, 56 [Boardman, *Archaic* no. 237]) is stated by Furtwängler to have a mask of silenesque type attached behind; but the mask belongs to the aegis and not to the helmet. (*Margin*: That it is a helmeted youth and not the usual combination of heads, is shown, against De Ridder (*Revue critique* 1920, 10, 182), by the crest.)

Our head is terminated below the neck by a row of pellets. This is a very common termination for heads and foreparts on archaic Greek coins, but it is less common on gems: examples on archaic Greek scarabs in Copenhagen (F., pl. 8, 71 [Boardman, *Archaic* no. 118]) and in Paris (F., pl. 6, 66), and on a Greco-Phoenician scarab from Iviza with a bearded head in three-quarter profile [Boardman, *Ibiza* no. 110]. In the free period, the row of pellets is ousted by the curvilinear cut. The hair is treated in the same manner on a green jasper scarab from Tharros in the British Museum with a youthful head wearing a helmet (F., pl. 7, 45 [*Tharros* pl. 60c]).

The style is almost as Greek as that of no. 13.

Beginning of the fifth century.

[See on no. 9. These combined heads are a major feature of the series, as also on Persian-period finger rings and occasionally in Greek art.]

The style is pure Greek of the Greco-Phoenician class.

Beginning of the fifth century.

[See on no. 9. This is one of the most Greek motifs in the series, deriving from late archaic Greek scarab subjects.]

13. [27.660]

From Iviza (Vives, *La necrópoli de Ibiza* 71, no. 358). Formerly in the Kennedy collection (sale catalogue no. 212, 2). Vives, pl. 23, 6; Perez-Cabrero, *Ibiza arqueológica* 28, no. 1.

Scarab. Green jasper. [16 x 13 x 9 mm]

The beetle as in no. 11.

Hatched border. A naked youth running with a cock on his left arm and a bow and arrows in his right hand. The hair hatched, save over the forehead and where it is gathered up behind; fillet, with two loose ends in front, each terminating in a tiny pellet, and the like at the back. The inner marking of the body precise and hard: the arch of the ribs begins low down, and contains five bosses representing the prominences of the rectus abdominis.

For the style, compare the green jasper scarab, from Tharros, in the museum at Cagliari, F., pl. 15, 47, and another from Iviza (*LHG* Pl. A, 13 [Boardman, *Ibiza* no. 172]): in both the arch of the ribs is low as in ours.

13 *bis.* [27.765]

From Iviza (Vives, *La necrópoli de Ibiza* 71, no. 358). Formerly in the Kennedy collection (sale catalogue no. 213, 1). Vives, pl. 23, 17; Perez-Cabrero, *Ibiza arqueológica* 28, no. 3.

Scarab. Green jasper. [16 x 12 x 8 mm]

The beetle as in nos. 11 and 13, but the rump only lightly flattened.

Hatched border. Herakles holding his club in one hand and a bow with two arrows in the other. Naked, beardless: the hair short and pelleted.

More careful than the Herakles on the green jasper scarab from Tharros in the British Museum [*Tharros* pl. 63a], but greatly inferior to nos. 12 and 13 in the present collection. Beginning of the fifth century.

[See on no. 9. A very common subject in the series. In the east Herakles was assimilated to Melkart.]

Greek: Archaic

14. [27.668]

Found at Corneto. F., pl. 6, 46.

Scarab. Banded agate, black, white, and grey.

The beetle very delicately wrought. Carinated. Vertical hatched border. Recurving winglets. Hatched border right round the thorax. The clypeus goffered. Hatched border round the edge of the plates, and also on the legs. Between the elytra, three lines: from each of the outer ones a small spiral springs near the top.

Pellet border, continued by a simple line below the ground band. Ground band diagonally hatched and counter-hatched. The Struggle for the Tripod. Herakles, wearing the lionskin, holds the tripod in his left hand and his club in his right, and looks back on Apollo who is pursuing him and grasping the tripod. Apollo has plain long hair and a kind of chlamys. The knees of both figures are strongly marked: the toes, except on Apollo's right foot, are rendered by pellets. The genitals are not indicated. The legs of the tripod straddle.

The snake may be Python, introduced to locate the action. Furtwängler, however, compares the two snakes on the Etruscan chariot (*Margin*: from Perugia).

Pure Greek scarabs with a vertical border are rare: later examples in the Story Maskelyne collection (F., pl. 6, 52; *Burlington Catalogue* pl. 108, O 49 [Boardman, *Archaic* no. 371]), and in the British Museum (F., pl. 9, 34 [*BM Gems* no. 513]). It is possible that our stone, like no. 35 *ter* should be called Etruscan rather than Greek. (*Margin*: Certainly Etruscan.)

Mid sixth century.

[Boardman, *Archaic* no. 79; Zazoff, no. 584, Archaic Style. The earliest 'Etruscan' scarabs were most probably made by Greek artists and include subjects which are shared in the Greek repertoire, but the decorated sides to the plinth of the scarab will long remain characteristic of manufacture in Etruria, where the scarabs are treated as much as jewellery as for sealing purposes.]

15. [23.595]

Bought in Paris, 1902. *Gemmes et médailles antiques, vente a l'hôtel Drouot 24-26 mars 1902* pl. 1, fig. 18 (no. 26).

Scarab. Jasper, black and red. [13 x 10 x 6 mm]

The beetle moderately careful. Carinated. No vertical border: no winglets. Hatched border right round the thorax. The elytra are not separated, but there is a small palmette on the elytra half-way along the thoracic border.

Hatched border. A silen and a nymph dancing: in the field, a wreath. The silen has horse's hooves: his head is frontal: he holds lyre and plectron. The knees and the muscles of the lower leg are faintly indicated. A vertical depression near the middle of the forehead (see no. 16). The beard hatched. The nymph wears a chiton and a wrap: long hair, plain on the skull, in straight strands behind. It is suggested in the sale catalogue that she holds castanets, but more probably her hands are empty, with the thumb separate from the rest of the fingers and these combined, in early archaic fashion, into a single curved line: compare the hands of Deianeira on the London scarab (F., pl. 6, 39 [Boardman, *Archaic* no. 75]).

Mid sixth century.

[Boardman, *Archaic* no. 88, Plump Satyr Group; *GGFR* pl. 304. The horses' hooves for the silen are an east Greek feature, and it was in east Greece (Ionia) that most of the Greek archaic studios for gem engraving were located.]

16. [27.667]

Formerly in the Boulton collection (sale catalogue no. 4, 1).

Scarab. Translucent sard. [16 x 11 mm]

The beetle rough. Slightly ridged. No vertical border: no winglets. Two lines along the lower edge of the thorax. Between the elytra, a line which ends above in a triangle inscribed with a line parallel to one of the sides.
 Hatched border. Silen running with oinochoe and kantharos. Horse's hooves, no tail, head frontal, beard hatched. A vertical groove in the middle of the forehead. Little inner marking: between chest and hip merely three streak-like prominences, one above the other.

The same subject, but the head in profile, on a contemporary scarab in the British Museum (F., pl. 8, 20; a replica pl. 63, 5 [Boardman, *Archaic* no. 84, cf. 85]), and on a scarab in Corneto (*Annali* 1885, pl. G-H, 33 [Boardman, *Archaic* no. 89]: similar, but apparently without the oinochoe [*ibid.*, no. 98] F., pl. 7, 60). The silen's tail is omitted, to prevent overcrowding of the design, on the London scarab and the replica; on a Berlin scarab which is allied to them ([*ibid.*, no. 179] F., pl. 8, 2); on the Corneto scarab and its fellow; and on a rock-crystal scaraboid from Cyprus in Berlin (F., pl. 8, 1 [Boardman, *Archaic* no. 208; *AGDS* II, no.

177]). (*Margin*: Tailless silen also red figure cup in BM, Hoppin, 2, 289 [*ARV* 129, 22]; red figure column krater Naples RC 132 [*ARV* 233, 1]; later Attic red figure stemless cup Louvre G 638.) The vertical groove on the forehead, separating the temples, reappears in our no. 15, in the scarabs F., pls. 8, 33 and 8, 4 [Boardman, *Archaic* nos. 87, 93]) and also in F., pls. 8, 61 and 15, 70 [*Thorvaldsen* no. 4; Boardman, *Archaic* no. 230], and in the relief silen on the back of the pseudo-scarab signed by Syries in the British Museum [*ibid.*, no. 352]. (*Margin*: Vertical groove on forehead: Munich Perseus vase by the Berlin painter FR pl. 134, 1 [*ARV* 197, 11]; gorgon on coin of Neapolis, Babelon pl. 55, 15 and of Eretria *ibid.* pl. 31, 7-8 and 13-17; gorgon on bronze boss, *Le Musée* 2, pl. 10.) The same rendering of the kantharos in the Berlin scaraboid (F., pl. 8, 1); less summary in F., pl. 8, 20 [Boardman, *Archaic* no. 84]: the kind of vessel meant is shown by the scarab ([*ibid.*, no. 97; Boardman, *Ionides* no. 1] F., pl. 8, 19) formerly in the Beugnot, now in the Ionides collection.

In style our stone most resembles the Berlin scaraboid (F., pl. 8, 1) and the scarab F., pl. 8, 33 [Boardman, *Archaic* no. 87].

Mid sixth century.

[Boardman, *Archaic* no. 102, Slim Satyr Group.]

17. [23.577]

Bought in Athens, 1901. Formerly in the Postolakka collection. Imhoof-Blumer and Keller, *Tier- und Pflanzenbilder* pl. 26, 44; F., pl. 63, 1, and, drawn, III, 102; Perrot, *Histoire de l'Art* IX, 26, fig. 28, after Furtwängler's drawing.

Scarab. Sardonyx, discoloured, now dark brown with creamy yellow patches. [19 x 13 x 9 mm]

The beetle summary. Carinated. No vertical border. The winglets rendered by two strokes. Along the lower edge of the thorax, a hatched border with a V-shaped dip in the middle. The elytra not separated.

Cable border. A silen bestriding a sphinx and seizing her by the hair. The silen has horse's hooves; head frontal; hair and beard hatched, tail striated: between chest and hip, four semi-elliptical prominences, one above the other. The sphinx is wingless, and very long in the body, both no doubt for the sake of the design:

hair hatched.

If the stone were later, the representation might be interpreted as a parody of Oedipus consulting the Sphinx, like the pictures on South Italian vases (Crusius, *Festschrift für Overbeck* 103, 3; Hartwig, *Philologus* 56, pl. 1 [*LIMC* VII, *s.v.* 'Oidipous' nos. 70-2]) and, as early as the second third of the fifth century, on an Attic oinochoe in Berlin ([*ibid.*, no. 68] *AA* 1891, 119; *Philologus* 56, 4); but in the sixth century it is perhaps preferable to assume, with Furtwängler, a parallel story: it is not impossible, however, that the representation was not founded on any myth, the design being a mere contamination of two favourite figures.

A composition which bears a fundamental resemblance to ours is the group of a naked youth attacking a naked woman on a sard, presumably a cut scarab, from Cyprus in New York (*LHG* Pl. A, 1 [Boardman, *Archaic* no. 111]). The New York stone, though less careful than ours, is so close in style that it might not unreasonably be ascribed to the same artist: common to both the modelling of breast and body, the shape of the thigh, the female head and hair, the neglected feet.

That the form assumed by our Sphinx's hair is not due to the silen's action is shown by the hair of the woman on the New York sard, and in the youthful head, which seems almost like an excerpt from that stone, on a sard scarab of the same style in the Cabinet des Médailles (*Collection Pauvert de la Chapelle* pl. 6, 75; F., III, 445, fig. 224 [Boardman, *Archaic* no. 112].

Mid sixth century.

[Boardman, *Archaic* no. 110; *GGFR* pl. 307; its relationship to no. 111, cited by Beazley, may suggest that the theme is basically erotic.]

18. [27.669]

Bought in Athens, 1917.

Scarab. Sard, streaked with white. [13 x 10 x 7 mm]

The beetle summary. Slightly carinated towards the rump. No vertical border: no winglets. Along the lower edge of the thorax, two lines. A line between the elytra.

Hatched border. A bearded man running with a lyre in his left hand and a cock in his right. Long plain hair.

The arch of the ribs prominent: within it four bosses one above the other. The modelling drier than in the preceding stones. Somewhat similar in style, a chalcedony scarab in the Louvre (F., pl. 6, 37 [Boardman, *Archaic* no. 212]).

Addendum: A naked youth running with cock and lyre is the subject of a green jasper scarab, more archaic in style than nos. 11-13 *bis* which is at present in the market [*Cambridge* no. 16].

Mid sixth century.

[Boardman, *Archaic* no. 211, Dry Style.]

19. [27.672]

Bought in Brighton.

Scaraboid. Chalcedony. [18 x 15 x 8 mm]

Line border. A Gorgon, or possibly an Erinys, running with a snake in her hand. She has wings, not recurved, and wears a short chiton with kolpos: her hair is gathered up at the back of the neck and has a few rough striations on it.

A replica on a rock-crystal scaraboid from Corinth in the British Museum (*LHG* Pl. A, 8; F., pl. 6, 61 [Boardman, *Archaic* no. 205]). Furtwängler is wrong in describing the London figure as bearded and as wearing a corslet.

Rude work. Second half of the sixth century.

[Boardman, *Archaic* no. 204, Dry Style; *GGFR* pl. 335. This is presumably an unfriendly demon, more probably Erinys or Eris than a Gorgon whose face is invariably frontal at this date.]

20. [27.671]

Formerly in the Evans collection. Bought in Paris from Rollin and Feuardent, 1911.

Scaraboid. Chalcedony. [18 x 11 mm]

Line border. A young male figure, with recurved wings on shoulders, head and heels, running with a lyre and a head fillet in his hands. The hair hatched: thick at the back of the neck. The chest frontal, all below in profile: four bosses, two and two, for the prominences of the rectus abdominis.

The head-wing, which is attached immediately to the head and not to a cap, might speak for Hermes, whose head is winged on an Attic bell-krater, of about 400 BC, in the Villa Giulia (FR pl. 20 [*ARV* 1339, 4]), and occasionally later; the lyre also would not be inappropriate: but the object in the left hand is probably a fillet rather than a plectron with its cord, and lyre and head fillet point to Eros: on the early representation of this god, see no. 33.

Second half of the sixth century.

[Boardman, *Archaic* no. 172; *GGFR* pl. 333. The head-wing is an east Greek feature.]

21. [27.670]

From the Bruschi collection at Corneto. F., pl. 6, 47.

Scarab. Translucent sard. [13 x 9 x 7 mm]

The beetle very delicately wrought. No vertical border. Winglets, recurved. Round the sides and the lower edge of the thorax, a hatched border. The head, clypeus, and plates cross-hatched. On the thorax, two spirals springing from the lower part of the hatched border. Between the elytra, two lines terminating above in a triangle inscribed with a horizontal line. The outer line of each elytrum ends in a spiral near the rump.

Pellet border. Herakles leading one of Diomedes' horses: his bow-case hangs from the border. He holds the horse's bridle with his right hand and his club in his left: lionskin: elbow, knees, and calves carefully rendered: four bosses, ranged two and two, on the body below the chest. The horse's mouth is wide open, with the upper row of teeth indicated, and the skin about the mouth is creased accordingly. The mane striated: the forepart of it distinguished from the rest, as if blown back by the wind. The tail striated, with loose ends rendered by diagonal lines against the background. The headpiece of the bridle rendered by small pellets.

The same subject, differently treated, on a sard scarab, of somewhat later style, in the British Museum (F., pl. 8, 59 [*BM Gems* no. 720; Zazoff, no. 689]). Similar compositions to ours on a chalcedony scaraboid in the

British Museum (F., pl. 9, 15 [Boardman, *Archaic* no. 137]), on a sard scarab, closely resembling the last, in the museum of Corneto, and on an archaic coin of Erythrai (Gardner, *Types of Greek Coins* pl. 4, 32): less like, on coins of Ichnai (Babelon, *Traité* pl. 49, 12 and 14). The matter of horse-tamers has been discussed by A.B. Cook in *JHS* 37, 123-5, with reference to an archaic Attic relief in Cambridge: see also Zahn in *Jdl* 23, 179. A further parallel to our horse's gait on the scarab (F., pl. 8, 64 [Boardman *Archaic* no. 138; *AGDS* IV, no. 22]).

The hair on the horse's forehead is treated in much the same way on the archaic ivory plaques, of Ionian style, collected by Pollak (*RM* 21, pl. 15, 2 and pl. 16, 2): the ivory horses, however, have a topknot as well.

On the horse's head and dotted headpiece, see no. 28. Second half of the sixth century.

[Boardman, *Archaic* no. 268, related to the Semon Master.]

22. [27.674]

From Cyprus. Formerly in the Higgins collection (sale catalogue, 1904, no. 56). Cesnola, *Salamina* 158, fig. 162; F., pl. 10, 2.

Sard, slightly convex, set in a gold ring. [16 x 13 mm]

The stone is perforated, and in the two perforations are bolts ending in nail-heads which secure the stone in a setting decorated with two bands of cable pattern in wire. At either end of the setting a ring is applied into which the ends of the hoop are inserted. The present hoop is modern; and Mr. Higgins said that he had had the setting lowered because it covered too much of the gem.

Hatched border, flattened at one end and discontinued at the other. Herakles and the Lion. Furtwängler makes the stone horizontal, and if it is so placed the version of the subject is that which is preferred by artists of the later archaic period (see Reisch in *AM* 12, 118-30, and Robert, *Die antiken Sarkophagenreliefs* III, 120-2). Cesnola, supposing that the flattening of the border is intended to provide a ground line, places the stone upright: if he is right, two motives are contaminated, the horizontal already mentioned, and the upright motive (Walters, *History of Ancient Pottery* I, pl. 32 [*ABV* 254, 3]). Furtwängler's arrangement is adopted in our plate, but the other is possible.

Herakles has his arms clasped round the lion's neck, throttling it: his beard pelleted; his hair cross-hatched, with two rows of pellets for the lower edge. The lion has one forepaw at Herakles' knee, and one hindpaw close to Herakles' forehead: his mouth is wide open, with the teeth showing: the pucker of his nose rendered by pellets: short bristling hairs all along his back as far as it is visible: two rows of short hairs arranged herring-bone fashion along his belly, one row against the body, the other against the background.

The figure of Herakles recalls the archaic relief from Lamptrai in Attica published by Reisch, the earliest example of the horizontal motive in marble (AM 12, pl. 3, 1), and a red-figured cup in the manner of Oltos (Pottier, Album des vases du Louvre pl. 73, F 128 [ARV 58, 50]): both these about contemporary with our gem. The lion resembles the lion on the later scaraboid from Cyprus, no. 34 in the present collection, to which the reader is referred.

Last quarter of the sixth century.

[Boardman, Archaic no. 254; GGFR pl. 366, the Semon Master. If the vertical orientation is preferred, as here, the subject is one that appears on a very few other gems and rings, rather than vases, and may have been an east Greek innovation, taking the wrestling motif to an extreme, and in human terms.]

23. [27.766]

From the Bruschi collection at Corneto.

Pseudo-scarab. Black steatite, hand-engraved. [11 x 8 x 5 mm]

The convex part in the form of a youthful face which has the appearance of wearing a kind of cap or helmet: the rump and the hind legs of the beetle are also represented. Half-way along each side, a circle with the centre deeply incised. The fringe of hair hatched. No vertical border.

Hatched border. A man driving a biga. The wheel has four spokes. The mane is rendered by an outer arc with short transverse lines. Very rough work.

For the style, compare the steatite face-scarab in the British Museum (F., pl. 8, 14 [Boardman, Archaic no.

591]): for the mane, besides the last, a sard scarab from Greece in Berlin ([ibid., no. 329] F., pl. 8, 62), and another, with a biga, of finer work than ours, in the British Museum ([BM Gems no. 479]; F., pl. 8, 55).

Egyptian scarabs with a face substituted for the beetle occur as early as the end of the Middle Kingdom (Hall, Catalogue of Egyptian Scarabs in the British Museum I, xiv). Porcelain [faience] face-scarabs, mostly Greek or Phoenician imitations of Egyptian, have been found at Naucratis (Petrie, Naucratis I, pl. 37, 4, compare pl. 38, 8-11; Ernest Gardner, Naucratis II, pl. 18, 55 and 59-61), at Olbia (RA 18 (191 1), 21, fig. 2), at Delphi (Homolle, Fouilles de Delphes V, 25, fig. 100), and at Carthage (see Musée Alaoui supplement, 353, no. 197). [A.F. Gorton, Egyptian and Egyptianizing Scarabs Type XXVIII]. Greek face-scarabs, in sard, F., pl. 8, 30: in steatite, F., pl. 8, 11,: where the face is a silen's, and F., pl. 8, 14, where there are two faces [Boardman, Archaic nos. 143, 352, 591]. The type was known to the Etruscans also: in the Corneto sard, F., pl. 17, 49 [Zazoff, no. 1176], the beetle is replaced by the face of a youth with a fillet in his hair. From a similar stone, a brown jasper fragment, found at Falerii, in the Cabinet des Médailles (Babelon, Collection Pauvert de la Chapelle pl. 10, 161): the face is in the same style as the Corneto face. In the British Museum sard, F., pl. 8, 31 [Boardman, Archaic no. 610], which is probably Etruscan rather than Greek, a silen's head is substituted for the beetle.

Second half of the sixth century.

[Boardman, Archaic no. 590. The head scarabs are especially popular in Etruria and Cyprus; this, from its material, could well be Greco-Cypriot.]

24. [27.673]

Scarab. Light greenish steatite. [16 x 12 x 9 mm]

The beetle rough. Strongly ridged. No winglets or vertical border. Along the lower edge of the thorax, a line merely. The elytra not separated.

Hatched border. A silen tuning his lyre. His action is rendered with some precision: he rests the lyre on his left thigh, steadying it with his left hand, and turns the peg with his right: his head is thrown back. He has horse's ears, human feet, and a tail which encroaches on the border and is covered with thin lines arranged, roughly, herring-bone fashion. His beard is long and bushy: lines run down it lengthwise, and shorter lines, set at an angle to the others, indicate the thinner edge of the beard. His hair falls in long locks over his shoulder, and is plain except in front, where it starts back from the forehead in a striated mass. He is ithyphallic. The toes are not indicated. Inscription, very hastily written, ONESIMOS.

The inscription is hard to make out, for the letters are hastily formed and the surface of the soft stone is scratched and worn. The omicrons are of irregular shape, the second one loop-like. The nu is slanting, and the second and third strokes do not touch. The epsilon is indistinct owing to an abrasion, but two cross-strokes and part of the back are visible. The sigmas are pretty clear. The iota is short and perhaps slightly curved. The first two strokes of the mu are thin and shallow, the third missing, the fourth short, thick, and deep.

For the subject, compare the scarab in Boston, of Etruscan free style, with a naked youth seated on a rock and tuning his lyre [98.734; Boardman, *GGFR* pl. 374].

On a scarab of light green steatite, the same material as ours, in the Louvre (*LHG* Pl. A, 5; F., pl. 6, 35 [Boardman, *Archaic* no. 346]) Furtwängler read ONE...ES, which he interpreted as Onesilos, a name attested from Cyprus. The inscription, like that on our stone, and for the same reasons, is difficult to decipher. The writer reads ONESIMOS on the imprint. The nu and the epsilon, which are both slanting, are quite clear, and the slightly curving iota. The mu is also certain: the first two strokes are long, thin, and shallow, the other two short, deep, and thick. The omicrons seem to be shaped as loops open below; the upper portion of both has almost disappeared. The form of the first sigma is doubtful, as a crack runs through the upper part: the top of the second is rubbed away.

The subject of the Louvre scarab is a young warrior testing an arrow. The style certainly resembles that of our stone, especially in the furrowed thighs, the big loose knees, the heavy upper arm, and the feet. Moreover, the letters of the inscription are produced in the same manner. Everything tends to show that the two stones are by the same hand, and that Onesimos is the name of the author and not the owner; which might be inferred, if other arguments were wanting, from the illegibility of the inscriptions.

It may be objected, that an artist's signature is not probable on a gem of second-rate quality. This argument is always a bad one, and that it has no validity in Greek art could be shown by many instances: sufficient to cite the amphora signed by the vase-painter Polygnotos (*Monumenti dei Lincei* 9, pl. 1 [*ARV* 1107, 7]); and, in gems, the pseudo-scarab with the signature SYRIES EPOIESE in the British Museum (F., pl. 8, 11 [Boardman, *Archaic* no. 352]; the inscription, *JdI* 3, 195-7). That stone is particularly relevant to the present case, for it is of the same, not extremely common, material, and the style, not to speak of the lettering, is clearly akin. The inscription is beyond doubt the artist's signature, since the proper name Syries is followed by *epoiese*. Syries is conjectured by Röhl and by Furtwängler to have been a Euboean, because although his name is Ionic in form, he writes it with three-stroked sigma and epsilon. On the ground of his stylistic affinity with Syries, we should be inclined to place our artist in the same quarter of Greece. Moreover, like Syries he uses epsilon where an Ionian of Asia Minor would have used eta, and two of his sigmas are three-stroked, while the other two are doubtful. The form of his name says no more than that he was not a Dorian. There is nothing to prove that he was not an Athenian: indeed, his silen is more closely akin to Attic silens than most on gems; and his archer has many fellows on Attic vases. If one inclines to Euboea rather than to Attica, it is because of his affinity with Syries. A third stone may be attributed to Onesimos, from its resemblance, already noticed by Furtwängler, to his scarab in the Louvre: namely, the greenish steatite scarab in Berlin, with a warrior drawing his bow (F., pl. 8, 12 [Boardman, *Archaic* no. 347]).

Last quarter of the sixth century. Furtwängler places Syries in the middle of the sixth century (*JdI* 3, 197), but that is undoubtedly too early.

[Boardman, *Archaic* no. 345; *GGFR* pl. 351. These 'Island Scarabs' are a well-defined class of the later sixth century which uses the material of the older archaic Island Gems, and differs from contemporary scarabs from east Greece mainly in being hand-cut, without use of the drill, giving them a more sculptural appearance. A third Onesimos signature is known: Boardman, *Archaic* no. 348, and others attributable to him from their style: *ibid.*, nos. 347, 349, 350.]

25. [27.675]

Bought in Athens, 1898. F., pl. 64, 8.

Ring of pale gold, with engraved bezel. The hoop quadrangular and very thin. [16 x 8 mm]

A light-armed warrior: a bearded man, wearing boots and pointed cap with a flap in front of the ear, holding spear and wicker pelta. The right leg is frontal, with the foot seen at full length; the left leg is in profile and passes behind the right: the figure is to be thought of as moving towards you. The long hair is plaited horizontally at the back of the neck.

(*Margin*: cf. gold ring, Zervos, *Rhodes* 190. fig. 385 (Rhodes, coll. Casullis).)

End of the sixth century.

[Boardman, *GGFR* pl. 440.]

26. [27.676]

From the Evans collection: bought in 1911.

Scarab (or less probably scaraboid), cut. Chalcedony, rosy brown. [18 x 15 mm]

Hatched border. Ground line. Athena walking, with spear and shield. Crested helmet, chiton, himation passing over both arms; long aegis with the gorgoneion in profile; the serpent fringe of the aegis visible on either side of the himation: plain necklace. A row of pellets for the hair on the forehead: the hair which escapes from the neck-piece of the helmet is cross-hatched. The gorgoneion also has a row of pellets on the forehead: the mouth is wide open and the upper lip protrudes beyond the nose: the head has almost lost human semblance.

A similar Athena on three archaic Etruscan scarabs (F., pl. 16, nos. 9-11 [Zazoff, nos. 25, 353-4]): himation and aegis similar on another (*ibid.*, 13 [Zazoff, no. 357]). Compare also the archaic Greek scaraboid of rock-crystal, British Museum 494 (*LHG* Pl. A, 6 [Boardman, *Archaic* no. 244]). The profile gorgoneion is paralleled on a hydria of Etrusco-Ionian style (*Jahreshefte* 13, pll. 5-6) and on an archaic scarab from Cyprus in the British Museum (F., pl. 6, 56 [Boardman, *Archaic* no. 237]; see on no. 12).

End of the sixth century.

[Boardman, *Archaic* no. 239; *GGFR* pl. 381, Group of the Leningrad Gorgon. This late archaic group is distinguished by the extreme detail of dress. The way Athena's aegis is worn, like a cloak, and the head and neck of a sea monster (*ketos*; not a profile Gorgon as

Beazley suggests) attached to it at the neck, are unusual, but are features picked up also in Etruscan glyptic.]

27. [21.1194]

Said to have come from Aegina. Formerly in the Prokesch-Osten and Tyszkiewicz collections. *Collection Tyszkiewicz* pl. 24, 11; F., pl. 8, 38, and, enlarged, pl. 51, 11; Bulle, *Neue Jahrbücher* 1900, pl. 1, 14.

Scaraboid, cut. Chalcedony. [20 x 15 x 6 mm]

Hatched border. An archer: a naked youth, kneeling, three-quarter back view, drawing his bow. The hair cross-hatched: the edge in front pelleted: a roll at the edge behind, into which the vertical lines of the hair extend.

Compare the archer on an even finer scaraboid in the Southesk collection, which is probably by the same hand (*LHG* Pl. A, 10; F., pl. 9, 23, and, enlarged, pl. 51, 14 [Boardman, *Archaic* no. 248]): for the attitude, the slinger on an archaic red-figured cup in Leipsic (Hartwig, *Meisterschalen* pl. 18, 1; Hoppin, *Euthymides and his Fellows* 83). (*Margin*: Also Cilician coins, Babelon, pl. 106, 15-24.)

Probably by Epimenes: see no. 28.

About 500.

[Boardman, *Archaic* no. 247; *GGFR* pl. 356; see on no. 28.]

28. [27.677]

From the Tyszkiewicz collection. Count Tyszkiewicz told the present owner that it was certainly found in the Egyptian Delta and perhaps at Naucratis. F., pl. 9, 14; enlarged, pl. 51, 7; drawn, II, 44. Bulle, *Neue Jahrbücher* 1900, pl. 1, 13. Perrot, *Histoire de l'Art* IX, 18, fig. 19, after Furtwängler's drawing; Fowler and Wheeler, *Greek Archaeology* 387, fig. 308.

Scaraboid. Sapphirine chalcedony. [19 x 17 x 9 mm]

Hatched border. A naked youth holding the bridle of a

restive horse. Signed by the artist, EPIMENES EPOIE (*Epimenes epoiei*). The youth is in three-quarter backview, with the right leg seen from behind: his hair cross-hatched, with the lower edge pelleted. The horse's mane and tail pelleted; pelleted topknot. The mouth open with the teeth showing; the lips puckered; three creases on the neck; single lines, studded with pellets, for the headpiece of the bridle; ornamental peytrel rendered by a long line with a series of V-shaped appendages; three short lines, each tipped with a pellet, running out from the lower extremity of each.

A fairly accurate facsimile of the inscription is given on Furtwängler's drawing. The iotas and the first stroke of the pi are long. The cross-bars of the epsilons have an upward tendency: twice, the vertical stroke projects above and below the cross-bars, and once below only. The straight lines of the omega run diagonally. Similar representation of the E and O sounds occurs on archaic inscriptions from the Cyclades and Thasos: in Attica only from about 470 to 450 BC; the artist cannot have been an Athenian.

Two other works may be attributed to the engraver Epimenes. The first is a scaraboid which resembles ours in every comparable point: the Southesk archer from Naucratis (*LHG* Pl. A, 10 [Boardman, *Archaic* no. 248]). The material of that stone is said to be white marble, but Furtwängler calls it burnt sard and John Marshall pronounced it to be discoloured chalcedony. The second is the archer scaraboid no. 27 in the present collection, a less exquisite piece than the other two, but in the same style.

All three stones have the three-quarter backview, and the signed stone presents one leg from behind. The artist, therefore, has the same conception of form in space as the Attic vase-painters of the riper archaic period, the period which is inaugurated by Phintias, Euphronios, and Euthymides (see Hartwig, *Meisterschalen* 154-61: Beazley, *VA* 27-8). Epimenes appears to be slightly younger than those pioneers, but older than the later archaic painters to whom the style was no innovation, the Brygos painter, for example, and his contemporaries, the degree of whose archaism may be compared to that of the Greek stones nos. 30 and 31, and the Etruscan nos. 40 and 41, in this collection.

A third stone which appears to bear some resemblance to the work of Epimenes is the scaraboid of rock-crystal, with a seated youth making a helmet, which has recently been acquired by the Munich collection: exactly how close it stands to our stones cannot be determined from the not very clear reproduction in *AA*

1917, 35 [Boardman, *Archaic* no. 284; *AGDS* I, 1, no. 204]. (*Margin*: not close at all! For the head of the youth cf. stele from Abdera, Perrot, VIII, 357.)

It is natural to begin by equating Epimenes with Attic vase-painters, because they have left more and clearer examples of this style than any other body of artists. Of course it is traceable in other classes of monuments. It has not hitherto been found on Ionian vases produced beyond doubt in the eastern part of the Greek world, in particular not on Clazomenian vases, for the three-quarter backview noted by Duemmler on the London vase from Aeolian Kyme (*RM* 3, 161 and pl. 6) exists, as may be seen from Mansell's photograph, in the illustration only. The style is also unknown in Caeretan hydriai, which are sometimes thought to have been made by Ionians working in the West. We come upon it at last in full swing on the notable amphora in Würzburg republished not very long ago by Klein (Gerhard, *Auserlesene Vasenbilder* pl. 194; *Jahreshefte* 13, pll. 5-6). This vase also was no doubt made by an Ionian in Etruria. Turning from vases to wall-painting, we find what we are looking for in the Tomba delle Bighe at Corneto, where the decoration was probably executed not merely under Ionian inspiration but by Ionian hands (Weege, *JdI* 31, 105-53). (*Margin*: Also Tomba della Scimmia at Chiusi.) Coins offer fewer or less obvious instances than gems: examples, such designs as the discobolos on the early coins of Cos (Gardner, *Types* pl. 4, 28; *JHS* 27, 30) and the horseman on the early coins of Kelenderis (Gardner, *Types* pl. 4, 26). In sculptured relief, examples are still less frequent: but the stele carved by the Ionian Alxenor of Naxos (Perrot, *Histoire de l'Art* VIII, 361) looks almost like a drawing by Douris translated into stone. (*Margin*: Cornice of the Old Artemisium at Ephesus; frieze of the Siphnian Treasury at Delphi.) The legs are similarly foreshortened on a Melian clay relief in the British Museum (*BM Catalogue of Terracottas* pl. 19, 2). The style which we have been following up belongs essentially to the history of drawing and not to the history of sculpture; low relief or intaglio in whatever material, occupying an intermediate place between the two arts, but partaking almost more of the first than of the second. The parallel development in sculpture proper does not require illustration here.

For the peytrel, and the dotted headpiece of the bridle, Furtwängler (II, 96) has already referred to Clazomenian vases and sarcophagi. We have encountered the dotted headpiece on the stone no. 21: it is also found on the sarcophagi in London (Murray, *Terracotta Sarcophagi* pll. 1-7) and in Berlin (*Antike Denkmäler* II, pl. 58); on fragments of a Clazomenian hydria in Athens and Brussels (*AM* 23, pl. 6), on a Clazomenian vase in London (*Antike Denkmäler* pl. 2, 21, 2), on a neck-amphora of the same fabric from Kertch (*Izvestiya Imperatorskoi Arkheologicheskoi Kommissii* 9, 1904, 85), and on a Clazomenian fragment, from Naucratis, in Oxford; and as late as the ripe archaic period in a representation of Hades carrying off Persephone on Locrian clay reliefs (*Bollettino d'Arte* 3, 467, fig. 37; *Ausonia* 3, 171). The dots represent metal studs set in the leather straps: a more precise rendering is found on Assyrian reliefs. In the great mosaic from Pompeii, the horses of Darius and Alexander have the headpiece heavily studded (Winter, *Das Alexandermosaik aus Pompeji* pl. 1; Springer, *Handbuch der Kunstgeschichte* I, pl. 13). (*Addendum*: Studded headpiece: also in an architectural clay group in the Villa Giulia, from an archaic temple at Falerii.)

A peytrel of the same type as ours is worn by horses on the Clazomenian sarcophagi in Berlin (*Antike Denkmäler* II, pl. 26) and in London (Murray, *Terracotta Sarcophagi* pl. 5), and on the Clazomenian vase from Aeolian Kyme in the British Museum (*RM* 3, pl. 9). The other peytrels cited by Furtwängler and by Rossbach (in Pauly-Wissowa, *s.v.* Epimenes) are not of this type. Furtwängler sees a floral motive in our example, but there is nothing floral either here or in the cases quoted above. These bands must be textile (or possibly leathern), tasselled, perhaps, but not necessarily, enriched with beads. Tasselled peytrels of the same type are worn by Assyrian horses, for instance on a relief from the Palace of Ashur-nasir-pal at Nimrud (*Assyrian Sculptures in the British Museum* pl. 17, 1). In the Alexander mosaic, the horses of Darius wear a plain band, evidently of stuff, perhaps silk, with a single tassel in front on the breast (Winter, *loc. cit.*). (*Addendum*: The nearest Attic peytrel: Attic calyx-krater of free style in Corneto (phot. Alinari 26041, 1) [RC 4195: *CVA* Tarquinia 2, pl. 13, 3].)

The horse on our stone has traits in common with the earlier horse on no. 21, but the treatment here is far freer and more spirited. Broadly speaking, it belongs to the same family as the horses on the sarcophagi and the vases of Clazomenae (for example, *Antike Denkmäler* II, pl. 26; Murray, *Terracotta Sarcophagi* pll. 1-7; *Antike Denkmäler* II, pl. 58; *ibid.*, pl. 56, 3). More closely akin, because bolder and more masterly, the horse and the ass on the Caeretan hydria in Berlin (*ibid.*, pl. 28). Furtwängler compares our horse with those on the marble frieze attributed to the Treasury of the [Siphnians] at Delphi, and the resemblance is undeniable: see, in especial, Homolle, *Fouilles de Delphes* IV, pll. 9-10. Comparable also the horses on

coins of Erythrai (Babelon, *Traité* pl. 12, 10 and 11), and the earlier horses on the ivory plaques, of Ionian style, published by Pollak (*RM* 21, pl. 15, 2 and pl. 16, 2: see his p. 323). These Ionian horses, whether carved or painted, are distinguishable from their Attic fellows, more reticently elegant, by their emphasized points, by their fierier mettle and haughtier allure. The horse of Euphronios (FR pl. 22 [*ARV* 16, 17]) is one of the few Attic works which the horse of Epimenes brings to mind.

With regard to groups of horse and man, see the reference quoted on no. 21. A group painted on the wall of the Tomba delle Bighe at Corneto (Weege, *JdI* 31, supplement to 138) so far resembles ours that the youth is seen in foreshortening from behind.

About 500 BC.

[Boardman, *Archaic* no. 246, and pp. 92-94 on Epimenes; *GGFR* pl. 355. J. Boardman, *Intaglios and Rings* (1975) no. 22, for a further attribution to Epimenes (now, Malibu, J. Paul Getty Museum 81.AN.76.22; Boardman, *GGFR* pls. 1023, 1025) and pp. 12-13 for the problems of attribution.]

29. [23.578]

Formerly in the Naue collection at Munich. F., pl. 6, 30.

Scaraboid, cut. Chalcedony. [19 x 13 mm]

Hatched border. A griffin holding a youth, dead or overcome, between its paws. The wings of the griffin are straight. Spiny comb; long straight ears, the ends now broken away; bulging forehead without horn; short stout beak, jaws open with teeth and tongue showing; goggle eye; ruff at the throat, with curving lines on it. The youth's hair striated, combed forward in front and downwards behind: the lower edge pelleted. His left hand is open with the back showing; his right arm raised with the hand hanging behind the head, as in nos. 37 and 38.

Furtwängler speaks of this stone in his History (III, 104), and points out that the representation is probably to be regarded as a variant of a common theme, a youth felled by a sphinx.

A naked youth attacked by a griffin is the subject of a bronze relief from Palestrina, Greek work of the late fifth century, in New York (*Monumenti* IX, pl. 31, 3; Miss Richter, *Greek, Etruscan, and Roman Bronzes in the Metropolitan Museum* 62, no. 94), but there the youth carries a sword and is probably therefore an Arimaspian.

Beginning of the fifth century.

[Boardman, *Archaic* no. 252; *GGFR* pl. 361, the Semon Master. The artist seems to specialize in such floating scenes of struggling pairs, one of them often a winged figure (Eros, sphinx; Boardman, *Archaic* nos. 250, 251).]

30. [21.1195]

Bought at Castrogiovanni (Enna) in Sicily. F., pl. 61, 15.

Scarab, cut. Sard. The lower part missing: chipped on the head and above the shield. [14 x 11 mm]

Hatched border. A young warrior bending over to pick up his helmet: his shield on his arm: the left leg frontal. In the field, the letter A, very large, no doubt the first of the owner's name. The hair cross-hatched: the lower edge rendered by two rows of pellets.

The same subject and design on a sard scaraboid, with a Cypriote inscription, in the De Clercq collection [*LHG* Pl. A, 7; Boardman, *Archaic* no. 260], and also on two archaic Etruscan scarabs (F., pl. 20, 6; *Burlington Catalogue* pl. 110, M 24; *Cook* pl. 2, 40: and F., pl. 20, 7; [Zazoff, nos. 59, 951]); close, a fragmentary scarab, late Etruscan or early Italiote, in Berlin (*Berlin* pl. 7, 376); a somewhat similar design on an Italiote stone (F., pl. 23, 68 [Zazoff, no. 954]). (*Margin*: Same subject also free Etruscan scarab, *Cat. Dr. B. et M.C.* pl. 25, no. 299.) Compare also the youth lifting a discos on a scarab from Cyprus in the British Museum (F., pl. 9, 6 [Boardman, *Archaic* no. 215]) and on an archaic Etruscan scarab in the Cabinet des Médailles (*Collection Pauvert de la Chapelle* pl. 6, 87; F., III, 449, fig. 232 [Zazoff, no. 366]).

Beginning of the fifth century.

[Boardman, *Archaic* no. 261. The stooping type was used for many comparable figures in late archaic glyptic and was especially favoured in Etruria.]

31. [27.682]

From Cyprus. Bought from Mrs. W.T. Ready in 1917.

Scaraboid, cut. Sard, brownish. The stone has been pared all round, especially at the sides. [17 x 16 mm]

Hatched border. Ground band of pellets between two lines. Achilles and Penthesilea. Achilles pierces the falling Amazon in the right side with his spear: with his left foot he treads on her ankle: his right leg frontal, slightly bent at the knee. Shield on arm, Corinthian helmet, chlamys fastened below the neck with a brooch: sword suspended from a baldrick at his side. Beardless; the hair, as far as visible, pelleted; three pellets indicate a slight whisker, four the pubes. The right leg of Penthesilea is frontal, and slightly bent at the knee; the right foot is seen at full length: in her left hand she holds a bow, in her right the spear about to drop: short chiton, girdled, and drawn up so as to expose the pubes, which is rendered by four pellets: peaked cap with a thin flap in front of the ear: plain necklace and circular earring: a large quiver with arrows in it at her side. The hair over her brow rendered by a row of pellets: behind, long and striated. Her dress presents two difficulties: the first is the two short horizontal lines between her breasts, which do not fit into the system of folds: it is conceivable that they represent a clasp fastening back the short sleeves from the shoulders, but such a clasp is without analogy. The second is the two curved lines, one at either wrist: at first sight they look like bracelets, but the width, and still more the irregularity, of the curves suggest the ends of sleeves on closer scrutiny. The Amazon would be wearing a sleeved undervest, reaching not much farther than the waist, in addition to her chiton. Just such a costume is worn by the Amazon who grasps her battle-axe with both hands on a red-figured calyx-krater in New York (FR pll. 118-19 [*ARV* 616, 3]).

In the field, behind Achilles, a star. A star is often placed in the field on gems (for example, F., pl. 8, 8 and 9 [Zazoff, no. 74; *BM Gems* no. 620]) and on coins, without determinable significance.

A somewhat similar Achilles and Penthesilea on a red-figured hydria in New York, the work of the Berlin painter in his early period (*JHS* 31, pl. 9 [*ARV* 209, 169]). The figures on the stone are somewhat more limber, thanks mainly to the bending of the frontal legs at the knee. On the stone, the collapse of Penthesilea is complete: on the vase, as in other Attic representations (fragmentary cup in the Cabinet des Médailles, *Monumenti* II, pl. 11, 2 [*ARV* 428, 16]: compare the calyx-krater in the Louvre, Millingen, *Peintures de vases grecs* pl. 49 [*ARV* 590, 12]), the Amazon is still able to extend her hand in appeal.

A parallel to the position of Penthesilea's legs is not easily found: the profile leg is usually more fully fiexed, as for instance in the group, akin to ours, on the hydria by the Eucharides painter in the Vatican (Gerhard, *Auserlesene Vasenbilder* pl. 202 [*ARV* 229, 38]).

The same exergual line on archaic coins of Laos and of Sybaris (Gardner, *Types* pl. 1, 10 and 11).

The indication of the female pubes is very rare apart from Attic red-figured vases. There also, but hardly on gems, parallels can be found for the indication of the veins on the frontal foot.

Early fifth century.

[Boardman, *Archaic* no. 255, the Semon Master. This is an exceptionally detailed narrative scene for the period and a rare example of the gem-engraver's art borrowing from the narrative repertoire of other arts, such as vase painting.]

32. [27.680]

Whelan reported that the ring was certainly found at Paphos. It was bought from a Dutch priest who was said to be a kinsman of the Duke of Norfolk. According to Ready, who had the first offer of it, the priest had purchased most of his antiquities at Amathus, but had added some at Larnaka. F., pl. 61, 30.

Sard scarab in a gold ring.

The beetle rough. Ridged. No winglets. Along the lower edge of the thorax, a pair of lines, interrupted in the middle of the stone. The elytra not separated. The hoop of the ring octagonal: band setting enriched with egg pattern, inlaid with white, red, and blue enamel, between a plain and a globulated border.

Hatched border. Eros flying with a sprig in either hand. Recurved wings. A wrap over both arms. The hair short and plain, with the lower edge pelleted. The arch of the ribs prominent: within it four bosses, arranged two and two.

Eros, in his earliest representations, is commonly associated with music, as in no. 33, and with plants or flowers as here.

> In season too Eros comes; when the land blooms, waxing with spring flowers, then Eros leaves the most beautiful island Cyprus to go down among men bearing seed to earth.
> Theognis, vv. 1275-9.

See no. 33.

Early fifth century.

[Boardman, *Archaic* no. 274. See no. 33.]

33. [27.767]

Bought in 1907 from a Carian who said it came from Caria.

Scaraboid, probably of discoloured sard, in a gold ring. The hoop of the ring circular, with wires twisted round it at the ends and passing through the stone, which is kept in place by two eyelets in the form of a four-pointed star covered with globules. [15 x 11 x 7 mm]

Hatched border. Eros flying with a wreath in one hand and a lyre in the other. Recurved wings at shoulder and ankle. Long hair, striated, and at the neck cross-hatched: over the brow a row of pellets: long locks falling on the breast. The upper part of the shoulder wings pelleted: pellets for the dark markings on the tortoise-shell body of the lyre.

A replica, on a sard scarab, was at one time in Mr. Cowper's possession ([Boardman, *Archaic* no. 273] *LHG* Pl. A, 4). The same design on a sard, set in a ring, which was formerly in the Newton Robinson collection (sale catalogue, pl. 1, 20) and on a stone which was once in W.T. Ready's hands. Similar, no. 32 in the present collection, and a stone of somewhat different style in Dorpat ([Boardman, *Archaic* no. 276] F. III, 103, fig. 71). The type culminates in the sard scaraboid from Cyprus in New York (*LHG* Pl. A, 3 [Boardman, *Archaic* no. 250]), where a winged youth is carrying off a naked woman who holds a lyre. (*Margin*: A winged naked youth holding a little woman, Etruscan bronze statuette of early free style in Florence.) Whether the youth on the New York stone can be called Eros is doubtful, for Eros is not seen following after women till the middle of the fifth century, and it is not in his original nature to do so, for he is the deification of the Eromenos, of the pursued and not the pursuer: but a better name can hardly be found.

Earlier than all these, the scaraboid no. 20.

The first quite certain representations of Eros are to be found on Attic red-figured vases of the later sixth century (Beazley, *VA* 7). Almost contemporary with these, Eros running with a flower and a lyre on a Greek bronze mirror in the British Museum (*BM Catalogue of Bronzes* pl. 17, 1): his feet are winged as in no. 20 and in the present stone. (*Margin*: Black figure fragment of pinax, Athens, Acropolis. Greek mirror from Vonitza in Berlin, *Jahreshefte* 18, 57-60.) Later, the coins and statues mentioned by Thiersch in *JdI* 30, 179-92.

Early fifth century.

[Boardman, *Archaic* no. 272; *GGFR* pl. 371. See no. 32. This was a common motif on late archaic gems and finger rings.]

34. [21.1196]

From Golgoi in Cyprus. Bought from W.T. Ready in 1897. F., pl. 61, 17.

Scaraboid. Chalcedony. [17 x 13 x 7 mm]

Ground line. A crouching lion: above him an eagle flying with a serpent in his talons. The teeth and tongue of the lion showing: puckered nose. Short bristling hairs all along the back. The mane rendered by two rows of short lines, one along the neck, the other on the breast, with a series of longer lines between them, slightly undulating and approximately horizontal. The body of the eagle and the uppermost part of his wings pelleted: vertical lines round his neck. The snake ringed.

A lion very like the present one, though more archaic, on no. 22, which also came from Cyprus. Similar also the chimaera on a rock-crystal scaraboid in London (*LHG* Pl. A, 9 [Boardman, *Archaic* no. 447]). The mane is rendered in the same manner on all three stones.

A lion with a flying eagle above is found on a series of Cypriote coins which has been assigned to Amathus (Hill, *BM Coins of Cyprus* pl. 18, 3-10, pl. 1, 6-15, and pl. 2, 1; Babelon, *Traité* pl. 132, 18-23, and pl. 133, 1-7), but in these the lion is couched on his hind-legs,

and the coins, even the earliest of them (Hill, pl. 18, 3), are rather later than the stone. Closer, an earlier coin attributed to the same locality, of which Hill publishes a poor specimen (pl. 18, 1) and Babelon a better (pl. 132, 11): here the mane, at any rate in the forepart on the obverse, resembles that on the scaraboid. In another group of Cypriote coins, assigned to Golgoi, the attitude of the lion is the same as on our stone: and the earliest of these lions (Hill, pl. 13, 5: a better specimen, Babelon, pl. 27, 20) bears considerable resemblance to ours: the back is bristly, and the mane appears to be rendered in the manner described. This coin is dated "before 480" by Hill; and "450 BC" seems a little too late for the earliest of the Amathusian series. Another lion not unlike ours, in treatment as in pose, is that on a coin of Hyele (*BM Coins of Italy* 304, no. 2; Babelon, pl. 68, 11), which, from the likeness of the female head on the obverse to the Arethusa on the Syracusan Damareteion, may be dated about 480.

For the bristly back, see no. 65.

About 480.

[Boardman, *Archaic* no. 428, the Aristoteiches Group. The style is rightly associated by Beazley with Cyprus where a distinctive and related Group of the Cyprus Lions can be distinguished, *ibid.*, 130-132.]

35. [27.681]

According to memory from Greece.

Scarab. Clear sard. [16 x 12 x 7 mm]

The beetle fairly careful. Carinated. No winglets. Along the lower edge of the thorax, a hatched border. Between the elytra a line.

Hatched border. A bull rousing himself.

Bulls of this type are common on archaic and early free gems. Other examples on sard scarabs in the Wyndham Cook and De Clercq collections ([Boardman, *Archaic* nos. 521, 483] *LHG* Pl. A, 14; *Cook* pl. 2, 33: De Ridder, *Collection De Clercq* VII, pl. 20, no. 2873, from Tortosa), on a rock-crystal scaraboid in Boston [01.7545; Boardman, *Archaic* no. 524] *LHG* Pl. A, 15; fragmentary inscription, retrograde, THE.LESE..), on a sard scarab formerly in the Sarti collection (*Vendita Sarti* pl. 28, no. 431), and on another, of very poor work, in the British Museum; on an Etruscan sard scarab in New York [*New York* no. 191]; and, somewhat barbarized, on two scaraboids of black jasper in the Southesk collection ([Boardman, *Archaic* no. 482] *Southesk* pl. 17, O 34 and O 28): the latest and finest member of the series is a sard scaraboid from Tanagra in Berlin [Boardman, *Archaic* no. 526; *AGDS* II, no. 169]. A similar bull, grouped with other figures, on sard scarabs in Berlin (F., pl. 8, 58 [*AGDS* II, no. 211]) and in the Southesk collection ([Boardman, *Archaic* no. 125] F., pl. 6, 29; *Southesk* pl. 1, A 17), on a sardonyx scarab in the Story-Maskelyne collection [now Cambridge; Boardman, *Archaic* no. 371; *Cambridge* no. 44], on a sard scarab from Gela in the Evans collection [now New York; Boardman, *Archaic* no. 407] and on a chalcedony scaraboid from Thebes in Boston [98.720; *ibid.*, no. 450]. Compare also the Acheloos on a sard scarab in London (F., pl. 9, 5 [Boardman, *Archaic* no. 253]). The same type on archaic coins of Cyzicus (Babelon, *Traité* pl. 176, 41 and 42).

A sheep in the same attitude on no. 35 *bis*.

On the inscribed scaraboid in Boston, the action of the bull is explained by the presence of a gadfly on his hind-quarters.

First third of the fifth century.

[Boardman, *Archaic* no. 522, the Fine Style.]

35 *bis*. [27.689]

From Stimnitza near Dimitzana in the Peloponnese. Formerly in the Evans collection: acquired in 1919.

Scarab or scaraboid, probably the latter, cut. Bluish chalcedony mottled with white. [16 x 12 mm]

Hatched border. A ewe getting up from the ground. Inscription, retrograde, giving the owner's name, ERMOTIMOEMI (*Hermotimou eimi*). The ewe is shorn save on the neck, where the wool is indicated by pellets. Long tail passing between the legs: creases on shoulder and elbow: large eye.

The attitude is common in bulls on gems: see no. 35. Walking rams on two Ionian stones, both more archaic in style than ours: a plasma scarab in the British Museum [Boardman, *Archaic* no. 131] and a chalcedony scaraboid in the Cabinet des Médailles [Boardman, *Archaic* no. 518]: both bear owner's names, Mandronax and Bryesis.

The inscription is written in small, neat characters. The upright of the first epsilon overlaps the cross-strokes above and below.

First half of the fifth century.

[Boardman, *Archaic* no. 516, the Fine Style.]

Etruscan: Archaic

35 *ter*. [21.1197]

From the Evans collection: acquired in 1919: originally bought in Rome.

Pseudo-scarab, the beetle replaced by a figure of Dionysos in relief. Clear sard. [13 x 10 mm]

No vertical border. The god is running in archaic posture to the left: his head is frontal: in his right hand a drinking horn, in his left a big vine branch with clusters, leaves, and tendrils, which passes above his head and hangs down as far as his right heel. Ionic chiton, with hatched borders at sleeves and ankles: mantle over both shoulders. Long even striations for the pleat-like folds: in the mantle, every other pleat is hatched. The outline of the hair above the forehead is a series of arcs convex to the face. The spade beard and the long moustache are hatched vertically. Goggle eyes: hatched eyebrows. For such pseudo-scarabs, see F. III, 79, 91, and 178-9; also our nos. 23 and 44: the figure of Dionysos is unique.

Pellet border, which stops at the ground line. Exergue filled with triangles hatched and counter-hatched. The subject is one of Herakles' adventures. The hero moves quickly to the right: opposite him is a smaller man with knees and body bent, and right hand raised, open and in profile. Herakles' right hand grasps this person's left: the left arm of Herakles is extended, with the forearm concealed behind the other's body. Behind Herakles stands Athena, holding her spear in her left hand, and raising her right with the index finger extended upwards and the other fingers closed: behind the other

man, a woman, whose right hand is raised, with the fingers spread out, holding a flower composed of a bud between two tendrils, and whose left arm is bent at the elbow with the hand open, in profile, and thumb upwards.

The figures are very short. The cheeks, except Athena's, are so modelled, that the heads seem, at first sight, to be helmeted. The limbs of Herakles are powerful, with copious inner marking; his knee-caps, ankles, and elbows are rendered by pellets. His eye is set very high. A row of pellets for the hair over his fore-head: no beard indicated. He wears a short chiton, striated, the lower border vertically hatched; over the chiton, a lionskin. His opposite has a long garment passing over his right shoulder and leaving his left shoulder free: this is no doubt a himation: if he is wearing a chiton under it, it is not indicated. The chin is pointed and therefore bearded. The hair is plain: it falls in a long mass behind: it is bounded by a plain curved line in front of the ear, and by a plain straight line high on the forehead: a pellet marks the ear. Athena is clad in chiton, mantle, both striated, and long snake-fringed aegis. The crown of her head is chipped away: but it is almost certain that she wore no helmet. Her hair is striated, and falls in a mass behind: over the forehead, short locks terminating in small pellets. The other female figure wears the same costume as Athena, save the aegis: her mantle has a hatched border. The skull is plain: behind the ear, three locks of hair, the outermost pelleted, the others plain: stephane, vertically hatched in front of the ear.

The interpretation principally depends on the person

with whom Herakles is engaged. It seems clear, from the attitude of this person, that the encounter is not an amicable one. The face is bearded. Moreover, the hair begins noticeably higher up on the forehead than in the other figures: this suggests incipient baldness and hence old age: the figure may therefore be Nereus, the old man of the sea.

The contest of Herakles and Nereus is represented on a number of monuments from the later part of the sixth century and onwards: though not elsewhere in the same scheme as on our gem. The female figure behind Nereus may be his wife Doris, but Doris might be expected to show dismay: Hera?

The style of the stone may perhaps be called Etruscan rather than Greek. If it is Etruscan, it is one of the earliest Etruscan gems.

Second half and probably third quarter of the sixth century.

(*Addendum*: For the style, compare the sard scarab number 15260 in the Museo Archeologico at Florence (young warrior holding helmet).)

[Boardman, *Archaic* no. 77 and pp. 162-163. This is the name piece of the Group of the Boston Dionysos, on which see J. Boardman, *Intaglios and Rings* [1975] 38-39, on no. 121; *GGFR* pl. 1033 (now Malibu 81.AN.76.121). This is probably the earliest Greek studio established in Etruria which has a sufficiently distinctive style to relate to origins in the east Greek world. It has been studied by several scholars over the years, notably by P. Zazoff (*JdI* 81 [1966] 63-78), in Zazoff, 17-19, and by J. Spier (in *Periplous* 330-335). *AGDS* I no. 672 may be an addition - possibly a cut scarab.]

36. [21.1198]

Bought in 1900.

Scarab. Murky sard. [15 x 11 mm]

The beetle careful. Winglets. Vertical egg border. Round the sides and the lower edge of the thorax, a hatched border, with a rectangular space left plain half-way along the lower edge. The clypeus goffered: the plates cross-hatched. A line between the elytra.

Pellet border, which stops at the ground line. Exergue

filled with triangles hatched and counter-hatched. A naked youth led off by two winged females clad in chitons. The hair plain, and rolled up at the back of the neck. Four round bosses for the rectus abdominis. Rather than encumber his composition, the artist has given the females but one wing each.

The females would seem to be death demons: a parallel representation is to seek, but a somewhat similar group on an Etruscan tombstone of free style (Grenier, *Bologna villanovienne et étrusque* 447) is clearly a descent to the underworld: a youth is being hurried off by two males, one winged, one carrying a torch: see also Ducati, *Monumenti dei Lincei* 20, 607-12.

End of the sixth century.

[Zazoff, no. 415, Strong Style.]

37. [21.1199]

From Corfu. Bought from Madame Heimpel, daughter of Rhousopoulos, in 1901.

Scarab. Sard. [14 x 10 x 7 mm]

The winglets almost rubbed away. Triple hatched vertical border. A hatched border, now very indistinct, round the sides and the lower edge of the thorax. Between the elytra, probably three lines.

Hatched border. Ajax dead. A naked bearded man, body and right leg frontal, his right hand behind his head, has fallen on his sword, which passes through his left side: a female figure moves quickly towards him and covers him with a large cloth. She wears a chiton, girdled, with short kolpos: the general outline of the right leg is shown through the cloth. Her hair, which is plain, falls in a heavy mass behind and is tied near the end. Pellets on the upper part of the wings. The hair of Ajax reaches to his shoulders and is filleted and hatched. His left arm raised, with the hand at the crown of the head: his right foot seen at full length.

In the Ajax of Sophocles (915 ff.) Tecmessa spreads a garment over the disfigured corpse of her husband:

> I shall cover him completely with this cloak folded about him, since none that was a friend could bear to look upon him...
>
> [trans., Lloyd-Jones]

34

The figure on the stone is winged, and therefore cannot be Tecmessa. It is not unlikely that Sophocles took the motive, Tecmessa covering the body of Ajax, from an earlier, say an epic poem; that the representation on the stone is derived, in the long run, from the same source; and that the engraver, or a predecessor, added wings to the female figure on the analogy of kindred scenes where divine beings are busied with the dead or dying, as, for example, on the stones nos. 36 and 38 in the present collection. It is winged youths, and not mortals, holding a heavy cloth, who are painted on the walls of the Tomba della Pulcella at Corneto, one at each side of the alcove in which the inmate of the tomb reposed (*Antike Denkmäler* II, pl. 43).

Although the stone is traced to Corfu, the style is Etruscan rather than Greek.

Beginning of the fifth century.

[Zazoff, no. 333, Strong Style. The subject now on a Brygos Painter cup in New York, *Paralipomena* 367, 1 *bis*.]

38. [21.1200]

Bought by Tyszkiewicz in Naples. P.J. Meier, *Annali* 1883, 213; *Collection Tyszkiewicz* pl. 24, 8; F., pl. 16, 22. A rough sketch in F. Parkes Weber, *Aspects of Death and Correlated Aspects of Life* 651, fig. 111, and *Aspects of Death in Art and Epigram* 379.

Scarab. Sard. [16 x 12 x 8 mm]

The beetle careful. Slightly ridged. Winglets. Vertical egg border. Round the sides and the lower edge of the thorax, a hatched border, interrupted by a triangular depression half-way along the lower edge. Round the head, outside it, two rows of dots. A line between the elytra.

Hatched border. A dead youth borne by two winged figures, one female and one male. The corpse is naked, the pose parallel to that of Ajax on no. 37: the hair hatched, and the lower part of it falling vertically from the neck (compare no. 37). The male bearer is naked, the female clad in chiton and himation. The hair of both filleted and hatched: in the male, done up into a little roll at the back of the neck, in the female reaching to the shoulder and worn zazzera-wise. The upper part of the wings pelleted.

The disposal of Memnon's body is depicted in Attic vase-paintings of the early fifth century (Löwy, *Zur Aithiopis* in *Neue Jahrbücher* 1914, 81-94: earlier literature is cited by Löwy; see also Riezler, *Weissgrundige Attische Lekythen* 9-10, and Wilamowitz-Moellendorff, *Aischylos, Interpretationen* 245, n. 3 [*LIMC* VI, 455-8]). The representations, as Löwy shows, divide into two classes corresponding to two different moments in the story. In one class, the winged goddess Eos is lifting her son, still dripping with blood, from the field of battle, or bearing him away in her arms (cup signed by Douris, Pottier, *Douris* 41: pelike by the Syleus painter, Beazley, *VA* 66 [*ARV* 434, 74 and 250, 24]). In the other, it is two winged youths, Hypnos and Thanatos, who are raising the body, now washed and anointed, to carry it to that remote country where Memnon is to enjoy the immortality granted him by Zeus (cup in the British Museum, *Wiener Vorlegeblätter* D, pl. 3, phot. Mansell 3168; calyx-krater in the Louvre, *Monumenti* 6/7, pl. 21 [*ARV* 126, 24 and 227, 12, a body of Sarpedon]).

Löwy, in his brilliant article *Zur Aithiopis* (p. 82), conjectures that the engraver of our stone has fused the two moments, and that our female is to be called Eos. Before this interpretation is accepted, two other Etruscan scarabs must be considered. On the Morrison stone (F., pl. 16, 23; *Morrison Catalogue* pl. 1, 46 [Zazoff, no. 35]), one of the bearers is female as in ours, and the other male; but in the later and rougher stone in the British Museum (*BM Gems* no. 680 [Zazoff, no. 240]) both are female. A like variation of sex is observable in another class of monument: a bronze cista-handle, of archaic Latin style (*Catalogue de la Collection Alessandro Castellani* Rome, 1884, pl. 8, no. 282) is formed of two armed and winged male figures carrying the body of a young warrior: and on another cista-handle (Reinach, *Répertoire de la statuaire* II, 521, 2) the winged bearers are both female.

It may be taken that Eos does not appear on the London stone or on the last-named cista, for a pair of Dawn-goddesses is out of the question. This does not imply that our female is not Eos, for the type may have been reinterpreted and diversified later: but it makes the identification doubtful. Our female may be a death-goddess.

We have left out of account those examples in which the bearers are wingless and therefore presumably mortal, in particular the handle-groups on Prenestine cistae (for example, Reinach, *loc. cit.*, IV, 322, 2, now in New York, with male bearers: *ibid.*, II, 322, 1, one bearer female: *ibid.*, II, 521, 1, *Bollettino d'Arte* 3, 179,

181, and 183, two warriors bearing a woman): for by the time they were made the group had become a decorative type without mythical significance.

Beginning of the fifth century.

[Zazoff, no. 36, Early Strong Style.]

39. [27.720]

Bought in Perugia, 1896-7. F., pl. 61, 19.

Scarab. Banded agate, bleached, now white and sky-blue. [13 x 10 x 7 mm]

The beetle careful. The winglets reduced to humps. Vertical cable border with pellets in the loops. Round the sides and the lower edge of the thorax a hatched border, interrupted half-way along the lower edge. The clypeus and the plates dotted. Between the elytra two lines.

Pellet border. Small exergue, with egg pattern: the right foot of the figure passes over this and rests on the border. Achilles, beardless, bending and drawing a cloak over his shoulder with both hands. On the ground in front of him a Corinthian helmet. Inscription ACHILE, retrograde. The hair hatched, worn zazzera-wise and filleted. The pubes indicated by three small pellets.

The position of the legs, one frontal with the foot fore-shortened, the other crossed behind it, is particularly frequent in red-figured vases of the ripe archaic period, though it is found some decades earlier, for example on the calyx-krater by Euphronios in Berlin (*Archäologische Zeitung* 1879, pl. 4; Hoppin, *Euthymides and his Fellows* pll. 20-1 [*ARV* 13, 1]).

Early fifth century.

[Zazoff, no. 328, Strong Style.]

40. [21.1201]

From Vulci. Formerly in the possession of Campanari, later in the Evans collection. F., pl. 16, 60, and, enlarged, pl. 51, 1.

Translucent sard scarab in a gold sepulchral ring. Cracked across. The hoop is hollow, oval outside and flattened inside: it is soldered to two shields, of the type shown in Marshall, *BM Finger Rings* xliv, D ii, through which the pin passes: the stone is secured by two rings between stone and shields. [16 x 15 x 7 mm]

The beetle careful. The winglets reduced to humps. Vertical border of egg pattern surmounted by a thin band into which the uprights of the egg border are produced. Round the sides and the lower edge of the thorax, a hatched border with a semi-circular dip half-way along the lower edge. Head, clypeus, and plates dotted. Between the elytra, three lines.

Pellet border. An athlete pouring sand on his thigh. He kneels on a heap of sand, with left thigh frontal, left leg from knee to ankle foreshortened away, and left foot in three-quarter profile, a common attitude on red-figured vases of the ripe archaic period (cup by the Colmar painter, *Le Musée* 3, 55; cup by the Panaitios painter, Hartwig, *Meisterschalen* pl. 15, 2 [*ARV* 144, 3 and 316, 4]). The hair short and pelleted.

First quarter of the fifth century.

[Zazoff, no. 1571, Strong Style.]

41. [27.717]

From the Boulton collection (sale catalogue no. 3).

Scarab. Murky sard. [13 x 11 x 8 mm]

The beetle careful. The winglets reduced to humps. Vertical egg border, surmounted by a hatched border. Round the sides and the lower edge of the thorax a hatched border with a triangular depression half-way along the lower edge. The head (barring the eyes), clypeus, and plates dotted. A line between the elytra.

Hatched border. Ajax falling on his sword: behind him, the scabbard: the hilt is planted on the ground, symbolized by the hatched border, and the point directed towards the hero's ribs. The left leg frontal, and the right leg crossed behind it; as in no. 39. The massive forms present a contrast to the slender elegance of the contemporary figure on no. 39. The long hair, which is filleted, and the trim beard are hatched: the hair hangs down in front of the head and recalls the hair on no. 38. The nipples at the corners of the pectorals: the linea alba indicated from navel to pubes. The hands more formal than the rest of the figure.

The same subject on two Etruscan scarabs of free style, one in the British Museum (*LHG* Pl. A, 19: *BM Gems* no. 635 [Zazoff, no. 334] F., pl. 17, 32),the other in the Wyndham Cook collection (*LHG* Pl. A, 20; *Burlington Catalogue* pl. 110, M 127; *Cook* pl. 2, 41 [now *New York* no. 172; Zazoff, no. 337]). The motive is different in all three: in our stone the figure is made frontal in the taste of the ripe archaic period. An earlier moment is represented on a scarab in Copenhagen (F., pl. 64, 38 [Zazoff, no. 280]), which bears a Latin inscription and is poorly executed in the globolo style. Other versions of the suicide of Ajax are discussed by Milani in *Bollettino d'Arte* 2, 361-8: the excellent bronze statuette in Florence, found at Populonia, which is published by Milani (*ibid.*, pl. 2 and 362: also in *Notizie degli Scavi* 1908, 208-9, and in *AJA* 1909, 208) is Etruscan work of the same period as our gem [*LIMC* I, 328-32].

A seventh-century representation of the same subject on a lenticular gem of green serpentine in the Evans collection [Boardman, *GGFR* pl. 264]: it was found at Peraia near Corinth and bears the retrograde inscription HAHIWAS.

First quarter of the fifth century.

[Zazoff, no. 335, Free Style.]

The left thigh is frontal, the rest of the left leg foreshortened away: for this motive see Jacobsthal, *Göttinger Vasen* 51: one of the earliest examples is on the psykter signed by Euphronios (FR, pl. 63 [*ARV* 16, 15]), and it is common on ripe archaic vases.

The same subject on an Etruscan mirror from Cervetri in the British Museum (627; *Monumenti* VIII, pl. 33), and often on Etruscan and Italiote stones. Nearest ours, the coarser scarab in Copenhagen (*LHG* Pl. A, 17; F., pl. 64, 26 [Zazoff, no. 68] and F., II, 291), where the leg, however, is not foreshortened as in ours and others. Examples and variants; F., pl. 19, 38-9; pl. 19, 36-7; pl. 20, 39; pl. 19, 35 and 40 [Zazoff, nos. 590, 594, 602, 604, 601, 228, 164]; and Gabrici, *Monumenti dei Lincei* 22, pl. 116, 10. For the craft, compare the scarab F., pl. 18, 13, and the Boeotian kotyle in Oxford (Gardner, *Ashmolean Vases* pl. 26). The subject is discussed by Furtwängler (F., III, 197), but his conclusion is open to doubt: the representation is probably to be connected with Herakles' western voyage (Pindar, *Nemeans* 3. 38). [*LIMC* V, nos. 337-41].

First quarter of the fifth century.

(*Addendum*: There are two sard scarabs with Herakles on the raft in the Castellani collection at Rome.)

[Zazoff, no. 589, Strong Style.]

42. [21.1202]

Bought in Rome, 1912.

Scarab. Sard: partially translucent. [13 x 11 x 8 mm]

The beetle careful. Winglets. Vertical egg border, surmounted by a hatched border. Round the sides and the lower edge of the thorax, a hatched border. The parts about the head broken away. Three lines between the elytra.

Pellet border. Herakles lying on a raft, which is supported by amphorae half-submerged. With his right hand he holds the end of the sail, as well as his bow and arrows; in his left hand his club, as if he were steering with it: his left hand rests on a little doubled cushion. Beardless: short hair, full at the neck, hatched, with faint pelleting over the forehead.

43. [27.718]

From Chiusi. Bought in 1914.

Scarab. Banded agate. [14 x 11 x 7 mm]

The beetle careful. The winglets reduced to humps. Vertical egg border. Round the sides and the lower edge of the thorax, a hatched border. Head, clypeus, and plates dotted. Between the elytra, three lines.

Pellet border. Herakles, beardless, drawing water in a pointed amphora from a fountain, the spout of which is in the form of a lion's head: behind him, his club and his bow with the string loose. Inscription HERCLE, retrograde. The hair short, and cross-hatched with the lower edge pelleted.

The subject, Herakles at the fountain, is common on gems ([*LIMC* IV, *s.v.* 'Herakles' nos. 1322-8 and V, *s.v.* 'Hercle' nos. 81-97] F., pl. 8, 39, Greek: the rest

Etruscan and Italiote (F., pl. 17, 45; pl. 61, 23; pl. 19, 20; pl. 20, 25: compare also pl. 19, 19 and 22 [Zazoff, nos. 547, 680, 559, 67, 773, 562]).

An agate scarab, of excellent Etruscan workmanship, in the museum at Corneto resembles ours in style (*LHG* Pl. A, 16 [Zazoff, no. 1178]): a naked youth, inscribed PELE, Peleus, is dropping oil from an aryballos into the palm of his hand: squatting on the ground in front of him, his little negro attendant who holds his sponge.

First quarter of the fifth century.

[Zazoff, no. 554, Strong Style.]

44. [27.719]

Bought in Rome, 1909.

Pseudo-scarab, the beetle replaced by a siren in relief. Banded agate, brown and white. [12 x 10 x 6 mm]

No vertical border. The siren is very carefully wrought. Both head and body are frontal: the fists are close together, one under each breast: the legs are also folded up symmetrically. Sleeved chiton with the border at the neck hatched. Long hair, filleted, and falling in a heavy mass on either shoulder.

Several siren-scarabs are mentioned by Furtwängler (pl. 8, 23 and III, 178-9): there are two others in the Southesk collection (*Southesk* pl. 2, A 36, and pl. 1, A 2 = F., pl. 20, 11 [Boardman, *Archaic* nos. 603, 606]). The head is usually in profile.

Pellet border. Warrior running and looking round, with spear and shield. Short chiton, leather corslet, helmet with cheek-pieces. On the skull of the helmet, a spiral; on the forehead-piece, an eyebrow. A row of pellets where the crest is attached to the helmet: two others, between lines, across the waist of the corslet. The corslet has a border, vertically hatched, at the neck. The long hair escapes from the helmet behind.

First quarter of the fifth century.

[Boardman, *Archaic* no. 602; Zazoff, no. 961, Strong Style.]

45. [23.579]

From Arezzo: Furtwängler says Chiusi, wrongly it seems. Formerly in the Evans collection. F., pl. 20, 12.

Scarab. Murky sard. [13 x 9 x 8 mm]

The beetle careful. Winglets. The vertical border reduced to a single uneven line. Round the sides and the lower edge of the thorax, a hatched border. The parts about the head broken away. A line between the elytra.

Pellet border. Eros flying down with a taenia in his hands. The hair hatched, filleted, and worn in a long zazzera.

First quarter of the fifth century.

[Zazoff, no. 407, Transitional Style.]

46. [21.1203]

From the Bruschi collection at Corneto: bought in 1896. F., pl. 61, 24.

Scarab. Opaque sard. [16 x 13 x 10 mm]

The beetle careful. The winglets reduced to humps. Vertical egg border, surmounted by a hatched border. Along the lower edge of the thorax, a hatched border, which may have extended to the sides, but here the surface has suffered. Three lines between the elytra.

Hatched border. Jason, swallowed by the dragon, or perhaps issuing from its mouth. Beardless; petasos; sword in right, shield in left.

A scene from the same story on a red-figured cup, painted in the later manner of Douris, in the Vatican (*Monumenti* II, pl. 35; phot. Moscioni [*ARV* 437, 116]): the hero's name is given as Jason.

First half of the fifth century.

[Zazoff, no. 760, Strong Style.]

Greek: Free Style

47. [27.691]

Furtwängler says that Dr. Töpffer acquired the stone from Sparta about 1890, but that it was known many years previously. Later in the Tyszkiewicz collection. *Collection Tyszkiewicz* pl. 24, 6; F., pl. 10, 3; *Tyszkiewicz Sale Catalogue* pl. 27, no. 286; Perrot, *Histoire de l'Art* IX, 28, fig. 30, from a drawing.

Sard, slightly convex; cut down at the back. [18 x 14 mm]

Line border, stopping at the ground line. Apollo with sceptre, hawk, and spray of laurel, accompanied by a roebuck. He stands with both feet frontal, the right knee slightly bent, and the left side of the body consequently a little higher than the right. A short cloak over his shoulders. A pellet at either end of his sceptre. The toes rendered by pellets. The eye large and in profile, with a stroke below it to model the cheek. The hair worn zazzera-fashion, with a fillet: striated, the edge pelleted.

Figures with both feet frontal do not occur so early as figures with one foot frontal and one in profile: one of the earliest instances is the woman on a cup by the Panaitios painter in London (FR, pl. 23 [*ARV* 318, 2]). The bent knee marks a later stage, that of the marble youth from the Acropolis at Athens who has been associated with Kritios; the statues of the Olympian pediments; and the vases of the Niobid painter and the Villa Giulia painter (see Beazley, *VA* 142).

A figure of a young man, inscribed Kastor, in the same position as our Apollo, is engraved on a glass scaraboid from Spata in Attica (not Sparta, as Furtwängler says) which was formerly in the Evans collection (*LHG* Pl. A, 23; F., pl. 12, 23 [Boardman, *GGFR* fig. 216]): it is somewhat later than our stone, for the attitude is freer and the modelling less hard.

Sceptres topped with a plain knob are less common than might be expected: the instances quoted in Daremberg and Saglio (*s.v.* sceptrum) do not bear examination. A golden sceptre which may be said to be of this type was found at Taranto and is preserved in the British Museum (Marshall, *BM Catalogue of Jewellery* 232, no. 2070, fig. 65): it is surmounted by a glass quince surrounded by leaves.

The spray, no doubt meant for laurel, characterizes the god as Katharsios (Overbeck, *Apollo* 309).

The hawk is associated with Apollo by Aristophanes and other writers: the references have been collected by A.B. Cook (*Zeus* I, 241). Apollo appears with a bird on certain coins, which are cited by Froehner in *Collection Tyszkiewicz*, for example, on those of Themistocles (Babelon, *Traité* pl. 88, 3), but where the nature of the bird can be made out, it seems to be not a hawk but a crow or raven. On the archaistic relief in Turin (Schrader, *Jahreshefte* 16, 23 and 26) only the wing of the bird is preserved. On a late archaic cup in the Villa Giulia (a tiny reproduction, useless for this purpose, in *Bollettino d'Arte* 10, 337), the bird which Apollo holds is called a raven by Savignoni, but the present writer took it to be a hawk, if not an eagle, on account of its hooked beak.

The date of the stone cannot be far removed from that of the pedimental sculptures at Olympia. The gem which stands nearest to ours is perhaps the chalcedony scaraboid from Cyprus, with Hades and Persephone, in New York (F., pl. 9, 32 [Boardman, *GGFR* pl. 451]). Ours is somewhat harder in style.

Between 470 and 460.

[Boardman, *GGFR* pl. 455.]

48. [23.593]

Formerly in the Bourguignon collection. Bought by Bourguignon in Constantinople. F., pl. 61, 32.

Gold ring with engraved bezel. The hoop quadrangular. [16 x 11 mm]

Short ground line. Hermes, clad in a chlamys, resting his left elbow on an Ionic pillar: in his right hand a phiale, in his left a kerykeion. The hair short and pelleted. Volutes, echinus, fluting, torus, and plinth of the column are all indicated: the plinth in perspective.

An early example of what later became a favourite motive in gems and in other works of art: one instance out of many, the Herakles on a scaraboid in Berlin (F., pl. 10, 41 [*AGDS* II, no. 156]).

A Hermes in the same attitude and with the same attributes as ours is engraved on a sard scarab from Taranto, of free Etruscan style, in the museum at Lecce (*LHG* Pl. A, 22 [Zazoff, no. 728]). Hatched vertical border; a hatched border round the sides and the lower edge of the thorax; two lines between the elytra. A little dolphin is engraved on the thorax: compare the female head engraved on the back of a sard scarab in the British Museum, and the head of Bes on another in Boston (F., pl. 20, 10 [98.735; Boardman, *Archaic* no. 613]).

It is generally considered, that the Polycleitan Narcissus and the Berlin Amazon are among the earliest sculptures in the round, in which a pillar forms an integral part of the composition; but it is not surprising that various collocations of man and pillar had been made by painters long before: so on archaic red-figured vases (amphora in Petrograd, mentioned in Beazley, *VA* 57, no. 1 [*ARV* 279, 1]; pelike in Copenhagen, mentioned in *JHS* 36, 128 [*ARV* 184, 27]; cup in London, Hartwig, *Meisterschalen* pl. 34;

Beazley, *VA* 93, fig. 61 [*ARV* 371, 24]); in the free period, nearer the date of the statues, on a cup in Miss Lamb's collection (*JHS* 38, 35, fig. 8 [*ARV* 1299]); on another in the Villa Giulia (*Monumenti dei Lincei* 24, 895 [*ARV* 1177, 1]); and on an oinochoe in the British Museum (*Guide to the Exhibition illustrating Greek and Roman Life* 112, fig. 97 [*ARV* 1175, 17]).

Hauser held that our ring showed marks of Peloponnesian style.

About the middle of the fifth century.

[Boardman, *GGFR* pl. 663, the Waterton Group of Early Classical rings.]

49. [27.686]

Bought in 1908 from a Greek, who alleged that it came from Delphi.

Scaraboid. Yellow jasper, mottled with chalcedony. [21 x 17 x 9 mm]

Ground line. Apollo, naked, moving towards the tripod and extending his right hand over one of the rings: his bow in his left hand. The long hair, which is covered with thick, irregular striations, seems to be plaited behind in transverse plaits, something like that of the discobolos on the archaic relief in Athens (Conze, *Die attischen Grabreliefs* pl. 4). A single lock passes in front of the ear and falls on the breast. The arrangement over the brow is hard to make out: a wreath is impossible because there is no trace of it behind the ear; a metal stephane would explain the pointed projection in front, but is objectionable on other grounds; some such effect would be produced by two long locks of hair, one in front of each ear, lifted and tied over the forehead; but locks so tied (Furtwängler, *Meisterwerke der griechischen Plastik* 678-81, and *Intermezzi* 5-6) are not found elsewhere in combination with long hair at the back of the head.

The tripod has leonine feet and stands on a ground line of its own: the bowl is rounded, with the upper edge curved, and the two lateral rings are also in perspective.

The thick-set, heavy figure brings to mind certain early coins from North Greece (Gardner, *Types* pl. 3, 1-2 and 4-6) and the Herakles on a coin of Thebes (*ibid.*, 45). The forms of thigh, knee, and calf suggest the sixth century; but the upper part of the body is foreshortened with moderate accuracy, and the forms of it belong to a later period. The cutting is deeper and the modelling broader than in early stones. The back hair, if rightly explained above, is dressed in a sixth century fashion, but the treatment of it is not contemporary with the coiffure.

The figure is probably an imitation of an earlier Apollo, and was probably not made before 460 or 450.

An Apollo in a somewhat similar attitude forms part of a 'Contest for the Tripod' on a sard scarab in the Cabinet des Médailles (F., pl. 10, 18), which shows, in Furtwängler's words, "free style with old-fashioned elements purposely retained." It is possible that our Apollo is derived from a representation of the Struggle for the Tripod: this might explain the action of the figure.

For the two ground lines, an early coin of Kaulonia may be compared (Gardner, *Types* pl. 1, 1).

[Boardman, *GGFR* pl. 452.]

49 bis. [27.697]

From Melos. Formerly in the Evans collection: acquired in 1919.

Scaraboid. Rock-crystal. [25 x 21 x 10 mm]

Hatched border. Uneven ground line. Two Amazons, one seated on a rock with a spear in her left hand, her right raised as if greeting the other, who rides slowly towards her, holding the reins in her left and a short goad in her right. Both Amazons wear the same costume: a sleeved and trousered garment, cross-hatched to suggest the lozenge pattern; over it a short chiton, pulled up a little to cover the girdle; soft shoes; and a high cap of soft material with two flaps and a peak. Striations for the folds of the chitons. The horse is a strong cob: the ears are pointed forward; the mouth open: the tail somewhat unevenly striated.

The seated Amazon may be compared with the figure of Paris, seated, and clad in Oriental costume, on a red-figured pyxis lid, datable to the third quarter of the fifth century, in the museum at Copenhagen (Dumont-Chaplain, *Céramiques de la Grèce propre* pl. 10 [*LIMC* VII 'Paridis Iudicium' no. 40]). Compare also the Amazons on a hydria of Lucanian style in Naples (3241; *Archäologische Zeitung* 1856, pl. 89 [*LCS* 36,

137]).

Second half, and probably third quarter, of the fifth century.

[Boardman, *GGFR* pl. 474, around Dexamenos.]

50. [23.580]

Said to have been found in a tomb at Kara in Attica about 1860. It passed into the hands of Admiral Soteriades, and was later in the possession of Rhousopoulos; then in the Evans collection. Stephani, *Compte rendu* 1868, pl. 1, 12; a poor drawing. King, *Antique Gems and Rings* I, 400: a mere caricature. Furtwängler, *JdI* 3, pl. 8, 8; Evans, *RA* 32 (1898), pl. 8, 2, enlarged, but reversed; F., pl. 14, 3, and, enlarged, pl. 51, 8; Hekler, *Greek and Roman Portraits* ix, fig. 1, enlarged; Delbrueck, *Antike Porträts* pl. 58, 1, enlarged; Fowler and Wheeler, *Greek Archaeology* 391, fig. 318.

Detailed discussions of the stone by Furtwängler in *JdI* 3, 201-2, and F., III, 138, and by Evans in *RA* 32 (1898), 337-55 "The Athenian Portrait-Head by Dexamenos of Chios". On Evans's identification of the portrait as Cimon, see F., III, 138, and Bernoulli, *Griechische Ikonographie* I, 100-1.

Scaraboid. Yellow jasper mottled with red. Line border. [21 x 17 x 6 mm]

Portrait head of a bearded man. Above, the artist's signature, retrograde, in two lines, DEXAMENOS EPOIE.

Facsimiles of the inscription are given by Furtwängler (*JdI* 3, 201) and by Evans (*loc. cit.*, 344). Evans notes that the form of the xi is Chiot: but it also occurs on Attic red-figured vases. The second upright of the nu higher than the first. The upright of the epsilons tends to project beyond the cross-bars. Broad alpha with horizontal bar.

The lips parted: the eyebrows meeting. The beard rendered by long undulating lines, the hair, which is scanty in front and worn full at the nape, by groups of the same, which produce a fleecy effect; the shorter hairs on the forepart of the skull engraved on the flat surface of the stone. The eyeball prominent; the line marking the exterior side of the iris is nearly straight; the eyebrow is rendered by slanting lines, nearly straight, on a ridge; the fold of skin above the upper eyelid indicated. Two curved lines, in a horizontal direction, starting at or near the anterior point of the upper lid, mark the upper profile lashes: three, the uppermost faint, from the lower lid, the lower profile lashes. The rest of the lashes, upper and lower, represented by short lines with a downward direction. Four very fine sharp lines for the wrinkles on the forehead, three for the creases at the back of the neck, three others between hair and eye.

Since the stone is by Dexamenos, it must have been produced within not very many decades of the signed scaraboid in Cambridge (F., pl. 14, 1 [Boardman, *GGFR* pl. 467; *Cambridge* no. 53]), which has severe elements and can hardly be much later than 450. Our stone is generally admitted, by reason of its style, to be not earlier than the Cambridge stone. Within the limits thus set there has been some difference of opinion. Evans places it as early as 450, Delbrueck about 430, Furtwängler and Hekler between 430 and 420. Precision is difficult on account of the scarcity of analogous representations and the highly personal character of the style.

Evans (*loc. cit.*, 348-50) pays particular attention to the minutely careful presentment of the eyelashes, and remarks that a similar rendering of the upper profile and the lower vertical lashes is found on the Damareteion, struck in 479, and on 'transitional' coins of Syracuse, but is less pronounced on the earliest signed coins, while on the earliest of Euainetos' tetradrachms, struck about 425, the lashes have ceased to appear, although there are faint vestiges of lower eyelashes on coins signed by Eumenes, and on the decadrachm by 'the new artist' (Evans, *Syracusan Medallions* 28). The lower lashes are also indicated in the head of Zeus on an Elean coin (Evans, pl. 8, 4), but here the upper profile lashes are lacking, and the exact date of the coin is uncertain, although it is generally placed about 450. The upper profile lashes alone are still indicated on one of Cimon's decadrachms (Evans, *Syracusan Medallions* pl. 2, 8), therefore after 413.

A somewhat similar rendering of lower vertical and upper profile lashes is prevalent on Attic vases of about 460 to 450 (for example, Beazley, *VA* 163 [*ARV* 987, 1]; Riezler, *Weissgrundige attische Lekythen* pl. 36 [*ARV* 998, 161]; FR, II, 264, fig. 94A [*ARV* 991, 61]), but is also found later, for instance, on a nuptial lebes in New York which cannot be earlier than 430 (*Bulletin of the Metropolitan Museum* 11, 255 [*ARV* 1126, 6]).

These coins and vases, however, supply no counterpart

to the peculiar treatment of the upper lashes, carried over on to the surface of the eye itself so as to point downwards and not upwards. (*Margin*: But cf. the white Glaukon lekythos in Bonn, *JHS* 16, pl. 4 [*ARV* 1582, 23]) The same, accompanied by upper profile lashes and lower vertical lashes, both as in the coins and the vases, on a white lekythos in Athens (Riezler, *op. cit.*, pl. 90 [*ARV* 1383, 12]); but this vase cannot be much earlier than the end of the fifth century. Both sets of vertical lashes as in our head, on an Etruscan mirror, of still later date, in the Vatican (Gerhard, *Etruskische Spiegel* pl. 287, 3) and on an oinochoe of barbaric Campanian style in the British Museum (F. 526; Walters, *BM Catalogue of Vases* IV, 222). It must be admitted that the treatment of the eye affords no conclusive evidence for a date as high as 450. It should also be remembered that Dexamenos, with his passion for minute finish, might well insert details which the art of his time, with its eye on the whole rather than the parts, was tending to chasten away: further, that it is probable, from his interciliary hairiness, that the sitter had prodigiously thick eyelashes as well, which led the artist to pay special attention to that feature, and to produce a rendering of it which surprised his contemporaries and which he himself would not have thought credible before he took the portrait in hand.

For the present it seems best to date the stone in the third quarter of the fifth century.

The existence of strongly individualized portraits at so early a date in Greek history would not have seemed probable from the Cresilaan Perikles, but might have been divined from the heads of Charon on Attic white lekythoi and from the head of an elderly warrior on the krater, already mentioned, in New York (FR, II, 264, fig. 94A; Buschor, *Griechische Vasenmalerei* 183 [*ARV* 991, 61]). Another portrait head, not much later if at all than ours, on a gold ring in Berlin (F., pl. 10, 35 [Boardman, *GGFR* pl. 220]). A third, of much slighter workmanship, on a gold ring found in a tomb at Kertch and now in Oxford (*LHG* Pl. A, 29 [Boardman, *GGFR* pl. 670]): the objects supposed to have been found with it would allow a fifth-century date; but Professor Rostovtsev states that the apportionment of the objects from Kertch in Oxford rests on highly untrustworthy information. The rough scaraboid, no. 51 in the present collection, also seems to have the character of a portrait. Evans makes the attractive suggestion, that such portrait gems as ours, preserved as family treasures, may have sometimes been consulted by later Greek sculptors for their presentations of long-dead worthies.

This may be thought an appropriate place to put

together those stones which stand a fair chance of being by Dexamenos. The ascriptions have all been made by Furtwängler, with the exception of the Bowdoin stone; but not all his ascriptions have been included.

Chalcedony scaraboids:

Cambridge, from Greece. A seated woman and her maid. Signed. F., pl. 14, 1 [Boardman, *GGFR* pl. 467; *Cambridge* no. 53].

Petrograd, from Kertch. Flying heron. Signed. *LHG* Pl. B, 3; F., pl. 14, 4 [Boardman, *GGFR* pl. 468].

[Boston] Lewes House, probably from Greece. Heron. [Here, No. 66.]

[Boston] Lewes House, from Messenia. Horse. [Here No. 67.]

[Petrograd] from Kertch. Bolting horse. F., pl. 14, 15 [Boardman, *GGFR* pl. 475.]

Scaraboids of yellow jasper mottled with red:

Petrograd, from South Russia. Heron and grasshopper. Signed. Evans, *RA* 32, 1898, pl. 8, 3; F., III, 137 [Boardman, *GGFR* pl. 469].

[Boston] Lewes House, from Attica. Portrait head. Signed. [Here No. 50.]

[Paris, Cabinet des Médailles, de Luynes 200.] Griffin attacking horse. F., pl. 31, 3 [Boardman, *GGFR* pl. 579].

Rock-crystal scaraboid:

Mrs. Cockerell, from Greece. Seated woman playing the harp. F., pl. 14, 20 [now *BM Gems* no. 529; Boardman, *GGFR* pl. 472].

Sardonyx scarab:

British Museum. Flying goose. F., pl. 14, 2 [Boardman, *GGFR* pl. 489].

Barrel of banded agate:

Bowdoin College [491]. Heron. *LHG* Pl. B, 4: see no. 66.

[Boardman, *GGFR* pl. 466, and discussion, pp. 194-199, with other attributions, and in *Burlington*

Magazine 1969, 591-595. Beazley's list of attributions to the artist has stood the test of time. The similarity of the head to others, beardless, attributed to Dexamenos, opens the question whether this is a portrait rather than a characterization favoured by the artist. He once names his home, Chios, which could suggest that the gem was cut or commissioned away from home. M.-L. Vollenweider, adds a gem with a cricket, *Revue Numismatique* 16 (1974) 143-148.]

51. [23.596]

From the Boulton collection, 1911 (sale catalogue no. 4, 3).

Scaraboid. Cloudy sapphirine chalcedony, discoloured at the back. [14 x 10 x 6 mm]

Line border. A woman's head. Sakkos, plain necklace. Apparently a portrait, but the roughness of the work makes this rather uncertain. The mark near the neck in the imprint is due to damage in the stone.

Probably late fifth century.

52. [23.581]

Bought from Charles Newton-Robinson in 1901. F., pl. 12, 43.

Scarab. Sard. A chip has destroyed part of the eye and forehead, another the lower part of the head behind the ear. [21 x 15 x 9 mm]

The beetle careful. Slightly ridged towards the hump. No winglets or vertical border. A hatched border all round the thorax. The elytra separated by two lines which curve apart before they reach the border of the thorax; two short lines start from these near the top and meet at the thoracic border.

Head of a negress. She wears a headdress consisting of an ample kerchief wound tightly round the head turban-wise; the tip of the securing end visible; the frizzled hair showing in front and behind. Pendant earring in the general form of a lotus-bud terminating in a pellet. Necklace of pellets, representing beads, with a pendant in front, part of which is now missing. The Venus rings indicated.

Warm, rich modelling, recalling the decadrachms of Kimon.

End of the fifth century.

[Boardman, *GGFR* pl. 530, after Dexamenos.]

53. [23.594]

Bought from Lambros in 1902.

Gold ring with engraved bezel. The hoop nearly circular. [18 x 10 mm]

Short ground line. Erotostasia: Aphrodite weighing two Erotes; a third Eros at her feet. She stands with her right leg frontal and bent at the knee. Ionic chiton, low-necked, bordered above by two lines: dotted himation, in which the left arm is concealed.

The attitude of the minute Erotes on the scales is not easy to establish: the left-hand one seems to be sitting with his right shin frontal, his right thigh foreshortened away, and his left leg doubled and in profile: the right-hand one nearly frontal and on hands and knees, something like the Eros on an Attic pelike of the fourth century in Petrograd (FR, pl. 70 [*ARV* 1476, 1]). All three have the long thin wings which came into fashion in the third quarter of the fifth century.

A similar representation, on a Campanian hydria in London, has been published, after Mansell's photograph, by Studniczka (*JdI* 26, 140 [*LCS* 414, 538]). The vase-painting shows that the concealed arm of our Aphrodite is resting on her hip and holding up the gathered folds of her himation. So also on a gold ring from Syracuse in the British Museum with a female figure, shown to be Aphrodite by the dove which flies to her, and Eros kneeling at her feet, busy with her sandal [Boardman, *GGFR* pl. 716].

Another Erotostasia, on a krater in Athens, is mentioned by Nicole in his supplement to the *Catalogue des vases peints du Musée National d'Athènes* 246, no. 1105 [*ARV* 1456, 1].

Subjects like ours have been collected and discussed by Studniczka (*loc. cit.*, 139-41 [*LIMC* II, Aphrodite, 120; III, Eros, 883]).

Later fifth century.

[Boardman, *GGFR* pl. 666, the Waterton Group; for its shape, perhaps slightly earlier than Beazley suggests.]

54. [21.1204]

Bought in Athens, 1903.

Gold ring with engraved bezel. The hoop quadrangular. [28 x 22 mm]

A rider striking with a lance at a spotted fallow deer. The deer is also attacked by a hound; in front of the horse's head, a flying bird of prey. The rider wears a short chiton, girdled, and a chlamys: hair and chlamys blown back. The horse's mane rendered by short strokes on a ridge, with a longer forelock: the lines on the tail arranged V-wise.

The rider seems, from the breast, to be female: if so, the choice lies between an Amazon and a heroine, for Artemis does not ride on horseback. Stephani gives two instances of Artemis mounted on a horse (*Compte rendu* 1860, 45-9); but the figure on the Attic bell-krater is Selene or rather Nyx, not Artemis, and that on the coins of Pherai Hecate (Percy Gardner, *BM Coins of Thessaly* 47-9).

(*Margin*: Rostovtsev compares the silver bowl from Solokha and thinks fourth century; thinks the figure male - Alexander or another prince - and so the eagle.)

End of the fifth century.

[Boardman, *GGFR* pl. 680, Classical, Heavy Rings.]

55. [23.582]

Bought in Athens. F., pl. 65, 4.

Scaraboid. Chalcedony. [36 x 21 x 12 mm]

Ground line. A two-horse chariot wheeling round: the action is described by Furtwängler (F., II, 297). The charioteer is beardless, and has shortish hair with free striations: the lower part of his long chiton is blown back. The horses are of the same general type as those on the coins of Syracuse from the later fifth century onwards: small heads with hogged manes, powerful cylindrical bodies, solid hindquarters. Ours are somewhat longer in the barrel, possibly owing to the shape of the stone. Horses of similar breed on a chalcedony scaraboid in the Cabinet des Médailles (F., pl. 9, 54 [Boardman, *GGFR* pl. 479]).

The manes are rendered by short strokes set on a ridge and projecting a little beyond it.

The head of the hither horse is in perspective, the upper part being more prominent than the lower, and the orbit of the off eye visible. This foreshortening of the horse's head occurred in painting of the Miconian period, for it is found on the Amazon krater in Bologna (FR, pll. 75-6 [*ARV* 891]), but it was probably not used in sculptured relief till rather later. The Echelos relief in Athens has it (Kekulé, *65tes Winckelmannsprogramm* pl. 2), but not the Berlin relief of like subject (*ibid.*, pl. 1), which Kekulé considers somewhat earlier than the other and nearly contemporary with the Parthenon frieze. It appears on Syracusan and Tarentine coins towards the end of the century (Evans, *Horsemen of Tarentum* pl. 2, 6), and probably, less pronounced, on an earlier gem than ours, the scaraboid in Petrograd attributed to Dexamenos (F., pl. 14, 15 [Boardman, *GGFR* pl. 475]).

The hither horse has all four feet lifted and advanced, while the off horse has its hind legs thrown back with its hind feet on the ground. This motive occurs on decadrachms by Kimon and Euainetos (Evans, *Syracusan Medallions* pll. 8-9) and also on subsequent Syracusan issues, but not apparently earlier. This would suggest that our stone is not older than 413: considering its over-refinement, it might be a decade or two later.

[Boardman, *GGFR* pl. 561, after Dexamenos.]

56. [27.700]

Said to be from Asia Minor. Bought in London, 1898. F., pl. 64, 5.

Scaraboid. Amethystine chalcedony. [22 x 19 x 10 mm]

The child Eros seated on the ground playing with a goose, which lifts its wings. Below, a pair of knucklebones, with which he was playing until the goose came to look. Eros has short hair: an amulet is slung round his shoulder on a string. The sole of the right foot is visible, but the artist has not ventured to

foreshorten the lower leg away.

A somewhat similar Eros, more compactly rendered, on the sard signed by Phrygillos (F., pl. 14, 6 [Boardman, *GGFR* pl. 529]). Kindred studies of child life on a sard conoid in the British Museum (F., pl. 10, 30 [Boardman, *GGFR* pl. 848]), on a convex sard (F., pl. 61, 29), and on a sard pendant, from Athens, in the British Museum (F., pl. 13, 17 [Boardman, *GGFR* pl. 615]); on Attic toy oinochoai; and in the marble statuette of a girl with a duck, from Tanagra, in Berlin (Furtwängler, *Collection Sabouroff* I, pl. 35).

For the sole of the foot, compare the convex stone mentioned above, and a Theban coin with the infant Herakles (Gardner, *Types* pl. 7, 23).

Eros is playing with a goose on a bronze repoussé relief, of Greek work, in the British Museum (no. 308). (*Margin*: Also on a bronze relief in the Louvre, De Ridder, *Bronzes du Louvre* pl. 88, no. 1841.)

End of the fifth century or beginning of the fourth.

[Boardman, *GGFR* pl. 604, Fourth Century Common Style.]

57. [23.583]

Bought in Naples, 1899-1900. Roscher, *Lexikon s.v.* Palladion, 1330, fig. 5.

Scaraboid. Blood sard. [20 x 17 x 9 mm]

Palladion. In the field, a bucranium, denoting the sanctuary. Ionic chiton, Ionic himation from the right shoulder; helmet with three crests; plain necklace. The spear in false perspective; the device a wheel. A knotted and tasselled fillet hangs from the spear, and another from the inside of the shield. The base on which the image stands is circular or oval, and bears the letters AD, no doubt the beginning of the owner's name. A long lock of hair, rendered by pellets, escapes from the helmet on either side of the face. The knees are emphasized in the archaic manner. The figure is to be taken as striding towards the spectator, in the attitude of the Athena from Herculaneum, for part of the right leg disappears behind the left, and the hatched paryphe ends at the knees.

The figure is comparable with the Athene Polias of Pergamon on a Pergamene coin (*JdI* 3, 46; Roscher, *loc. cit.*, fig. 6). That it does not reproduce a real archaic statue is shown by the triple crest. It may or may not have been inspired by a particular archaistic image. (*Margin*: Cf. bronze statuette from Athens, *BM Cat. Bronzes* pl. 29, no. 191.)

An analogous image on a sard of the free period (F., pl. 13, 16).

Fourth century.

[Boardman, *GGFR* pl. 599, Fourth Century Fine Style.]

58. [27.703]

From Cythera. Bought in 1898. Formerly in the possession of Rhousopoulos.

Scaraboid. Smoky chalcedony. [28 x 24 x 12 mm]

Ground line. Diomed carrying off the Palladion. The youth steals forward with the little statue in his left hand and his sword in his right: a cloak on his left arm. The hair short with free striations.

A similar design on coins of Argos (Gardner, *Types* pl. 8, 35), which are placed in the first half of the fourth century: a date which will fit our stone. Another version of the same subject on a glass scaraboid (F., pl. 13, 8 [*AGDS* I, 1, no. 325]). A modification of our type is a favourite subject on Greco-Roman gems (see no. 125).

[Boardman, *GGFR* pl. 596, Fourth Century Fine Style. The subject was surprisingly popular on gems for a very long time, and has been exhaustively studied by J.-M. Moret, *Palladion*.]

59. [23.601]

Bought in Sicily, 1907.

Bronze ring with engraved bezel. The hoop slightly ridged inside. The surface corroded. [19 x 13 mm]

Ground line. Eros dog-bodied. The combination is centauric, that is to say, the creature has two pairs of shoulders; but the bestial part seems canine rather than equine: leonine is possible, for ancient representations of lions were often modelled on the dog (Schröder, text to Brunn-Bruckmann, nos. 641-5). That the upper part is a demi-Eros is shown by the wings in conjunction with the plump childish body.

The action is difficult to interpret owing to the condition of the ring: both arms are extended, the right hand apparently bent down with the fingers together as if sprinkling or the like: there seems to be a tall slender object under the left hand, but the corrosion makes certainty impossible.

A kindred figure on a convex sard formerly in the Evans collection (F., pl. 66, 3): here the creature holds a stick, and wears wrap, pilos, and sword: Furtwängler recalls the bearded daemon on a sard which was once in the Morrison collection (F., pl. 10, 52).

The canine Eros might seem to be a symbol of love without shame; but the attributes on the Evans stone make such an interpretation of ours improbable.

Fourth century.

[Boardman, *GGFR* pl. 812.]

60. [23.597]

Bought from W.T. Ready, who wrote as follows: 'The stone was bought at Damanhour, and the Arab from whom it was bought said that it was found at this same place a few days before my client's visit there.' Ready vouched for the 'absolute straightforwardness' of his client, whose collection was moreover mainly Egyptian; but not for the Arab. F., pl. 61, 34.

Scaraboid. Sapphirine chalcedony. A big chip missing on the left of the engraving. [39 x 23 x 11 mm]

Coitus. See Ovid's *Ars Amatoria* 3, 775-6. The man's hair is short, with free striations. The woman wears a necklace, rendered by pellets, a bracelet, a circular earring, thin shoes, and a kerchief wound round the head with the hair escaping at the forehead and at the crown. Pellets for the hair, except in front of the ears.

Kindred motives in the Hellenistic clay relief found at Pergamon and published by Siegfried Loeschke in *AthMitt* 37, pl. 30, 4; and on an incised bronze mirror, of fine early fourth-century style, in the museum at Boston [Res.08.32c] (Six, *JdI* 20, 165-6, figs. 5 and 6).

Compare also no. 63.

Earlier fourth century. Probably Ionian: for the style, compare such stones as F., pl. 63, 10 and pl. 14, 30.

[Boardman, *GGFR* pl. 552, after Dexamenos.]

61. [21.1205]

From the Tyszkiewicz collection. Tyszkiewicz said that he obtained it from Greece: it is further known that he had it from Rhousopoulos. *Collection Tyszkiewicz* pl. 24, 14; F., pl. 31, 11.

Sard, slightly convex. The lower part missing. [24 x 19 mm]

Hatched border. Ground line. Theseus and the sow of Krommyon. The young hero, naked, his petasos slung behind his neck, presses his left knee on the back of the sow, while his right foot is on the ground. He appears to be passing a noose about the sow; but the details of the action are obscure. It seems clear that Theseus has slipped the cord round his body like the end-man in a tug-of-war, and that he has also attached the upper part of the cord to, say, the trunk of a tree: for the cord is seen under the right arm, following the modelling of the body, and again, drawn taut, to the left of the petasos. The lower part of the cord is held in the right hand: below the sow's mane it presents the appearance of a fork with three prongs which cease at the bristles of the ear. Below this the cord no longer appears.

Short hair in demi-crescent-shaped curls.

(*Addendum*: Mr. Gow objects that Theseus would be cut in two if the rope were as described. For the motive, he compares Pisanello's Venator Intrepidus.)

Fourth century, hardly earlier than the middle.

[Boardman, *GGFR* pl. 539, after Dexamenos.]

62. [27.704]

From Granitza in Doris. Bought from Rhousopoulos in 1898. F., pl. 14, 26.
Discoloured sard, now yellow: slightly convex. [23 x 17 mm]

Ground line. Cassandra clasping the image of Athena. She has just reached the image. Her garment, snatched up in haste, has fallen on to her legs, and she is trying to fling it round her again. Her rippling hair falls loose down her back. A bracelet on the left wrist. The archaistic statue wears a tight chiton, and an Ionic himation passing over the left shoulder and peaked at its lower edge; gorgoneion on the breast, so faint as to be barely distinguishable; crested helmet with three locks of hair escaping under the neck-piece; bracelet; shield on the arm; spear passing behind the head instead of in front, the artist having been unwilling to let it cross the face. The statue stands on a base of two degrees, the upper one round or oval, surmounted by a thin slab which projects on either side of the upper degree.

A Cassandra with body half-bared like ours, but without the motive of the hand holding the drapery, on a Campanian hydria in the British Museum (*Archäologische Zeitung* 1848, pl. 14, 1 [*LCS* 433, 538]).

Fourth century.

[Boardman, *GGFR* pl. 591, Fourth Century, Fine Style.]

63. [23.598]

Bought in 1911 from a Greek who said it came from Tripolitza in Peloponnese.

Scaraboid. Discoloured chalcedony. Engraved on both sides. [23 x 18 x 9 mm]

On the flat: ground line; coitus. On the convex: an eagle standing on a thunderbolt.

The hair of the youth hatched, combed forward in front of the ear, and backwards behind it: the lower edge, back and front, pelleted. The woman's hair is worn in a long pigtail, ending in a pellet, down her back; the pigtail faintly striated, the rest of the hair faintly hatched, with a row of pellets on the forehead. She wears thin shoes.

The technique resembles that of Greco-Persian stones, and the pigtail points to the same quarter. There is a Greco-Persian stone with the same kind of subject in the Cabinet des Médailles (F., pl. 12, 15-16

[Boardman, *GGFR* pl. 906]).

The eagle of Zeus standing on the thunderbolt does not seem to occur before the time of Alexander. There is no reason to suppose that the engraving on the back of our stone is not by the same hand as that on the front, though such cases occur, for instance, in a chalcedony scaraboid in Oxford (Duffield Osborne, *Engraved Gems* pl. 8, 20 and pl. 22, 9 [*Oxford* I, no. 174]), where the Aphrodite on the flat is of late fourth-century work, while the heads of Isis and Sarapis on the convex are an addition of imperial date. The date of our stone will be the later part of the fourth century.

Scaraboids engraved on both sides are rare. One of the earliest, a fifth-century piece, is a sard in Berlin (*Berlin* pl. 4, 173 [*AGDS* II, no. 166]), in which the sides also are decorated. Another, of black stone, found in a fifth-century grave at Kertch, is described by Furtwängler (III, 128) and figured by Stephani (*Compte rendu* 1877, pl. 3, 7 and 8 [Boardman, *GGFR* pl. 461]): the convex subject is Persian. A sard from Macedonia, now in New York (F., pl. 12, 38-9, and II, 60 [*New York* no. 73; Boardman, *GGFR* pl. 549]), resembles ours in having a bird on one side and a feminine scene on the other, and the style suggests the same region. A chalcedony in Boston (Duffield Osborne, pl. 6, 19) is Greco-Persian [03.1013; Boardman, *GGFR* pl. 964]. A yellow stone, apparently a discoloured chalcedony, in the British Museum (*BM Gems* no. 296), is perhaps the earliest of all, but is hardly pure Greek.

[Boardman, *GGFR* pls. 862, 996. The face subject is essentially Greek Style, within the Greco-Persian series and the woman is decidedly Persian as *ibid.*, fig. 298, pl. 906; comparable scenes with Persian males in the series are managed differently, as *ibid.*, pl. 1065. The device on the convex back is probably better regarded as a Hellenistic addition, whether or not it indicates approval of mixed marriages, such as Alexander favoured.]

64. [23.584]

Stated by Froehner to have been found in Greece. From the Tyszkiewicz collection (sale catalogue, no. 264). *Collection Tyszkiewicz* pl. 24, 18; F., pl. 12, 6.

Scaraboid. Banded agate. [21 x 16 x 7 mm]

Ground line. A zebu walking. In front of him a hoop-shaped mark. Froehner interprets this as the Phoenician

symbol for the figure 10, but it is difficult to see the object of inscribing 10 on a gem: Mr. Hill points out that the mark resembles the Cypriote symbol for *ko*.

A bull of very similar build and style on a sard scaraboid from Greece in Berlin (F., pl. 8, 47 [Boardman, *GGFR* pl. 870; *AGDS* II, no. 193]). Furtwängler classes the zebu as Greco-Persian, and the bull as Greek: but no oriental traits are discernible in either. Even if the hoop were a Phoenician symbol, it would not constitute a stylistic orientalism. The vertical marking on the hind-quarter might be considered Persian, but it is an old Greek as well as a Persian convention.

A plunging bull of kindred though coarser style on a scaraboid in the possession of Comm. Fausto Benedetti.

The zebu engraved on the convex surface of a chalcedony scaraboid in the Wyndham Cook collection (*Burlington Catalogue* pl. 112, O 96; *Cook* pl. 3, 57) is said by Furtwängler to be the oldest representation of the animal in Greek art. Our stone, however, is distinctly earlier.

Second half of the fifth century.

[Boardman, *GGFR* pl. 871, Greek Style Greco-Persian.]

65. [27.694]

Bought about 1895. Formerly in the possession of a priest at Taranto. F., pl. 9, 59 [once Evans' Coll.].

Sliced barrel. Banded agate; for the shape and material, see no. 77. [28 x 12 x 10 mm]

A lioness crouching for the spring. The mouth open with teeth and tongue showing: the nose puckered. The mane in lanceolations; short lines, representing bristly hair, all along the back; a tuft behind the elbow.

Lionesses are maneless: Rossbach therefore suggests (in Pauly-Wissowa, *s.v. Gemmen* 1077) that what seems to be a mane in our lioness is only the fur ruffled in anger. (*Margin*: A bronze lioness with mane from Corfu in London, BM 232, *Select Bronzes* pl. 4, 2.) But if the artist had intended to represent this, he would have chosen some other rendering: what we see is indistinguishable from a mane, and indeed, but for the dugs, no one would suppose the animal to be female. The artist had probably never seen the animal he depicts: his lion is essentially the old heraldic lion of the archaic stones nos. 22 and 34, uncorrupted by studies from nature. A lioness with a mane like ours on a scaraboid of lapis lazuli formerly in the Boulton collection.

The short bristle-lines along the back have already been remarked in the archaic lions from Cyprus, nos. 22 and 34. They also appear on a scarab from Pergamon (F., pl. 8, 43 [Boardman, *Archaic* no. 427]), the scarab F., pl. 10, 59 [Boardman, *Archaic* no. 414], a scarab from South Italy in the Cabinet des Médailles (*Collection Pauvert de la Chapelle* pl. 5, 52 [Boardman, *Archaic* no. 458]), a scaraboid from Cyprus in the British Museum (*BM Finger Rings* pl. 8, 295 [Boardman, *Archaic* no. 436]), a scarab from Gela in the collection of Sir Arthur Evans (F., pl. 6, 51 [Boardman, *Archaic* no. 407]), and a small scarab which was formerly in the Roger de Sivry collection. Further, on coins of Cyzicus (Babelon, *Traité* pl. 176, 23), of Amathus (*BM Coins of Cyprus* pll. 1 and 18), of Kition (Babelon, *Traité* pl. 130, 25), and of Akanthos (Gardner, *Types* pl. 3, 13); also in the griffin on certain coins of Teos (*BM Coins of Ionia* pl. 30, 7); on an Etruscan mirror, of early Ionian style, in the Cabinet des Médailles (Gerhard, *Etruskische Spiegel* pl. 292), and on an Etrusco-Ionian amphora, of the so-called Pontic style, at Corneto (phot. Moscioni, 8646).

From the instances given, the short bristle-lines would seem to be an Ionian characteristic and a mark of comparatively early date: in sculpture, however, the back-mane has a wider extension both in time and in locality.

(*Addendum*: Another lion with bristly back on a chalcedony scaraboid from Larnaca in the British Museum [Boardman, *Archaic* no. 436].

Maned lionesses. Mr. A.S.F. Gow writes:

> The artist of the button [our no. 3] knows more about lionesses than the artist of the sliced barrel [our no. 65], for he provides them with abdominal and not inguinal mammae, yet his lioness too is maned. I inquire therefore whether the mane may not have been regarded as common to the sexes. For instance Aristotle, *H.A.* II, 1 (498b.27), seems to class the lion as a maned animal without reference to sex. I add also that it is conceivable that lionesses were maned in Greece. Lions tend to lose their manes in

exceptionally hot districts, and Selous believes them to have been a northern animal which moved southward; so that when they extended farther north they were certainly hairier (as at the Zoological Gardens in London) and *may* all have had manes. See F.C. Selous, *African Nature Notes* 80ff.

The upshot is, it seems, that if there are unmaned lionesses in Greek art all this is perhaps of no importance. If there are not, a suspension of judgment would perhaps be wiser. In any case the barrel artist ought not to be rated too much, for apparently Aristotle makes worse mistakes (for instance, gives them two mammae), and seems never to have seen one (*De partibus animalium* tr. Ogle, 236), though they existed in Thrace in the fourth century at least. A different line of argument in a letter herewith from a zoologist.

The zoologist (Mr. M.D. Hill) writes: 'I can find no allusion to maned lionesses in any of the books I have looked at. The only suggestion I can make is that in the hotter parts of Africa lions often develop only the scrubbiest of manes, and thus the idea may have arisen that they were really lionesses and not lions at all. The confusion is not at all impossible as the genitalia are inconspicuous in both sexes as often as not.'

Second half of the fifth century.

[Boardman, *GGFR* pl. 520. Another feature of the eastern (Persian or Indian) lion is the belly hair, shown in eastern art, and so often in Greek, but which is absent on the larger African lion.]

66. [21.1206]

Bought in Athens, 1900. F., III, 446, fig. 228; Bulle, *Neue Jahrbücher* 1900, pl. 1, 20.

Scaraboid. Chalcedony.

Line border. Ground line. A heron standing on one leg. Assigned to Dexamenos, with great plausibility, by Furtwängler, on account of its resemblance to the heron stones with his signature in Petrograd: the scaraboid from South Russia, of yellow jasper mottled with red (Evans, *RA* 32, 1898, pl. 8, 3, reversed, and F.,

III, 137 [Boardman, *GGFR* pl. 469]); and the chalcedony scaraboid from Kertch (Evans, *loc. cit.*, pl. 8, 1, and F., pl. 14, 4 [Boardman, *GGFR* pl. 468]).

A replica of our heron, less fine, on a barrel, not sliced, of banded agate, presented to Bowdoin College by Mr. Warren (*LHG* Pl. B, 4). The Bowdoin heron might be a slighter work by the artist of ours, although the joints of the legs are not rendered in the same way. The same design, by different hands, on a sliced barrel of banded agate, from Athens, in Berlin (F., pl. 14, 11 [*AGDS* II, no. 181]), and on a sliced cylinder of the same material in Boston [98.721], which likewise came from Greece (F., pl. 9, 29 [Boardman, *GGFR* pl. 518]); also on two rougher scaraboids, one of chalcedony, from the Peloponnese, in Berlin (F., pl. 14, 17 [*AGDS* II, no. 180]), the other, of mottled jasper, in the Southesk collection (*LHG* Pl. A, 27; *Southesk* pl. 2, B 5 [Boardman, *GGFR* pl. 555]).

All these birds have been taken here for herons, though some of them have been called cranes or even storks. Ours and the Bowdoin bird are beyond doubt herons: the Boston bird and its Berlin companion have no aigrette on the head and no plume on the breast: the Southesk bird and its fellow in Berlin have the aigrette, but are longer in the neck than the others. The aigrette is not essential for an *erodios*: Dionysius says (*de avibus* ii, 18, quoted by D'Arcy Thomson, *Glossary of Greek Birds s.v.*): 'there are thousands of types...some have no lock (*plokamos*) on the head, on others some sort of crest (*bostruchos*) rises up'.

The heron, and birds which may be mistaken for it, are frequently found on gems of the later fifth and the fourth centuries. A heron, with aigrette, preening itself, on a fragmentary scaraboid of rock-crystal in Oxford [*Oxford* no. 106]: a chalcedony scaraboid of the same type in Petrograd (*Antiquités du Bosphore cimmérien* pl. 12A, 8): a standing heron or crane, with aigrette, on a sliced barrel of banded agate, in Mr. Warren's possession (*LHG* Pl. B, 2 [Boardman, *GGFR* pl. 518]); the uncommon elongation of the stone, not to speak of its style, would seem to place it in the fourth century. To the same period belongs the chalcedony scaraboid from the Forman and Newton-Robinson collections, which is now in Munich (*Burlington Catalogue* pl. 110, O 83; *Newton-Robinson Catalogue* pl. 1, 15; *Münchener Jahrbuch* 5, pl. B, 7 [Boardman, *GGFR* pl. 554]) with a bird drawing a bow: possibly a crane rather than a heron, the aigrette being very short. Probably somewhat earlier, a chalcedony scaraboid, from Cameiros, in the British Museum (F., pl. 11, 30 [Boardman, *GGFR* pl. 557]), with a bird feeding: a red-deer's antler is substituted for the aigrette to fill the

space above the head: the bird may well be a heron. Three stones may perhaps be grouped together: the sard scaraboid from Kastoria in Macedonia, now in New York (F., pl. 12, 38-9, and II, 60 [Boardman, *GGFR* pl. 549]); the pink quartz in Munich (*Münchener Jahrbuch* 4, pl. 2, 14 [*AGDS* I.1, no. 270]); and the chalcedony scaraboid, from Ithome, in Boston ([13.242] F., pl. 61, 39 [Boardman, *GGFR* pl. 492]). There remain the sard scarab in the Cabinet des Médailles (F., pl. 12, 46: perhaps a crane), the chalcedony cube in the Wyndham Cook collection (*Burlington Catalogue* pl. 112, O 95; *Cook* pl. 3, 61), and a rectangular stone, of banded agate, in New York [*New York* no. 124].

Rossbach thinks that the popularity of the crane with gem-engravers is due to its usefulness as a weather prophet (in Pauly-Wissowa, *s.v. Gemmen* 1074). The heron was similarly esteemed (Keller, *Die antike Tierwelt* II, 205-6). Moreover, it was sacred to Aphrodite (Collignon, *RA* 1875, 2). But the real reason for the appearance of the heron and similar birds is that they were domestic pets, cherished by the engraver's patrons, and admired and studied by the engraver. That they should be rare on gems before the middle of the fifth century, may be due to the increasing interest in woman and woman's life, which is a feature of that and the subsequent period (see the well-chosen remarks of Pottier, *Catalogue des Vases du Louvre* 1041-6). The birds were naturally the woman's familiars rather than the man's, since she stayed at home; and it is in scenes from the home life of women that they chiefly occur on vases. So, for example, on the Lecce pelike with Polyneikes offering the necklace to Eriphyle (FR, pl. 66 [*ARV* 629, 23]: for the artist, see Beazley, *VA* 155), where the crane standing between the two figures serves to show that it is in or near the lady's private quarters that the action takes place. So on the white alabastron, in the British Museum, with the signature of the manufacturer Pasiades (*JHS* 7, pl. 81; Perrot, *Histoire de l'Art* X, pl. 19 [*ARV* 98, 1]). The representation is in the manner of the Euergides painter (*JHS* 33, 347-55) and belongs to the later part of the sixth century, and is therefore an early specimen, painted on a woman's scent-bottle, of those scenes from the home life of women which became much commoner in later times. The bird standing between the two women seems to be a heron: Perrot, following Murray, is not of this opinion: 'a bird recognizable, by the aigrette on its head, as a crane.' Similarly in gems: on a chalcedony scaraboid, of the later fifth century, in the British Museum (F., pl. 13, 20 [Boardman, *GGFR* pl. 482]), a woman, resting on a warm day, is stroking the beak of a bird, which from its aigrette would seem to be a heron, but from its untidy appearance a crane;

on a stone in Petrograd (*Compte rendu* 1862, pl. 1, 12), a naked woman is standing at a laver caressing a long-legged bird; on a mottled jasper scaraboid of somewhat later style, in the Museum at Syracuse, a naked woman is offering an insect to a heron [Boardman, *GGFR* pl. 547], and on a sard cylinder, of the later fourth century, in Oxford, a woman is engaged with a bird of the same sort [*ibid.*, pl. 640; *Oxford* no. 123].

The popularity of the heron, in real life, may or may not have been partly due to its value as a weather prophet or as an associate of Aphrodite: its popularity in art is not due to either of these functions, but to its popularity in real life.

Third quarter of the fifth century.

[Boardman, *GGFR* pl. 490, after Dexamenos.]

67. [27.698]

Bought in 1895 from Hartwig. Formerly in the Postolakka collection at Athens, according to Imhoof-Blumer. Hartwig had it from Rhousopoulos, who said that it came from Messenia. Imhoof-Blumer and Keller, *Tier- und Pflanzenbilder* pl. 16, 37; F., pl. 14, 5, pl. 9, 31, and, enlarged, pl. 51, 9; Bulle, *Neue Jahrbücher* 1900, pl. 1, 21.

Scaraboid, cut. Smoky chalcedony. Chipped about the head. [20 x 16 mm]

Hatched border. A thin hatched band for the ground line. A race-horse walking, with broken reins. Both off-legs advanced in a correct walking attitude. Creases on the breast, on the elbow, behind the elbow, and near the top of the right fore-leg. The ribs very faintly indicated. The mane striated, the ends of the striations being on the flat surface of the stone: longer on the shoulder than on the neck. The tail long, and rendered by long undulating lines. Veins indicated on the belly and the hind-legs. The eye large: the head nervous. The hind-quarters extraordinarily delicate. A high-bred riding horse and not a chariot racer. English judges pronounce it herring-gutted and rather long in the back.

Inscription, in large letters, above, POTA; below, NEA. The omicron a trifle smaller than the rest of the letters. The first stroke of the pi curves slightly inwards. The first and third strokes of pi and nu are not parallel. The cross-bar of the tau comparatively short.

The nu oblique; the first stroke the longest. The alphas broad, especially the second; the bar horizontal. The cross-strokes of the epsilon at right angles to the vertical stroke, which projects a little above them. The inscription would seem to be the genitive of the owner's name, but the name Potaneas is unexampled.

Furtwängler compares the horses on two other scaraboids. One of the two was found at Kertch and is now in Petrograd (F., pl. 14, 15 [Boardman, *GGFR* pl. 475]): the horse has flung his rider and is bolting towards the post; the material is the same yellow jasper, mottled with red, which Dexamenos used for two of his four signed stones (see no. 50). To judge from the reproduction, the horse is very like ours and might be by the same hand.

The other scaraboid, of chalcedony, is in the Cabinet des Médailles (F., pl. 31, 3 [Boardman, *GGFR* pl. 579]), and represents a horse attacked by a griffin. Here also the resemblance is great, and the stone is quite possibly by the same artist as ours.

Furtwängler considers that our stone 'if not by Dexamenos, is by a greater master of the same time and group'. The lettering would not conflict with the ascription to Dexamenos.

Hatched ground lines are uncommon: earlier, on coins of Kelenderis (*BM Coins of Lycaonia, Isauria, and Cilicia* pl. 9, 2 and 3).

Second half, and perhaps third quarter, of the fifth century.

[Boardman, *GGFR* pl. 473, around Dexamenos.]

68. [27.693]

Bought in Athens, 1901.

Scaraboid. Chalcedony, bleached. [16 x 13 x 8 mm]

Hatched border. A hazel nut.

Realistic representations of vegetable life are known to be extremely rare in antiquity. A nature study so happy and so unaffected is most readily intelligible in a period not very far removed from that of Dexamenos.

Probably later fifth century.

69. [27.768]

Scaraboid. Streaked sard. [16 mm]

Line border. A mule (*Margin*: Donkey.) walking. Short- strokes for the mane and the hair on the tail.

Later fifth century.

[Boardman, *GGFR* pl. 463, Early Classical.]

70. [27.692]

Bought in Athens, 1911.

Scaraboid. Chalcedony. [16 x 12 x 7 mm]

Hatched border. Ground line; the surface of the exergue slopes in towards the border. A wild sow with two young. The mane terminates on the shoulder with a regular curve; a row of short bristles follows; then the long bristles of the rump. This rendering of the mane and back-bristles may be considered a development of that which Furtwängler maintained to be characteristically Ionian (*Goldfund von Vettersfelde* 23-4), but which also occurs on Attic vases, for instance, on an archaic red-figured cup in the Louvre (Hartwig, *Meisterschalen* pl. 3, 2 [*ARV* 117, 7]). A treatment resembling that on our stone, but with the termination of the rump-bristles not convex to the short hairs but concave in the earlier manner, on the Theseus cup by Douris in the British Museum: this detail is not given correctly in Gerhard, *Auserlesene Vasenbilder* pl. 234: see Mansell's photograph 617 [*ARV* 431,47].

A sard scarab with the same subject, of rather earlier style, is figured in F., pl. 7, 63 [Boardman, *Archaic* no. 541]: in his history (III, 105) Furtwängler mentions other wild sows, mostly earlier than ours.

Second half of the fifth century.

[Boardman, *Archaic* no. 554. A classical reprise of a very common late archaic subject for gems, probably an intimation of wealth and fertility.]

71. [27.696]

Bought from W.T. Ready in 1913.

Cylinder. Chalcedony. [20 x 11 mm]

A boar walking. The hair between mane and rump-bristles forms a thick striated roll.

Somewhat similar, but probably earlier, a wild sow on a sard scarab in the Wyndham Cook collection (F., pl. 63, 6; *Cook* pl. 2, 29 [Boardman, *Archaic* no. 549]): less like, a boar on a scaraboid of discoloured chalcedony in the Museum at Lecce (*LHG* Pl. B, 1).

Other stones with representations of boars are mentioned by Furtwängler: add the sardonyx scarab figured by Marshall, *BM Finger Rings* pl. 10, 346, a Greek stone set in a much later Etruscan ring; and a sardonyx scarab of similar style in Oxford [Boardman, *Archaic* nos. 537-8; *Oxford* no. 81].

Late fifth century.

[Boardman, *GGFR* pl. 914, Greco-Persian Group of the Leaping Lions; another boar on a cylinder is *Oxford* no. 179.]

72. [21.1207]

Bought from W.T. Ready in 1899.

Scaraboid, cut. Chalcedony. [18 x 14 x 6 mm]

Hatched border. Ground line. A goat walking. Hair indicated on breast and buttocks.

Almost contemporary, the walking goat on a rock-crystal scaraboid in the British Museum (*LHG* Pl. A, 28; *Collection d'un archéologue explorateur* pl. 2, 28). Later and broader in treatment, a grandly free and spirited goat on another scaraboid of the same material in the same collection (*LHG* Pl. B, 6 [*BM Gems* no. 591]). The goats on the coins of Ainos (*Nomisma* 4, pll. 4-5) are of stouter build.

Later fifth century.

73. [21.1208]

Bought in Athens about 1912.

Scaraboid. Agate. [20 x 15 x 9 mm]

Ground line. A goat standing. In the field, P , no doubt the initial letter of the owner's name. The goat is of heavier build than in no. 72, and is probably of somewhat later date.

Late fifth century.

74. [21.1209]

Formerly in the Boulton collection (part of no. 42 in the sale catalogue), but not bought till 1917.

Sard, no doubt a cut scaraboid. [22 x 17 mm]

Ground line. A fallow deer browsing.

A replica on a cut scaraboid of pale brown sard in Berlin (F., pl. 14, 13 [*AGDS* II, no. 172]): closely similar, a pale golden sard in Boston [99.357; Boardman, *GGFR* pl. 565], formerly in the Morrison collection (*LHG* Pl. A, 30): similar also, but rougher, a sapphirine chalcedony which was at one time in the Athenian market (*LHG* Pl. B, 8); a stone which belonged to Dr. Arndt in 1905 [tabloid; Boardman, *GGFR* 432, no. 68]; both presumably scaraboids: a discoloured scaraboid in Oxford [*Oxford* no. 197]; and a discoloured stone in Petrograd (*Compte rendu* 1865, pl. 3, 28). See also no. 75 in the present collection.

Late fifth century.

[Boardman, *GGFR* pl. 566, after Dexamenos.]

75. [21.1210]

Bought from a Greek in 1909.

Scaraboid. Rock-crystal. [24 x 19 x 10 mm]

Ground line, mostly covered by the representation of the terrain. The lower part of the stone has been routed out to produce the appearance of a grassy lawn. A fallow deer browsing: he is about to nibble one of the plants which grow round him.

See no. 74: the present deer is shorter in the body.

For the terrain concealing most of the ground line, compare the chalcedony scaraboid, from Greece, in

Boston [95.81], with a griffin attacking a fallow deer (F., pl. 31, 4 [Boardman, *GGFR* pl. 511]).

Late fifth century.

[Boardman, *GGFR* pl. 564, after Dexamenos.]

76. [21.1211]

Sent from Constantinople according to Froehner. From the Tyszkiewicz collection (sale catalogue no. 269).

Scaraboid. Black agate streaked with grey. [17 x 14 x 7 mm]

Line border. A bull-calf. His head is lowered and his tail a little raised as if he were slightly aggressive.

Calves of rougher workmanship, and in different attitudes, on chalcedony scaraboids in Lecce, in Bowdoin College (*LHG* Pl. B, 5), and in Berlin (F., pl. 11, 16 [*AGDS* II, no. 201; Boardman, *GGFR* pl. 913]).

Late fifth century.

[Boardman, *GGFR* pl. 504, around Dexamenos.]

77. [27.699]

Bought in 1902.

Sliced barrel. Banded agate, black streaked with grey. [17 x 9 x 7 mm]

A sandal seen from above. The subject possibly suggested by the shape of the stone.

A similar sandal, with an insect beside it, on a chalcedony scaraboid which was once in German private hands.

The vogue of the sliced barrel in Greek lands seems to have been a brief one: most of the Greek examples must be dated to the second half of the fifth century: the latest are probably not much older than the early years of the fourth. The stone given in *LHG* Pl. B, 2 [Boardman, *GGFR* pl. 519] stands apart from other sliced barrels by reason of its elongated shape. The earliest sliced barrel appears to be Berlin 331 (F., pl.

10, 32 [Boardman, *Archaic* no. 187]), which is still archaic. Far the commonest material is banded agate: other stones are very rare [Boardman, *GGFR* 409-410]. The Greek eye must have considered the material appropriate to the shape.

[Boardman, *GGFR* pl. 524 and pp. 199-200 on sliced barrels; another sandal gem, in Nicosia, is *ibid.*, pl. 513.]

78. [27.702]

Bought in 1911.

Scaraboid. Sard. [24 x 18 x 8 mm]

Hatched border. A coiled snake raising its head. The mouth closed with the tongue extended.

Later fifth, or fourth century.

[Boardman, *GGFR* pl. 503, around Dexamenos.]

79. [23.585]

Bought in Ruvo, 1898-9. This is the stone mentioned by Evans, *Syracusan Medallions* 120, n. 86, and after him by Sambon in *Corolla Numismatica* 279.

Scaraboid, cut. Sapphirine chalcedony. [29 x 19 x 5 mm]

Ground line. A plunging bull. The off fore-leg raised. The head in perspective, with the off ear and the orbit of the off eye showing.

A similar bull on a scaraboid of banded chalcedony in the Wyndham Cook collection (*LHG* Pl. A, 26; *Burlington Catalogue* pl. 110, M 122; *Cook* pl. 3, 62); a similar also on a scaraboid in Petrograd (*Compte rendu* 1860, pl. 4, 9), and on a stone, presumably a scaraboid, published by Cades. Of different style, a scaraboid of mottled chalcedony in Berlin (F., pl. 11, 31 [*AGDS* II, no. 171]) and the stone compared with no. 64. A pseudo-scarab with this bull on it in Petrograd (*Compte rendu* 1870-1, pl. 6, 21): a zebu in the same position on the convex side of a chalcedony

scaraboid in the Wyndham Cook collection (*Cook* pl. 3, 57). There are several Greco-Roman examples, the finest the chalcedony in the Cabinet des Médailles (F., pl. 45, 11). This bull is very common on Greek coins from the later part of the fifth century onwards.

The three-quartered head is already found in the bull on one of the metopes from the Temple of Zeus at Olympia (*Olympia* III, pl. 36).

About 400.

[Boardman, *GGFR* pl. 498, around Dexamenos.]

80. [21.1212]

From Sicily according to Froehner. Formerly in the Tyszkiewicz collection (sale catalogue no. 263). *Collection Tyszkiewicz* pl. 24, 16; F., pl. 9, 60.

Scaraboid. Yellow jasper mottled with chalcedony. [24 x 19 x 9 mm]

A pantheress crouching for an upward spring. The head raised, the mouth open with the tongue and the upper front teeth showing: the claws bared. The eye indicated by a pellet.

Froehner calls the animal a lioness; Furtwängler calls it a lioness in his description (II, 48), but a pantheress in his history (III, 145).

In style, our pantheress resembles the goat on a rock-crystal scaraboid from Lecce in the British Museum (*LHG* Pl. B, 6 [*BM Gems* no. 591]) and the walking bull on a rock-crystal scaraboid in the same collection (F., pl. 11, 32 [*BM Gems* no. 543]).

(*Addendum*: Mr. Gow considers the hind quarters wrong for a spring and supposes the animal to be stretching itself.

If the animal were canine we might compare the dog 'in a humble and affectionate frame of mind' shown in fig. 6 of Darwin's *Expression of the Emotions*.)

Late fifth century, or early fourth.

[Boardman, *GGFR* pl. 586, Plain Western Gems.]

81. [23.586]

Found in Egypt according to Froehner. Formerly in the Tyszkiewicz (sale catalogue no. 284) and Evans collections. *Collection Tyszkiewicz* pl. 24, 3; F., pl. 9, 28.

Scaraboid. Hyacinthine sard. The side low. [17 x 13 x 6 mm]

Carrier pigeon.

A dove of the same period on a convex sard, set in a gold ring, from Beyrut, in the British Museum (*BM Finger Rings* pl. 10, no. 350 [Boardman, *GGFR* pl. 625]): Marshall compares it with coins of Paphos. A flying dove on a rock-crystal scaraboid formerly in the Tyszkiewicz collection (sale catalogue no. 257) and now in Boston [98.723]. (*Margin*: Carrier pigeons in antiquity, J. Moeller, *BPW* 1905, 1436; Diels, *Antike Technik* 76.)

Earlier fourth century.

[Boardman, *GGFR* 409, no. 88, around Dexamenos. The pigeon is probably carrying a fillet, not a scroll or letter; there is a replica of this now in Malibu (81.AN.76.40) - J. Boardman, *Intaglios and Rings* (1975) no. 40, and one with the fillet unrolled in the Merz Collection in Switzerland, *ibid.*, fig. 8.]

82. [27.770]

Given by Mrs. John Marshall.

Silver ring with engraved bezel. The hoop quadrangular. [16 x 11 mm]

Ground line. The Nemean lion: a lion, mouth open, at bay, with a club above him. Part of the mane forms a ruff, rendered by a series of short thick close-set arcs: the rest is in long flame-like tufts. The looser skin on the belly is grooved off from the rest of the body. Short bristling hairs on the rump near the tail. The ribs pronounced.

Somewhat similar lions on fourth-century coins of Hyele and of Sicyon.

A couched lion, with a club above him, on an onyx, set in a ring, published in the *Dactyliotheca* of Abraham Gorlaeus (II, no. 115), where Gronovius compares

coins of Macedon, Messana, and Syracuse: the coins of Messana are bronze issues dated 357-288 (Head, *Historia Numorum* 155), those of Syracuse Agathoclean bronze dated 310-304 (*ibid.*, 182; Head, *Numismatic Chronicle* 1874, pl. 9, 3): the Macedonian coin is no doubt one of Archelaos I (413-399) with a lion's head and a club (Head, *Historia Numorum* 221).

Fourth century.

[Boardman, *GGFR* pl. 692, Classical Heavy Rings.]

83. [27.701]

Bought in Sicily, 1901.

Gold ring with engraved bezel. The hoop quadrangular. [20 x 12 mm]

A poor old donkey. His body is emaciated (with ribs, shoulder-blade, hips, and vertebrae protruding); except his belly, which is inflated, with swollen veins. The mane straggling and perhaps mangy: a sore on the neck. A study of decrepitude difficult to parallel among Greek representations of animals.

Earlier fourth century.

[Boardman, *GGFR* pl. 669, Classical Heavy Rings.]

84. [27.769]

Bought in Athens, 1910.

Scaraboid. Mottled jasper, red, black, and yellowish brown. [23 x 18 x 9 mm]

Ground line, swelling towards the middle. A tripod with a spiked cover on it: the lateral rings foreshortened: leonine feet.

A rather earlier scaraboid with a tripod, from Tanagra, in Berlin (Furtwängler, *Berlin* pl. 6, no. 306).

For the style, perhaps compare the scaraboid, of dark red jasper mottled with chalcedony, in Berlin (*Berlin* pl. 6, 320 [*AGDS* II, no. 185]), which is shown to be of the fourth century by the shape of the amphora represented.

Fourth century.
[Boardman, *GGFR* fig. 215, Fourth Century Common Style.]

85. [27.771]

Said to be from Athens. Formerly in the Evans collection. Bought in 1911.

Scaraboid. Bronze. [27 x 15 x 6 mm]

A griffin sitting on a club: in front of the griffin, starting from its forelegs, a horse's head, bridled. The griffin is of uncommonly massive build: the mouth open: the ears very slightly advanced: a sharp spiny comb on the neck: no ruff and no horn: the beak short: two folds on the neck below the beak.

A griffin with a club below its feet is found on a group of Abderite coins, both copper and silver (*Die antiken Münzen Nord-Griechenlands* II, *Thrakien* 33-4); here, however, the griffin is not seated as in our scaraboid, but either lying down or crouching to spring: this device is accompanied by the name or monogram of the magistrate, and sometimes by his symbol. A seated griffin is found on a copper coin of the period, but without the club (*Nomisma* 3, pl. 3, 12), and is very common on earlier coins of Abdera, often with a symbol added; and although the griffin usually has one paw raised, in one coin he has all four on the ground (*ibid.*, pl. 2, 40). The Abderite griffins tend to be massive like ours, and the comb is similarly short. The club coins belong to the latest group in the continuous series of Abderite issues. The continuous series is generally supposed to have ceased with the absorption of Abdera into the Macedonian Empire about 350 BC: the club coins would therefore date from the first half of the fourth century (Head, *Historia Numorum* 255-6; von Fritze, *Die autonomen Münzen von Abdera* in *Nomisma* 3, 22 and 25-6). Strack, however, believes that Philip II must have granted Abdera the privilege of continuing to issue coinage, and would therefore date the coins in question between 352 and about 323 (*Die antiken Münzen Nord-Griechenlands loc. cit.*). He adduces two arguments: first, that the standard on which the silver is struck is the Macedonian standard, slightly lowered in the interest of the royal mint; and, secondly, that the club is the badge of the Heraclid kings of Macedon, long employed on their own coins and now placed as a sign of suzerainty on those of a subject city. The fact on which the first argument is based must be left to the numismatist: with regard to the second, the suggestion that the club comes from Macedon is an attractive one; and if it is admitted, the inference as to date seems valid.

There are other instances of the ground line being replaced by a club, but only in Heraclean representations; for instance, on a coin of Tarsos, with Herakles and the lion (Evans, *Syracusan Medallions* pl. 5, 6), on a late Etruscan gem with Herakles shooting the birds (F., pl. 18, 69), and on an Italiote gem of Hellenistic style with Herakles pestered by Eros (F., pl. 27, 8). But the griffin has no connexion with Herakles. It can hardly therefore be a mere coincidence that the same design occurs on our scaraboid and on the club coins of Abdera: our scaraboid must be related in some way to the coins; dependent on them, for in the coins the club is explicable; and contemporary with them. The horse's head remains to be explained: it corresponds to the magistrate's symbol on Abderite coins, although this actual device does not occur on any of them.

It is conceivable that the scaraboid was the official or semi-official seal of an Abderite magistrate: but to assert this would be unwise, for here as elsewhere individual caprice must be taken into account. Whatever the exact explanation may be, it seems probable that the person who ordered the seal had the coinage, if no particular coin, of Abdera in his mind.

(*Addendum*: Mr. Gow writes: 'The material helps, I think. A magistrate wanting a seal which he could only use during his term of office might well have it of bronze and not of more costly and durable material.')

It must be admitted that the griffin is not of characteristic fourth-century type: if it is later than the fifth century, it must be archaistic.

A seated griffin, with all four paws on the ground, is engraved on a scaraboid which was at one time in German private hands.

Bronze scaraboids are rare: another in Berlin (Furtwängler, *Berlin* pl. 4, no. 146).

[Boardman, *GGFR* pl. 583, after Dexamenos. It is possible that the 'club' is simply a monumentalized base line, such as may also be seen on coins of Abdera.]

Etruscan: Free Style, and Italiote

86. [27.722]

Sent from Constantinople according to Froehner. From the Tyszkiewicz collection (sale catalogue no. 256). F., pl. 61, 20.

Scarab. Sard, translucent. [19 x 12 x 10 mm]

The beetle rather careless. Ridged, especially towards the rump. No winglets or vertical border. A hatched border right round the thorax. Between the elytra a line, with two short lines starting from it near the top and forming a triangle with the thoracic border.

Hatched border. Herakles and the lion. Herakles, naked, bearded, his left foot raised, his right tiptoe, has folded his arms round the lion's throat. The lion has one of his hind-legs raised with the paw pressing against Herakles' shin: his mouth is open with the teeth showing: his nose puckered: his mane rendered by short rippling lines, his shoulder by two quasi-circles each enclosing a boss, the whole resembling two units of a cable-pattern. The hair of Herakles short and pelleted, the beard in short thick strokes.

Similar though not identical designs on an Etruscan scarab (F., pl. 17, 57 [Zazoff, no. 665]), and on three Greco-Phoenician scarabs, two from Iviza (*LHG* Pl. A, 11-12; Vives, *La Necrópoli de Ibiza* pl. 22, 24; and pl. 23, 15 = Perez Cabrero, *Ibiza Arqueológica* 39, fig. 28 [Boardman, *Ibiza* nos. 232, 199]), and one, in Cagliari, from Sardinia (F., pl. 15, 75).

Similar also a bronze ornament in Berlin (Furtwängler,

Collection Sabouroff pl. 148).

Furtwängler has compared our Herakles and the lion with the Herakles and the boar on a sard scarab, found at Chiusi, in the British Museum (*LHG* Pl. A, 25; F., pl. 18, 30 [Zazoff, no. 115]), a brilliant comparison, for the style of the engraving is the same in every respect and the stones are very likely by one hand. The beetles also are similar, though the London beetle is more careful than the other and has the plates and clypeus hatched and three lines instead of one between the elytra: both lack winglets and vertical border: both have flat backs and a ridge towards the rump: in both the hatched border passes right round the thorax, and a short straight line runs to the thoracic border on either side of the elytric division: moreover, the elongation of the engraved side is common to both.

The absence of winglets and vertical border in large and careful scarabs like these would point to a non-Etruscan origin: perhaps also the presumed provenance of our stone. Moreover, the treatment of the lion's shoulder has no parallel in Etruscan work: it is Persian, as Furtwängler points out, and, outside of Oriental monuments (for example, Perrot and Chipiez, *Histoire de l'Art* V, 834), is confined to the Eastern part of the Greek world (F., pl. 11, 26 [Boardman, *GGFR* pl. 832], and III, 447).

These details, and the masculine compactness of design and modelling, make one hesitate to pronounce the stones Etruscan. They are placed here on account of their general analogy with Etruscan work: but it is possible that they are Greek of about 450 BC. If

Etruscan, they will hardly be much later.

[Zazoff, no. 666, Free Style.]

87. [23.587]

From the Bruschi collection at Corneto. F., pl. 61, 51.

Scarab. Murky sard. [13 x 10 x 8 mm]

The beetle careful. The winglets reduced to humps. Hatched vertical border. Round the sides and the lower part of the thorax, a hatched border, with a triangular space left plain half-way along the lower side. Two lines between the elytra.

Hatched border. A youth, with a cloak over his left arm, bends forward, holding a staff in his right hand with which he touches an open-mouthed grotesque head set on a rock. Short hair, striated. The modelling of the body soft and free.

The grotesque head is oracular: by touching it, the youth invites it to speak. Similar subjects are common on Etruscan and Italiote stones of free style, and are discussed by Furtwängler (III, 245-52 and 451-2). Compare particularly F., pl. 22, 2, and for the touching of the head with a stick, F., pl. 22, 7 and 8 [*AGDS* II, nos. 347-8].

Not earlier than the late fifth century.

[Zazoff, no. 1331, Free Style.]

88. [27.724]

Bought in Rome, 1911.

Scarab. Sard. [16 x 12 x 9 mm]

The beetle careful. The winglets roughly indicated. Vertical border of crossing lines, one set of lines twice as numerous as the other. A hatched border round the lower edge of the thorax. Between the elytra, two lines.

Hatched border. Herakles standing on rocky ground and
shouldering the firmament. On one side of him, the Hesperian tree: on the other, a rock with his club stuck

in it and his quiver tied to the club. A little plant grows from the rock between his legs. Inscription HERCLE, retrograde. Herakles is beardless: his short hair is in pellets. Big eye. Thick-set figure, powerful modelling, tighter than in no. 89. The same conception of form as in the cups of the vase-painter Aristophanes. The right leg is frontal, and bent at the knee. The firmament is represented by a curving mass set with the crescent moon, two big stars, one at either tip of the moon, and a number of lesser stars rendered by pellets.

The same subject, differently treated, on a sard scarab in Boston ([98.736] *LHG* Pl. A, 21 [Zazoff, no. 570]): Herakles with body and one leg frontal, his lionskin over his shoulders, supporting the firmament with one hand and holding his club in his left, while Atlas (ARIL) plucks the Hesperian apple from the tree: the firmament is set with sun as well as with moon and pellet stars: the engraving is in the free Etruscan style, but the original of the design is earlier than in our stone. A third rendering in one of the metopes from the Temple of Zeus at Olympia (*Olympia* III, pl. 40).

Early fourth century.

[Zazoff, no. 569, Free Style.]

89. [27.723]

Bought from an Italian about 1899. F., pl. 63, 23.

Scarab, cut. Murky sard. The outline of the lion's back missing and restored in gold. [19 x 14 mm]

Hatched border. Herakles throttling the lion: bow and club in the field: inscription HERCLE, retrograde. Herakles is beardless, and has short hair rendered with great freedom. Small pellets for the pubes. Heavy forms, massive modelling in the free style. The left legs of the lion press against the hero's thigh, the raised right fore-paw tugs at his arm. The mane is rendered by short lines: short lines for the hair along the belly.

The same design on a sard scarab in the British Museum (*LHG* Pl. A, 18; *BM Gems* no. 719; F., III, 188, fig. 126 [Zazoff, no. 108]). Two smaller versions have been in the Roman market: in one, the club and bow are placed as in our stone; in the other, the club is between the legs. The former bears the inscription CALANIC., Calanic(e), the last letter being doubtful [*LIMC* V, Herakles/Hercle 176-7]: it is the Greek *kallinikos* and Calanice is used instead of Hercle on an

Etruscan mirror (Gerhard, *Etruskische Spiegel* pl. 137).

The design has been discussed by Evans (*Horsemen of Tarentum* 53) and by Furtwängler (III, 188): it is borrowed from the Herakles and the Lion which makes its appearance, towards the end of the fifth century, on coins of Herakleia in Lucania and other cities.

Early fourth century.

[Zazoff, no. 669, Free Style.]

90. [23.599]

Bought in London, 1916.

Slightly convex. Sard. [16 x 12 mm]

Hatched border. Uneven ground line. Maschalismos: a man and a youth dismembering the trunk of a youth: the head lies on the ground, chin to right: the arms are still connected with the body, but one of the men is about to strike with a chopper. The youth wears a chlamys. The hair is short, with loose striations: the man's beard rendered by a row of pellets. Heavy but constricted forms.

Replicas, with slight variations, on a sardonyx scarab (F., pl. 21, 50 [Zazoff, no. 1111]) and a sard in the Southesk collection (*LHG* Pl. A, 24; *Southesk* pl. 2, A 30 [Zazoff, no. 1113]). A third version was in the Boulton collection and may be identical with ours. The subject of maschalismoi is discussed by Furtwängler (II, 209): a mythical prototype probably existed but is still to seek.

Italiote. Third century.

[Zazoff, no. 1112, Free Style; Martini, *Ringsteinglyptik* no. 25, Scarab Style.]

91. [27.725]

From the Boulton collection, 1911 (sale catalogue no. 26, 4).

Sard, translucent. Chipped at the sides and pared round. [18 x 15 mm]

A centaur about to hurl a krater. He is of the primitive type composed of a complete human body joined to an equine barrel and hind-quarters. The human body is powerful and heavy, with big pectorals and a large depression for the navel: the penis small, the legs in pure profile: the right ankle rendered by a pellet. The cheek-bone very prominent: the lower part of the face set back from the upper. A row of pellets for the lower edge of the hair, another for the beard: the hair on the skull is covered with lines nearly parallel to the contour of the head; three of these lines run out from above the nape to represent long loose hair. The lower part of the calyx-krater is broken away: round the mouth, a row of pellets, with a line below it: another row of pellets on the cul of the krater near the top. The right hand of the centaur is seen half-way along the upper side of the vessel: his left arm is bent and the fingers of the left hand are pressing against his side. The action of his legs is difficult to determine owing to the fragmentation of the stone: but he seems to be stooping in order to hurl the krater.

The centaur with human fore-legs, common in early Greek art (see *LHG* Pl. A, 2, an agate scaraboid in the British Museum [Boardman, *Archaic* no. 108]), is rare in the ripe archaic period and rarer afterwards. On red-figured vases, the cultivated Chiron sometimes has human fore-legs: as late as 460 BC, on the volute-krater, by the Niobid painter, in Naples (Schultz, *Die Amazonen-Vase von Ruvo* pl. 3 [*ARV* 600, 13]). Still later examples, the centauress on a Greek scaraboid, of early fourth-century work, in the Cabinet des Médailles (F., pl. 12, 41 [Boardman, *GGFR* fig. 207]), and the opponent of Theseus on a Greco-Roman gem of slightly archaistic style (Gori, *Museum Florentinum* II, pl. 59, 1; Reinach, *Pierres gravées* pl. 57: a pink paste of the same type, probably ancient, in the British Museum, *BM Gems* no. 3173). It is clear that the human fore-legs do not prove our centaur to be of very early date.

The body, powerful to heaviness, yet very fleshy, is not in the manner of the fifth century. Such bodies may be found in Italiote gems of the Hellenistic period, for instance, F., pl. 24, 41; pl. 27, 61; and pl. 23, 55. These three gems, and others of the class, have the same huge sunken navel as ours. The head of our centaur looks drier and more archaic than his body: this is also true of the Zeus and the giant on the Florence stone just mentioned, F., pl. 24, 41: and the haggard face, with its hollow cheeks, is characteristic of Italiote stones (F., pl. 18, 63 and 65; pl. 25, 3). The ends of the centaur's fingers are pelleted: and so are the ends of the giant's fingers on the Florence stone. The long bunch of hair at the nape of the centaur's neck recalls, though it does not reproduce, a fashion which is very frequently found on late Etruscan and Italiote gems (F. III, 195 and 223).

92. [27.726]

From Salonica according to Froehner. *Collection Tyszkiewicz* pl. 24, 15; F., pl. 20, 70; *Tyszkiewicz Sale Catalogue* pl. 27, no. 291.

Sard, translucent. Chipped below and pared round below and at the sides. [18 x 12 x 5 mm]

Uneven ground line. There was possibly a pattern, egg or the like, in the exergue.

Silen and goat. The silen, bald, bearded, wreathed with ivy, kneels with head and body frontal, the body being slightly tilted towards the spectator's right, his left arm round the neck of the goat, his right raised. The beard covered with vertical strokes ending in pellets. The tail, which looks somewhat like a goat's tail, flourished. The goat is kneeling on its fore-legs and one of its hind-legs is seen below the silen's foot: head frontal: heavy eyelids: pellets for the hair on the forehead: ringed horns: the coat rendered by thin diagonal lines.

The action of the right hand is made obscure by the paring of the stone. Furtwängler supposes that the silen is adjusting his wreath, but as far as can be seen, the palm of the hand, with the thumb in front of it, is turned towards the spectator, which is not the gesture required. The position of the thumb makes it a little unlikely that he is going to pat or smack the goat.

Froehner attributed the stone to a Greek artist of the fifth century, Furtwängler to an Italian of the third. The silen's tail if a goat's and not a horse's, is an argument, as Furtwängler observes, against an early date. Another is the position of the silen's legs: the left leg below the knee is invisible; the right is seen, somewhat foreshortened, in its whole length, and the foot is so far above the ground, on which the knees rest, that there is room for the goat's foot to appear between the toes and the ground line. This position, with the raised foot, is common on Italiote or very late Etruscan stones (F., pl. 21, 30, 31, and 49; pl. 23, 7: similar, but with the off leg in profile, F., pl. 23, 30, and pl. 64, 47: compare the Hellenistic stone F., pl. 34, 36). It does not seem to occur in the fifth century. There is something a little like it on a Greek relief which is ascribed by Lippold to the early years of the Peloponnesian war (Brunn-Bruckmann, no. 646, 1); but there the raised foot of the falling warrior is not resting on space, as in our silen, but on a dead body. The whole figure may be compared with that of Orestes on the fourth century Paestan bell-krater formerly in the Deepdene collection and now in the British Museum (Millin, *Peintures de vases grecs* II, pl. 68: the drawing reversed [*RVP* pl. 91]): Orestes' legs are so drawn that he seems to be floating in front of the omphalos.

A third argument, of a more general kind, is the nature of the relief in the imprint, for it lacks those quiet passages, formed by planes parallel to the original surface, which characterize Greek and especially earlier Greek relief: the frontal head of the silen, and the glimpse of the goat's hind-quarters, are not sufficient to rest the eye.

The rendering of the bodily forms recalls the centaur on no. 91: and here, as there, the head is drier than the body. Somewhat similar subjects are to be found on two Italiote stones (F., pl. 24, 29 and 30).

Greek: Hellenistic

93. [27.713]

Found at Chalkis in Euboea. Bought from Lambros in 1908.

Convex sard. [21 x 19 mm]

Ground line. Cassandra at the image of Athena. She kneels with bowed head, a sprig of laurel in her right hand, her left hand clasping the lower part of the image, which stands with left leg advanced on a rectangular pedestal set upon a plinth: the goddess wears a crested Corinthian helmet, and a long chiton, somewhat full about the ankles: a spear across her right shoulder; a shield on her arm, emblazoned with a gorgoneion. Cassandra's hair, wreathed with laurel, falls loose on her shoulders. She is naked save for a thin garment covering her left leg and passing behind her left shoulder and over the upper part of her arm.

The same figure, with the same drapery, is frequently used in Roman times: not, however, for Cassandra, but for Nike sacrificing a bull. In clay, on decorative plaques (Von Rohden and Winnefeld, *Architektonische römische Tonreliefs der Kaiserzeit* 82-9, the first type, left-hand plaques; Walters, *BM Catalogue of Terracottas* pl. 14, 1 and 2); in silver, on one of the jugs from Boscoreale in the Louvre (*Monuments Piot* 5, pl. 4: Reinach, *Répertoire de reliefs* I, 85, 3); in gems, on four pastes in the British Museum (*LHG* Pl. B, 9; Cecil Smith, *JHS* 7, pl. E, 6 (= F., pl. 36, 29), 4, 5, and 7 (= F., pl. 36, 31: the composition reversed [*BM Gems* nos. 3032-6]), and on stones published by Agostini (*Gemme antiche figurate* (1686) II, pl. 32: rock-crystal:

compared by him, on p. 18 of his text, with the clay reliefs mentioned above), by Gravelle (II, 77; Reinach, *Pierres gravées* pl. 80), by Furtwängler (pl. 30, 16), and in the *Southesk Catalogue* (pl. 5, D 9, sard, and D 10, red jasper).

The oldest of these monuments date from the first century BC. That the Nike and the Cassandra have a common origin cannot be doubted. The kneeling attitude with one arm drooping behind the body naturally occurs elsewhere; for instance, in a wounded Amazon on the Phigaleian frieze (slab 531) and in the Apollo on fourth-century coins of Sicyon (*BM Coins of Peloponnesus* pl. 8, 4): what distinguishes the Nike and the Cassandra from all such figures is, first, the position and arrangement of the drapery, and secondly the idea embodied in the form, which is the motionless moment immediately following extreme physical effort.

The numerous Greco-Roman, in the absence of earlier, parallels seem to place our stone in that epoch. The great warmth, vigour, and expressiveness of the modelling might speak for an earlier time: John Marshall considers it Hellenistic of about 300 BC: and it is placed here, provisionally, among the Hellenistic stones. It must be observed, however, that the big London pastes are admittedly Greco-Roman: and the lost originals, of which they are, after all, poor copies, cannot, for execution, have fallen far short of the present stone. True, they would have lacked its depth and majesty of feeling: but let it be borne in mind, that the type may very likely have been created, not by a gem-engraver, but by an artist in some other material, say a painter. If the original figure was a Cassandra, the engraver who copies it as a Cassandra may be able to preserve the spirit of the original: the engraver who copies it for a Nike, or rather copies a work in which the original figure was adapted to make a Nike, will forfeit the original spirit.

The original figure may have been either a Cassandra, or a Nike, or something else. That it was not a Nike, may possibly be inferred from its greater impressiveness as used for Cassandra: moreover, it is perhaps rather more likely that an alien figure would be used for a Nike, considering the great demand for figures of Victory, than that a Nike would be used for a Cassandra. There are faint indications that the original figure was a Cassandra, but no reliance can be placed upon them. First, the upper part of the body, the drooping arm with the laurel sprig, the bent head and flowing hair, all reappear in the Cassandra or Pythia on the Medici krater (Hauser, *Jahreshefte* 16, 38). The resemblance is probably not accidental. Secondly, the head of Cassandra may be compared with a laurelled bust, very likely of the same, which occurs on several Greco-Roman gems (F., pl. 38, 40 and 41; pl. 40, 10 and 14): but these are draped and filleted.

See no. 94.

[Boardman, *GGFR* pl. 1004; Plantzos, no. 626, later first century BC.]

94. [27.707]

Bought in Athens, 1915.

Double convex. Glaucous beryl of the kind called aquamarine. [24 x 19 x 10 mm]

Ground line. Cassandra clasping the image of Athena: a replica of no. 93. The spear is lacking, and the shield plain. The engraving is not so deep or so precise as in no. 93, but no less masterly and of more delicate charm.

The beryl is not used by gem-engravers until Hellenistic times. Double convex beryls, of Greco-Roman date, are in the Wyndham Cook collection (F., pl. 40, 3) and in the Cabinet des Médailles (F., pl. 48, 8).

[See no. 93.]

95. [27.711]

From the Tyszkiewicz collection. Said by Froehner to have been found in Phoenicia; but Naoum Mitri of Rhodes told John Marshall in 1905 that he had sold it to Tyszkiewicz and had bought it from a peasant at Adana near Tarsos. Furtwängler, *JdI* 4, pl. 2, 2; Froehner, *Collection Tyszkiewicz* pl. 24, 17; F., pl. 32, 31; *Tyszkiewicz Sale Catalogue* pl. 27, no. 292; Fowler and Wheeler, *Greek Archaeology* 399, fig. 327; Lamer, *Griechische Kultur im Bilde* 61, fig. 7.

Chalcedony, strongly convex. [33 x 26 x 9 mm]

Portrait of a Ptolemaic queen as Isis: a female head with the beginning of the chiton and himation indicated. Egyptian coiffure: the hair tightly coiled, with corkscrew locks, short over the forehead, long behind the ear: diadem, and in front of it the symbol of Isis, the sun cradled in a pair of cow's horns. Full chin and neck: the pupil, and the outer line of the iris, indicated by faint prominences. To the left, downwards, the inscription LUK.MEDES, perhaps the artist's name: no end-dots; the omicron reduced to a dot: a facsimile is given by Furtwängler (*JdI* 4, 81).

The features are idealized, but less than appears from the reproduction, in which the projecting chin and the characteristic nose, being engraved on the curve of the stone, are seen in fore-shortening. The queen represented must be either Berenike I or Arsinoe Philadelphos: Furtwängler considers Berenike I the more likely (*loc. cit.*, 80-4).

First half of the third century.

[Plantzos, no. 48, probably made in Alexandria.]

96. [27.709]

Formerly in the Ludovisi, later in the Tyszkiewicz collection. *Collection Tyszkiewicz* pl. 24, 4; F., pl. 32, 36; *Tyszkiewicz Sale Catalogue* pl. 27, no. 285.

Hyacinth. The back convex. [18 x 13 mm]

Portrait of a Ptolemaic queen: female head with clothing shown on the neck. Chin and neck full, with the Venus rings noticeable. Prominent eyeball; the pupil, and the outer line of the iris, in relief. The irregular nose is of the same type as in no. 95. Earring, consisting of a ring with a wire hanging from it strung with three drops, a larger between two smaller. Metal stephane with a diadem passing round the lower part of it. The hair elaborately dressed, apparently by the following process. The hair is parted from ear to ear so as to form a fringe: the fringe is turned back from the brow in even curls, the ends of which are covered with the stephane: the rest of the hair is taken back from the parting, a small coil formed at the back of the head, and the hair which remains brought forward again in the curls which are seen to the right of the coil. In contrast with this formality, the hair on the nape of the neck is lightly combed forward with a natural wave. A lady on a gold ring in Petrograd (F., pl. 32, 33) has dressed her hair on the same principle, but she lacks the formal Ptolemaic curls over the brow.

The type of stephane and diadem, not to speak of the hair-dress, is that worn by Ptolemaic queens on their coins. The features resemble those of Arsinoe Philadelphos, and Froehner is no doubt right in identifying the portrait as hers. The head is that of a woman who is still young, and the stone may therefore be attributed to the earlier part of the third century.

97. [27.710]

Said by Froehner to have been found at Suleimanieh in Turkish Kurdistan. From the Tyszkiewicz collection. *Collection Tyszkiewicz* pl. 24, 12; F., pl. 31, 24, and, drawn, III, 169; *Tyszkiewicz Sale Catalogue* pl. 27, no. 289.

Syriam garnet. The back convex. [27 x 22 mm]

Portrait of a middle-aged man: head and shoulders of a bearded man wearing a fez-like cap and a chlamys fastened with a bow. The lips parted, the eye salient, the pupil and the outer line of the iris marked by slight prominences.

With the fez, Furtwängler compares the headgear of certain barbarians on the columns of Trajan and of Marcus Aurelius. The headgear of the Trajanic figures, supposed by Cichorius to be Iazyges (*Die Trajanssäule* III, 143 and 151, and pl. 73), seems to differ from ours in having a lower rim, and is probably a helmet, whereas ours is a cap of felt or the like: the Aurelian headgear, which is taken to be Scythian (Petersen, *Die Marcussäule* pl. 56, 2), is flattened at the top.

A rougher but forcible replica of our head, in pale brownish chalcedony, was formerly in the Ionides collection and is now in the British Museum (*LHG* Pl. B, 10; *Burlington Catalogue* pl. 112, M 136 [*BM Gems* no. 1182; Plantzos, no. 133]): it is said to have been brought to England from Constantinople about sixty years ago. A.S. Murray considered ours to be a modern copy of the Ionides stone, which he wrongly described as a scaraboid (*Quarterly Review* 1901, 434); but ours is in good Hellenistic style.

Third century.

[Boardman, *GGFR* pl. 1000; Plantzos, no. 137.]

98. [27.716]

Bought in 1899 from W.T. Ready, who reported it to have been found on the Euphrates. Furtwängler says that it came from the East, and was at one time in the possession of Mr. Lau. F., pl. 31, 23, and, drawn, II, 154.

Clear sard. [18 x 16 mm]

Portrait of a man in Eastern costume: head of a clean-shaven elderly man, wearing a club-shaped torc and an Oriental head-dress: the collar of his garment indicated, the eyeball prominent, the forehead wrinkled. There is a circle in front of the ear, as if some one had begun to bore a hole.

The pupil is not marked: herein Furtwängler's drawing is misleading.

The head-dress is a conical cap of felt or leather, running down to a peak on the forehead, and furnished with three flaps. The central flap hangs down at the back of the neck and is seen in profile. The other two are folded together in front of the head. These tapering side-flaps, if they were not gathered up, would not fall smoothly in a vertical direction, as in many Eastern head-dresses, but, to remain smooth, would have to be brought diagonally forward towards the chin, where they might be tied together.

Experiment, kindly conducted by a friend, proves that the head-dress is accurately rendered. Its shape before, during, and after manipulation is shown in the accompanying figures [See plate following; from *LHG* figs. 1-3]. The directions for use are as follows:

(1) Place the object on the head, take the flaps and fold them back above the ears with the insides outwards, at

the same time folding down the upper edges of the flaps.

(2) Cross the flaps above the forehead peak, concealing the left-hand flap under the edging of the right-hand one.

(3) Bring the left-hand flap out again over the edging and tuck it in under the flap, leaving the tip curling out.

The head-dress has been compared by Furtwängler with that worn by Samos and other kings of Commagene on their coins (Imhoof-Blumer, *Hellenistische Porträtköpfe* pl. 6, 9, and 10; Macdonald, *Catalogue of Greek Coins in the Hunterian Collection* III, pl. 70, 20-2): but the resemblance, so far as can be made out from the poor specimens preserved, is limited to the conical caul, the flaps being differently shaped and differently disposed. A king of Persis gathers his side-flaps up over his forehead (Imhoof-Blumer, *Hellenistische Porträtköpfe* pl. 7, 27; Allotte de la Füye, *Corolla Numismatica* pl. 3, 3; Head, *Historia Numorum,* 824), but his whole head-dress is quite different from ours both in shape and in arrangement.

It can easily be understood, that the loose flaps of the various Eastern head-dresses were sometimes found troublesome, and were fastened either under the chin, or in front of the head, or behind it as in the archer from the western pediment of the temple at Aegina (Furtwängler, *Aigina* 210-11), or into an encircling band as on a sixth-century Attic cup (Pottier, *Album des vases du Louvre* pl. 73, F 126 [*ARV* 55, 13]): see also no. 99.

99. [27.735]

Bought from W.T. Ready in 1913.

Mottled sard. Roughly rectangular. The sides of the stone slightly convex. A very rare shape. (*Margin*: For the shape cf. crystal, Cab. Méd., with two ravens.) [23 x 20 mm]

Portrait of an Eastern ruler: head of a clean-shaven old man wearing a chlamys and an Oriental head-dress.

The head-dress bears a certain resemblance to that on no. 98, but it is worn farther back on the head, so that the fringe of hair on the temple is exposed; the peak in front is longer; and the side-flaps are differently

arranged. The horizontal line on the forehead below the hair is a fillet or diadem tied round the head before the head-gear is put on, and not afterwards, as in the coin of Persis referred to on no. 98 (Imhoof-Blumer, *Hellenistische Porträtköpfe* pl. 7, 27) or on Armenian and Parthian coins. The right-hand side-flap is lifted up and slung over to the left side of the head: the left-hand side-flap is similarly slung over to the right side of the head, where it appears in our stone as a broad sock-shaped projection above the ear.

Save for the flaps, the hood-like head-dress is somewhat analogous to that worn on coins attributed to Persis (*Corolla Numismatica* pl. 3, nos. 4, 6, &c.).

[This is probably modern.]

100. [27.714]

Formerly in the Ludovisi, later in the Tyszkiewicz collection (sale catalogue, no. 296). *Collection Tyszkiewicz* pl. 24, 5; F., pl. 33, 24.

Slightly convex. Clear sard. The crown of the head missing and restored in gold. [22 x 18 mm]

Portrait, perhaps of a Roman: a clean-shaven man with short hair and wrinkled forehead: the clothing shown at the back of the neck. The eyebrow rendered by short diagonal lines, the outer line of the iris by a raised arc; the pupil incised. Mis-shapen ear.

A paste after this stone, in the Stosch collection (fourth class, no. 323), was wrongly described by Winckelmann as antique (*Description des pierres gravées* 450).

101. [27.715]

From the Ludovisi and Tyszkiewicz collections. *Collection Tyszkiewicz* pl. 24, 10; F., pl. 33, 16, and, enlarged, pl. 51, 25; *Tyszkiewicz Sale Catalogue* pl. 27, no. 288; Hekler, *Greek and Roman Portraits* xviii, fig. 7; Delbrueck, *Antike Porträts* pl. 59, 2 (misprinted 1); Lamer, *Griechische Kultur im Bilde* 61, fig. 6.

Black jasper.

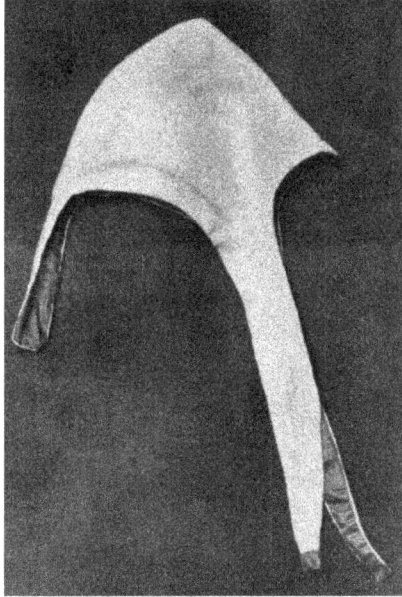

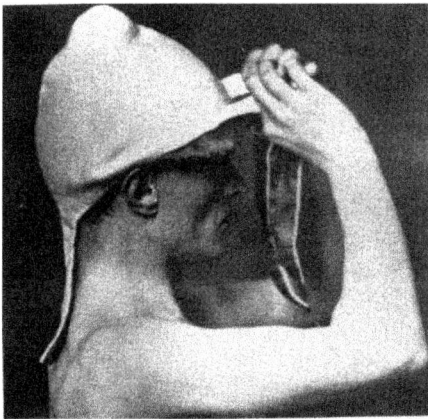

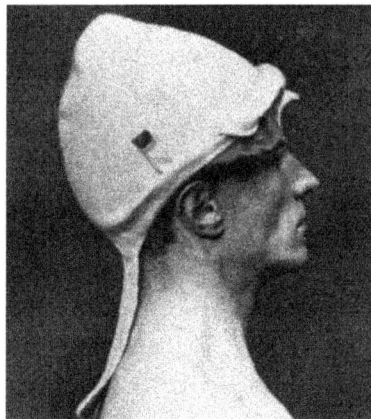

Beazley demonstrating the construction and
wearing of the leather cap worn by the figure on gem no. **98**.

Portrait head of an elderly Roman. The pupil and the outline of the iris in relief: thick eyebrow rendered by irregular, roughly vertical strokes: wrinkled forehead: misshapen ear: the hair somewhat woolly.

This is one of those gems which Furtwängler separates from the mass of Roman portrait gems and assigns to the Hellenistic period, and it is true that such heads as ours and the even finer one on the Carlisle chalcedony in the British Museum (F., pl. 33, 14, and pl. 51, 24 [*BM Gems* no. 1190]) are different from and superior to even such excellent Greco-Roman heads as that on no. 116 in the present collection. The superiority is not due to the stronger personality of the men represented, but to a combination of varied realism in the treatment of substance with the strength and understanding which charge the forms with compact and characteristic life.

The group of gems in question is studied by Furtwängler on F., pl. 33, 9, 14, 15, and 16; see also III, 165, and *JdI* 3, 108-9.

102. [21.1213]

Found in a tomb at Eretria (*ArchEph* 1899, 228). Formerly in the Evans collection. F., pl. 66, 4. At present on loan in the museum at Boston, where the other objects found in the tomb are preserved (*Museum of Fine Arts, Boston, Annual Report* 1914, 96). The accompanying picture shows one of the clay figures from the tomb [omitted here].

Convex garnet in a golden ring. Inside the hoop, CHAIRE. The same inscription on a scaraboid and two gold rings in the British Museum (*LHG* Pl. A, 9 [Boardman, *Archaic* no. 447]; Imhoof-Blumer and Keller, *Tier- und Pflanzenbilder* pl. 25, 40; *BM Finger Rings* nos. 85 and 102 [*BM Gems* nos. 174, 243]): CHAIRE KAI SU on a sard scarab in the same collection (F., pl. 9, 34 [*BM Gems* no. 513]). The ring is of the general type shown in Marshall, *BM Finger Rings* xlii, C xxvii. [29 x 24 mm]

Ground line. Aphrodite arming. The goddess stoops with both arms bent and the left one advanced and passes her left arm through the grip of the shield, holding the rim with her right hand. The spear rests against her left shoulder. She is naked from the thighs upwards, and her legs are nonchalantly draped: she has picked up her himation, placed an end against her flank, wound the garment round her legs from right to left, and passed the remainder in front of her breast and

over her left shoulder. The hair is parted in the middle and twisted up into a knot behind. The artist's signature, in two lines, GELON EPOEI: see F., II, 305.

An unsigned replica on a convex sard from Amrit in the De Clercq collection (*LHG* Pl. B, 7; De Ridder, *Collection De Clercq* VII, pl. 20, no. 2841).

The tomb from which the stone came is dated, on the evidence of the other finds, to the end of the third century (Kourouniotis, *ArchEph* 1899, 233-4).

For the style of the stone, Rossbach (in Pauly-Wissowa, *s.v.* Gelon (8)) compares a sard, set in a gold ring, from a tomb belonging to the cemetery of the ancient Trichonion in Aetolia (*ArchEph* 1906, pl. 4, 47). The design on the sard is a female figure, half naked, and seen in three-quarter view from behind, leaning on a column and holding a comic mask in her hand; across her shoulder, a streamered thyrsus, corresponding to the spear on our stone: Thalia according to Soteriades. Soteriades dates the Aetolian tomb to the beginning of the second century (*loc. cit.*, 74).

Another kindred design on a convex garnet in Petrograd (F., pl. 34, 17 [Plantzos, no. 427]): a maenad with oinochoe and phiale, a thyrsus against her shoulder. Also akin, Aphrodite with the eagle on a sard in the Chatsworth collection (F., pl. 38, 9), and Nike writing upon a shield on a paste in the British Museum (*JHS* 7, pl. E 8 [*BM Gems* no. 1128; Plantzos, no. 170]).

About 200 BC.

[Plantzos, no. 165, and 68-69 on Gelon.]

103. [21.1214]

Bought from W.T. Ready in 1897. From Athens according to the sender. F., pl. 61, 53.

Bluish chalcedony flecked with white. The shape approaches the rectangular, but all four sides are curved and the corners rounded off. [16 x 12 mm]

Border of diagonal strokes. A sea-pantheress attacking a polypus, which she grasps with mouth and paws. The polypus has three plain and two pelleted tentacles. The monster shows flippers at the right elbow and on the left shoulder.

Stones of this shape are not found before the Hellenistic age (F., pl. 22, 67; pl. 20, 71; pl. 25, 4; pl. 65, 39). The shape is derived, in the long run, from the scarab and scaraboid. The border of diagonal strokes, a degenerate variant of the hatched border, appears on Italiote stones of the Hellenistic period (F., pl. 23, 5, and pl. 20, 63) and on a very late scarab, of Hellenistic date, in the British Museum (F., pl. 65, 10 [*BM Gems* no. 565; Plantzos, no. 196]): not, it seems, later.

104. [23.600]

Brought from Athens, 1908, and said by the dealer, a trustworthy man, to be from Lesbos. A replica of, if not identical with, the stone published by Pietro-Vivenzio (*Gemme antiche per la più parte inedite* Rome, 1809, pl. 17), and after Vivenzio in a small anonymous work of which there is a copy in the library of Sir Arthur Evans (*Raccolta di trenta scelte incisioni in pietre dure appartenenti alcune al Real Museo Borbonico ed altre a private collezioni* Naples, 1845, pl. 17). Vivenzio describes the stone as a jasper in his plate, and as an agate in his text. (*Addendum*: The stone published by Vivenzio is also figured by Gargiulo in his *Recueil des monuments du Musée National et de plusieurs autres collections particulières* Naples, 1861, III, pl. 7, 1.)

Moss agate. [21 x 16 mm]

Ground line. Marsyas and Olympos. Marsyas seated on a rock: in front of him Olympos, a slender boy with short hair, holding a flute in either hand. Marsyas lays his left hand on Olympos' shoulder and extends his right arm as if to bring him nearer. His hair and beard are rough and his features rugged: a beast's skin on his lap and over his left arm. Olympos looks at Marsyas for guidance: a cloak over his right shoulder.

(*Margin*: The subject already in the Nekyia of Polygnotos (Paus. 10, 30, 9).) The representation of the same subject on a late Italiote stone (F., pl. 30, 36) must go back to the same original. Compare also the Pompeian painting, Herrmann, *Denkmäler der Malerei des Altertums* pl. 87. Marsyas teaching Olympos the flute is a pendant to the Chiron teaching Achilles the lyre, which is known from a Herculanean painting (Herrmann, pl. 82) and from engraved gems (F., pl. 24, 65 [*AGDS* II, no. 398]; pl. 43, 16; pl. 43, 10).

Perhaps late Hellenistic.

Greco-Roman

105. [27.733]

From Hadrumetum in Tunis according to Froehner. Formerly in the Tyszkiewicz collection. *Collection Tyszkiewicz* pl. 24, 13; F., pl. 50, 19, and, drawn, II, 242; Bulle, *Neue Jahrbücher* 1900, pl. 2, 53; *Tyszkiewicz Sale Catalogue* pl. 27, no. 290; Reinach, *Apollo* 81, fig. 117; Stuart Jones, *Companion to Roman History* 426, fig. 61, after Furtwängler's drawing.

Slightly convex. Sard, now milky in parts. [21 x 16 mm]

Augustus, as Neptune, mounting a chariot drawn by four sea-horses over a troubled sea: he is escorted by a young Triton and a dolphin. Above, the inscription POPIL ALBAN, giving the owner's name, Popilius Albanus.

The letters are end-dotted, the omicron rather large, the nu slanting, the beta thin with the upper loop smaller than the lower.

The chariot, conceived as emerging from the waves, is invisible save for a glimpse of the felloe, of one spoke, and of the upper edge of the car. The sea-horses have distended nostrils and tossing manes: they are finned at the elbow, and a girdle of weed, as commonly in sea-creatures, masks the commencement of the spinous tail. The Triton, seen to below the nipples, is shown to be swimming by his raised right shoulder: he seems to have big bestial ears like the marble Triton in the Vatican (Bulle, *Der schöne Mensch* pl. 219). The driver is naked save for a wrap which passes over the right shoulder and behind the back and is wound round the left arm: the left leg frontal; the hair short; a trident in the left hand.

In a general way, the representation may be compared with the Poseidon driving a pair of sea-horses on a paste in Berlin (F., pl. 37, 3), of which there is a smaller replica in the British Museum (*BM Gems* no. 2729). On the pastes, the chariot is not indicated at all: as in our gem, the rigid geometrical lines of the chariot would have marred the furia of the representation.

One of the few chariot-pieces comparable with ours for its fiery vigour is the Nike flying with a team of horses which is preserved in several examples, on a cameo in Petrograd signed by Rufus (F., pl. 57, 6 [Neverov, *Cameos* no. 37]) and on several intaglios (for instance, F., pl. 42, 5 [Zwierlein-Diehl, *Würzburg* I, no. 337]), and which was conjectured by Panofka, not without plausibility, to be the "Victoria quadrigam in sublime rapiens" of Nikomachos (see Furtwängler, *JdI* 4, 60-2).

The short hair and beardless face of the driver, perhaps also his youthful body, show that he is not Poseidon. The features are portrait-like and therefore mortal. At the period to which the gem belongs, no one but Augustus could have been figured as Poseidon: and the features, in fact, bear an unmistakeable resemblance to those of Augustus.

The gem most likely belongs to approximately the same period as those Augustan coins which display naval emblems in honour of the battle of Actium: that is, between 31 and 27 BC.

Another monument of the same kind, though of vastly inferior quality, is the cameo in Vienna published by Rossbach (*Aus der Anomia* pl. 3), on which Augustus, or his genius (F., III, 318), stands in a chariot drawn by four tritons.

106. [23.588]

Bought from Rhousopoulos, who said it came from Asia Minor. F., pl. 61, 68; Bulle, *Neue Jahrbücher* 1900, pl. 2, 51.

Sard. [13 x 9 mm]

Head of a boy satyr smiling. A skin tied round the shoulders. Tousled hair, half concealing the bestial ear: the lower lashes rendered by short strokes pointing vertically downwards: the iris prominent, in relief: bushy eyebrows represented by pellets disposed on a line.

The character is more pronounced than in the somewhat similar head on Hyllos' cameo in Berlin (F., pl. 52, 2 [Vollenweider, *Steinschneidekunst* pl. 80.1-3]), and ours consequently recalls more vividly the bronze head of a satyr in Munich (Wolters, *Illustrierter Katalog der K. Glyptothek* (1912), pl. 70): compare also the young satyr who offers a hare to a dog on a relief in the Louvre (Schreiber, *Hellenistische Reliefbilder* pl. 22).

107. [27.731]

From the Tyszkiewicz collection (sale catalogue, no. 300). F., pl. 61, 71.

Clear sard. [24 x 20 mm]

Ground line, swelling towards the middle. Theseus examining his father's sword. On the ground the shield: the device a gorgoneion framed in petals.

This design was extremely popular in Imperial times: further examples on a sard in the Cabinet des Médailles (*Collection Pauvert de la Chapelle* pl. 7, 100; F., pl. 38, 18) and on a lost stone (F., pl. 43, 31); on a yellow paste in the British Museum [*BM Gems* no. 3171]; on a red jasper in Berlin (Furtwängler, *Berlin* pl. 60, no. 8481); on the nicolo, no. 123 in this collection; on

another, set in a third-century ring, in the British Museum (Henkel, *Römische Fingerringe* 114, fig. 65 [*BM Gems* no. 1909]); on an onyx set in a silver ring found at Trèves (*Bonner Jahrbücher* 7, pl. 3. 1-2, figs. 4 and 5; Henkel, 114, fig. 66); on a paste, set in a third-century bronze ring, found at Augsburg, in Munich (*ibid*, pl. 78, 348, and pl. 48, no. 1254 [cf. *AGDS* I.3, no. 2710]); and on an onyx, set in a gold ring of about the same period, published by Abraham Gorlaeus in his *Dactyliotheca* (I, no. 96). Others, the antiquity of which cannot be vouched for from the illustrations, are figured by Agostini (*Gemme antiche figurate* II, pl. 100), by King (*Antique Gems and Rings* (1872), II, pl. 43, 5), by Gori (II, pl. 17, 1; Reinach, *Pierres gravées* pl. 51), and in the description of the Orleans collection (II, 52; Reinach, *op. cit.*, pl. 130). It is easy to understand the popularity of the design: a ring with Theseus examining his sword would make an excellent present for a young man beginning his military career.

The original was no doubt a work in the style of the fifth century, possibly in the manner of Polykleitos.

The petal frame on the shield recurs on the Berlin jasper and in the stone published by Gorlaeus. A shield like ours, emblazoned with a gorgoneion surrounded by petals, on an Italiote sard (F., pl. 22, 48). The petals also on a stone reproduced by Agostini (II, pl. 46) with a Venus Victrix of the same type as F., pl. 44, 78, on a late bronze relief with the same subject in Berlin (*JdI* 2, 203), and on a marble relief in Turin published by Rizzo (*Römische Mitteilungen* 25, pl. 8).

The figure of Theseus is grouped with another on a stone published by Furtwängler (pl. 42, 7).

108. [27.738]

Bought in Rome (?) 1912-13.

Golden sard. [16 x 14 mm]

Ground line, swelling towards the feet. A comic actor, masked, in the part of an old gentleman, holding a long knotted stick and stroking his beard. The left leg frontal. The hair hatched with the lower edge pelleted: the beard in rows of pellets. Sleeved under-garment, himation. Paunch.

A favourite design in Greco-Roman gems. Two examples are figured, and others mentioned, by Furtwängler (pl. 41, 48, and 50, and II, 198). Another was recently in the Paris market (*Gemmes et médailles antiques, 24-26 mars* 1902, 1, pl. 2, 3; *Collection Jules Sambon* pl. 24, 570). A similar design on a stone in Munich (*Münchener Jahrbuch* 4, pl. 2, 24 [cf. the paste, *AGDS* I.2, no. 1825]).

109. [21.1215]

Bought in Naples, 1912-13.

Slightly convex. Sard. [17 x 12 mm]

Ground line, swelling towards the hither foot. An archaic Apollo: he holds bow and arrows in one hand and in the other the fore-foot of a fawn which stands on its hind-legs in front of him. The head of the god is slightly bent. The body archaic: high chest, bulging calf, long feet, tight knees. The skull high. The long hair is hatched, and edged with pellets behind as well as before: two series of pellets represent loose locks falling on the breast: the fillet indicated.

The same design on a number of Greco-Roman stones (F., pl. 40, 1 and 2; Furtwängler, *Berlin* pl. 21, 2308; Millin, *Pierres gravées* pl. 6 = Reinach, *Pierres gravées* pl. 120; *BM Gems* no. 1310): facing left instead of right, on a chalcedony in the possession of Sir Edward Sieveking, considered by Cecil Smith, who published it, to be a cut scaraboid (*Proceedings of the Royal Society of Antiquaries* 1887, plate at 253, 1). (*Margin*: Now in Arndt collection; early Roman.) The archaic statue reproduced has been supposed to be the bronze Apollo Philesios by Kanachos at Miletus, but it is presumably that statue which is reproduced on Milesian coins (*BM Coins of Ionia* pl. 22, 9 and 10; Gardner, *Types* pl. 15, 15 and 16), and in these the fawn is not standing, as in our gem, but sitting on Apollo's hand. Cecil Smith (*loc. cit.*, 251-5) conjectures that the original fawn was lost during the sojourn of the statue at Susa, and that the statue was restored, on its return, after the similar Apollo of Kanachos at Thebes, the gems reproducing its first, the coins its second state.

The stone which most resembles ours is F., pl. 40, 2. The British Museum sard is a poor, watery work of later Imperial date.

110. [27.740]

An imprint in Cades, sixth century, 41; described in *Bullettino* 1839, 110, as "replica accuratissima dalla pietra posseduta dal duca di Blacas col nome di HEIOU. Corniola già degli eredi dell' avvocato Isola in Roma ora nella collezione Vannuttelli". The Blacas stone is now in the British Museum ([*BM Gems* no. 965] *LHG* Pl. B, 13; Inghirami, *Galleria Omerica* I, 107; Choiseul-Gouffier, *Voyage pittoresque* II, 177; Tischbein, *Homer nach Antiken* III, 3; Overbeck, *Galerie heroischer Bildwerke* pl. 16, 19). The inscription HEIOU is false, and Furtwängler condemns the stone as well (*JdI* 4, 71). If the Blacas stone is modern, so is ours, for the technique is exactly the same: but both stones appear to be ancient.

Slightly convex. Translucent sard. [18 x 15 mm]

Irregular ground line. The death of Dolon. Dolon, beardless, has sunk at the feet of Odysseus, and is begging for his life: with his right hand he clasps the hero's knee, and he stretches his left upwards as if towards the beard. Odysseus stands looking down at him, his sword, sheathed, held at his side in his left hand, for it is not he who is to slay Dolon, and his right hand raised with a gesture of detachment. At the other side of Dolon stands the youthful Diomede, his left leg planted on Dolon's thigh, his left hand at the Trojan's head, as if grasping it, and his naked sword ready in his right. Dolon wears a sleeved under-garment with a short chiton over it, a wolfskin cap, and a skin tied round his shoulders. Odysseus wears pilos and chlamys: Diomede has a cloak fastened at the neck, and his scabbard is suspended from a baldrick slung round his shoulder. The hair of Diomede is short and unkempt: the hair of Odysseus escapes from under the pilos above the ear; his beard is pelleted; and the pellet is used freely throughout the engraving.

The same subject, differently treated, on a stone published in *Annali* 1875, pl. Q, 4: whether antique or modern is uncertain from the drawing. The two figures on an Italiote paste in Berlin (F., pl. 33, 32) have been interpreted as Odysseus and Dolon. A brown sard in the collection of Mr. Henry Oppenheimer is a modern variant of the Heiou type: Odysseus holds Dolon's head and grasps his sword in his right hand: Diomede is wearing chlamys and helmet, and raises his sword point downwards. A variant on a sard from Cadiz in the British Museum [*BM Gems* no. 966].

111. [27.736]

From the Boulton collection (sale catalogue, no. 28, 1). An imprint in the Impronte dell' Instituto.

Sard. Fragment. [19 x 16 mm]

A centaur carrying a maenad on his back. His left arm passes behind the maenad, supporting her: in his right hand he holds a thyrsus, head downwards, the foot of which is lanceolate and the shaft tied with a streamer near the head which is now broken away. His hair is ruffled, his beard formally neat. The maenad's head is thrown back: her arm follows it, with the hand half open as if holding some object, now missing, between her fingers. The parted lips and the wrinkle in the forehead show her excitement. She wears a chiton with cross-bands on the breast: for this fashion, see Stephani, *Compte rendu* 1860, 80-2, and 1870-1, pl. 2, 4, and 53.

A kindred theme on two pastes, perhaps from a single stone, in Boston ([98.748] F., pl. 63, 45) and in Berlin (Furtwängler, *Berlin* pl. 31, no. 4084). A centaur has overtaken a maenad and caught her up on to his back: he holds a streamered thyrsus, the maenad a tympanum: our maenad may have held the same.

Another representation from the same cycle is preserved in a Pompeian painting and on an engraved stone: the maenad has leapt on to the centaur's back (Herrmann, *Denkmäler der Malerei des Altertums* pl. 93 and 139-40).

112. [27.780]

Paste, amethystine. Perhaps an ancient paste re-polished. [20 x 13 mm]

Ground line, partly broken away. A maenad, seen in three-quarter view from behind, rushing with head thrown back, in her right hand a thyrsus with a streamer round it, in her left a kantharos, and something else which is indistinct. Her chiton is fastened on the right shoulder and leaves her left shoulder free: the left-hand portion of the chiton is blown aside, so that her back, left leg, and right thigh are exposed, and between her legs, so that the lower part of the right leg is covered. A long wrap passes over her left arm, in front of the body, and over her right arm.

The same figure is found in bacchic reliefs on sarcophagi (Reinach, *Répertoire de reliefs* III, 359, 2; III, 326, 5; II, 61, 3). The motive of the drapery blown between the legs recurs in another type of maenad, that used by the new-Attic sculptor Salpion on his marble krater in Naples (Hauser, *Neuattische Reliefs* pl. 2, no. 24).

A somewhat similar figure on a paste in Berlin (F., pl. 36, 37), and on another in the British Museum.

113. [21.1216]

From Chalcedon according to Froehner. Formerly in the Tyszkiewicz collection. Froehner, *Collection Tyszkiewicz* pl. 24, 9; *Tyszkiewicz Sale Catalogue* pl. 27, no. 287.

Sard. Very deeply cut. [14 x 12 x 6 mm]

Head of Io, almost frontal. The hair filleted, parted in the middle, turned back from the face and falling loose behind. Necklace rendered by two rows of pellets joined by strokes and terminated below by lines tapering downwards. The nose somewhat aquiline. The lips parted: pathetic expression.

A similar head on a sard signed by Dioskourides (F., pl. 49, 9, and pl. 51, 17 [Vollenweider, *Stein-schneidekunst* pl. 67.1,4]) is identifiable as Io from the little horns in the hair. Furtwängler condemns the present stone as a copy of the other (II, 234), first, because the workmanship is coarse and bad, secondly, because the horns are absent: the engraver did not understand them in his original, and therefore omitted them in his copy.
 With regard to the first argument, most critics will consider the engraving good, not bad: the head has not the restrained perfection of Dioskourides' work, but the execution is masterly and the expression just. With regard to the second: the horns are clearly indicated, by bosses half-way between the parting and the sides of the head.

Ancient pastes of somewhat similar types in Berlin (Furtwängler, *Berlin* pl. 35, nos. 4928-32): another in Mr. Warren's possession [probably Boston 27.779].

114. [27.734]

Formerly in the Chesterfield, Bessborough, and Marlborough collections (Story-Maskelyne, *The Marlborough Gems* 46, no. 270). Natter, *Traité de la méthode antique de graver en pierres fines* (1754), pl. 16; Natter, *Catalogue des pierres gravées tant en relief qu'en creux, de My lord Comte de Bessborough* (1761), pl. 16, no. 40; Worlidge (*A select Collection of Drawings from curious antique Gems, most of them in the possession of the Nobility and Gentry of this Kingdom; etched after the manner of Rembrandt. By T. Worlidge, Ptr.* London, 1768), no. 1; Bracci, *Commentaria de antiquis scalptoribus* (1784), pl. 45; *Gemmarum antiquarum Delectus ex praestantioribus descriptus quae in dactyliothecis ducis Marlburiensis conservantur* (1845) II, pl. 34 = Reinach, *Pierres gravées* pl. 115; F., pl. 50, 4. See also Furtwängler, *JdI* 4, 57.

(*Addendum*: The Chesterfield Collection. Lord Chesterfield delivered the following admonition to his son in Rome (Letter CX):

> No piping nor fiddling, I beseech you; no days lost in poring upon almost imperceptible *Intaglios* and *Cameos*; and do not become a Virtuoso of small wares. Form a taste of painting, sculpture, and architecture, if you please, by a careful examination of the works of the best ancient and modern artists; those are liberal arts, and a real taste and knowledge of them becomes a man of fashion very well. But beyond certain bounds, the man of taste ends, and the frivolous Virtuoso begins.)

Strongly convex. Syriam garnet. [24 x 17 x 8 mm]

Sirius. The head and shoulders of a dog, frontal, with rays round the head. The mouth open; showing the tongue, the teeth complete, and the corrugated palate. Coarse hair in striated tufts. Shaggy pointed ears. The body smooth, save for light tufts on the breast. Round the body, a collar, inscribed with the artist's signature, GAIOS EPOIEI, with small end-dots: the cross-bar of the alpha was not noticed by Furtwängler. The deep red stone has a livid bluish hue where it is hollowed thin, which makes the dog's muzzle look pale and moist.

A somewhat similar design on a chalcedony, said to be ancient, in Berlin (Imhoof-Blumer and Keller, *Tier- und Pflanzenbilder* pl. 14, 3; Furtwängler, *Berlin* pl. 52, 7043). Natter copied our stone, which he greatly admired, and his copy is believed to be in Petrograd

(see Story-Maskelyne, *The Marlborough Gems* 46). A copy by Lorenzo Masini, of rock-crystal, is in Berlin (9243: *JdI* 3, pl. 3, 27). A modern sard in the British Museum (Dalton, *Catalogue of the Engraved Gems in the British Museum: Post-classical Period* pl. 30, 774) is not a copy, but a free imitation.

The dog seems to belong to the class called by Keller 'pseudo-Molossian' (*Jahreshefte* 8, 258-69; *Die antike Tierwelt* I, 112-13), reproduced by a grave-statue in the Ceramicus at Athens (Collignon, *Sculpture grecque* II, 383, and *Statues funéraires dans l'art grec* 241), by statues in the Uffizi (*Jahreshefte* 8, 267: see Amelung, *Führer durch die Antiken in Florenz* 15), and in a bronze head at Geneva (Deonna, *Catalogue des bronzes figurés antiques, Ville de Genève* pl. 3, no. 108); compare also the gem F., pl. 45, 20. The same type is used for Cerberus in a stone in the Wyndham Cook collection (*Cook* pl. 8, no. 199): and in a small bronze figure of Cerberus belonging to Mr. Henry Oppenheimer, the main head is pseudo-Molossian, while the two lateral heads are of long-nosed greyhound-like form. (*Margin*: See Furtwängler, *BPW* 1906, 19; 'lion head' *Magnesia* 136 is dog's head; and cf. same type as dogs of Hecate and Artemis on Pergamon frieze; dogs of this breed probably kept in sanctuaries of Artemis and Hecate; Sirius gem of same type.)

The treatment of the hair recalls the Hyperechios stone, no. 115.

[On the artist, Zwierlein-Diehl, *Würzburg* 103-104.]

115. [23.589]

Said to have been found in Macedonia, in a porus sarcophagus. Bought from Rhousopoulos in 1897. Rhousopoulos had known it for twenty years and before it was mounted; thought it genuine, and had made many efforts to buy it. The owner, who lived at Salonica, took it "to Europe", where it was condemned by Chabouillet (the same who condemned the flying heron by Dexamenos) and by A.S. Murray. In 1889, Furtwängler saw no sufficient reason for doubting the genuineness of engraving or inscription, but was inclined to think that the inscription was not the artist's signature, but the owner's name added subsequently (*JdI* 4, 647). In 1900 he said that the engraving and the inscription, "which doubtless designated the artist", seemed to be genuine (F., II, 241). Since 1900 a second stone with the name of Hyperechios has appeared, but has not been published, and is known to the writer from Sieveking's description only (in Pauly-Wissowa, *s.v. Hyperechios* (5)):

> The Berlin Antiquarium has recently acquired another work by Hyperechios, a red jasper, found in Egypt, with the head and shoulders of a bearded philosopher wrapped in a cloak. Both stones, which unmistakably exhibit the same style, are distinguished by remarkably deep cutting. The character of the inscription, the name, and the use of yellow jasper, point to a late period, perhaps the Antonine epoch.
> [*AGDS* II, no. 540.]

Furtwängler, *JdI* 3, pl. 11, 24; F., pl. 50, 6, and pl. 63, 34.

Yellow jasper. [22 x 17 mm]

Ground line, swelling to provide pedestals for the hither paws. A lion walking, wheeling round, with the head, which is undercut, nearly frontal. In the exergue, [H]UPERECHIOU, the letters end-dotted. The mouth open; the claws showing; the end of the tail raised. The off fore-paw presses less heavily on the ground than the others. Massive forms, thick legs and big paws; beetling brow and scowling expression; the ribs faintly indicated; a fringe of hair along the belly and in the hinder crutch, and a tuft on the elbow; the mane freely rendered in coarse striated tufts; outlying tufts, longer and finer, on the body near the mane.

A similar lion on another Greco-Roman stone (F., pl. 45, 25). Both animals are of the same type as the Barberini lion (Brunn-Bruckmann, no. 645), the later type based, unlike the earlier (see the stone no. 65), on study of the animal itself. Pliny states that Pasiteles made studies from living captive lions, no doubt circus animals. The subject of antique representations of the lion has been attended to by Schröder (text to Brunn-Bruckmann, nos. 641-5).

The outlying hair seems not to occur before the Greco-Roman period.

116. [27.741]

Said to be from Athens. Formerly in the Evans collection. Bought in 1911.

Translucent sard. The lower right-hand part missing.

[15 x 12 mm]

A portrait head of an elderly Roman wearing corslet and cloak. Close-cropped hair rendered by very short strokes. Crow's feet. The ear small. The brow drawn down, the lips tightly pressed together and the lower one protruding. Between the neck and the curving fold of the cloak behind it, a straight line, running diagonally, with a short transverse line at the top.

The portrait head on a lost sardonyx (F., pl. 48, 1) bears a certain resemblance to ours: in the field behind the head a nail point downwards. This suggests that the object on our gem between neck and cloak is the upper part of a nail. A third portrait, with similar features, though the shape of the head is different, is engraved on a sard in the British Museum (*LHG* Pl. B, 11; F., pl. 47, 64 [*BM Gems* no. 2043]), a replica of which, in chalcedony, was once in the Montigny collection (*LHG* Pl. B, 12; *Collection de M. de Montigny, Pierres gravées, vente 23-25 mai 1887* pl. 3, 325): in these, as in our stone, only the upper part of the nail is seen, the point being concealed behind the neck. (*Addendum*: Other versions of the man with the nail: Naples 25182, sard; Uffizi 3556, circular sard of Renaissance work.) The Stosch collection contained a modern paste (fourth class, no. 175), which Winckelmann described as a copy of a gem in the collection of Dr. Gavi at Florence (*Description des pierres gravées* II, 435): the Gavi stone seems to have been the one which is now in the British Museum. Winckelmann calls the head a portrait of Atilius Regulus, adding a reference to the *Imagines* of Fulvius Ursinus, no. 38. There is no Regulus, however, in the 1570 edition of Fulvius Ursinus: the figure on page 38 -- there is no other numbering -- is taken from a Mytilenean coin with the supposed head of Sappho. But in the *Illustrium Imagines ex antiquis marmoribus nomismatibus et gemmis expressae quae extant Romae maior pars apud Fulvium Ursinum*, published by Plantin for Theodorus Gallaeus in 1598, no. 38 is a head called "M. Atilius Regulus, apud Fulvium Ursinum in nomismate argenteo", which is presumably what Winckelmann meant, although it bears no resemblance whatever to the Gavi stone and lacks the identifying nail.

The London and Montigny stones are not above suspicion, but the sardonyx and our sard are beyond doubt genuine. The nail is hard to explain. It may be a gentile emblem such as are found on Roman coins: conceivably, but by no means probably, that of the Atilian gens. (*Margin*: The nail was sovereign against the falling sickness (see F.H. Marshall, *JHS* 24, 332-335).)

That the four stones, or the two, represent the same person cannot be said with assurance. That the great Regulus is figured on any or all of them is most improbable: the heads do not look like that of a long-dead hero.

It remains to account for Gallaeus's identification of the published head. Mr. Hill writes: "I have no doubt that one of the coins of L. Livineius Regulus is responsible for the engraving in Gallaeus. See Grueber, *BM Roman Republican Coins* III, pl. 57, 12-17. Some of these (15-17) have an unnamed head on the obverse, which Gallaeus or Ursinus has assumed to be the hero of the barrel story. But on others what seems to be the same head is labelled L. Regulus Pr."

117. [27.739]

Bought in England between 1914 and 1917.

Sard. [17 x 14 mm]

A portrait head of Julius Caesar wearing a laurel wreath tied with a fillet.

Comparable with certain coins figured by Bernoulli (*Römische Ikonographie* I, Coin plate 3, 57, and 62). The portrait may be posthumous, but seems to be ancient.

118. [21.1217]

Bought in London, 1916.

Slightly convex. Translucent sard. The eye chipped and the top of the head missing. [17 x 14 mm]

A portrait head of a middle-aged Roman, with the clothing indicated. Inscription, perhaps ancient, GNTS.

119. [21.1218]

Said to have been found in or near Rome. Bought in Rome about 1912.

Sard, set in a massive gold ring. The hoop circular. [33

x 15 mm]

The type of ring is early imperial (Marshall, *BM Finger Rings* xlvi, E xvi). It is not quite certain that the stone belongs to the ring.

A portrait head of an elderly Roman. Close-cropped hair rendered by short strokes. (*Addendum*: Naples 25224, a sard set in a gold ring, seemed to be a replica.)

120. [23.590]

Said to have belonged to a Bishop of Winchester. Bought in Edinburgh, 1915.

Brown chalcedony. Mounted in an eighteenth-century gold ring. [19 x 16 mm]

Portrait of an aged Roman.

121. [23.591]

From the Morrison collection: formerly in the possession of Saulini at Rome. *Morrison Sale Catalogue* pl. 2, no. 201; F., pl. 49, 24.

Black jasper. [16 x 12 mm]

Portrait of a young man: head, shoulders, and part of the chest, with the clothing indicated. His hair is combed down over his forehead, and he is allowing his beard to grow. Inscription, P.PLITINI, and below it SEPTIKILI. The letters end-dotted. The last letter is doubtful owing to the break in the stone. The vertical stroke is certain, but there seems to be a diagonal stroke starting from the upper dot, as if the letter were mu or nu. The third letter of the first line looks more like a lambda than an alpha, but it must be either a form or a miswriting of alpha. The upper and lower strokes of the sigma are parallel and the alphas seem to lack the cross-bar.

The second line presents difficulty. Furtwängler says that the lettering of the whole inscription, and the arrangement of it in two straight lines, connect it with the signatures of artists, and he supposes that our inscription, in which he read Septikiai, gives the name of the artist and not that of the owner. But there seems to be no instance of an artist signing with two names, and there is no reason why the owner's name should not sometimes have been written in the lettering here used: indeed, Furtwängler assumes this in the case of no. 105 in the present collection: and on the stone in the Evans collection signed by Felix, the name of the owner, Calpurnius Severus, is written in the same fashion as on our stone. Finally it may be asked what Furtwängler conceived the artist's name to be: speaking precisely, what nominative he formed from Septikiai.

Perhaps the best reading is P.PAITINI SEPTIKIAN, for *P. Paitini*(os or ou) *Septikian*(os or ou), the owner's name, P. Paetinius Septicianus. The abbreviation *Paitini*, instead of *Paitin* like *Popil* (no. 105), is curious, but presumably not impossible.

122. [21.1219]

Bought in England, 1917.

Amethyst. Slightly convex. Convex behind. [18 x 12 mm]

Portrait of Lucius Verus: head, shoulder, and part of chest.

123. [27.781]

Bought in Naples, 1898.

Nicolo. Bevelled edge. [15 x 11 mm]

Short ground line. Theseus examining his sword. A coarse late version of the type no. 107.

124. [27.783]

Formerly in the possession of Charles Dawson at Lewes.

Plasma, strongly convex, in a gold ring. An open space in the bezel below the stone. The hoop rounded outside, flattened inside, and thickened and thrice compressed on either side of the bezel. Rings of this shape, in metal, jet, or glass, are datable to the third and fourth centuries AD: examples are figured by Henkel (*Römische Fingerringe* pl. 49, nos. 1287-9; pl. 11, nos. 218 ff.; pl. 22, nos. 432 ff.; pll. 60-1 (jet), and pl. 64, no. 1736 (black glass imitating jet)). There is a glass specimen in the British Museum (Marshall, *BM Finger Rings* 233, fig. 159, and pl. 34, no. 5914); bronze specimens in this collection (no. 125), and, with engraved bezel, in Carlsruhe (Schumacher, *Beschreibung der antiken Bronzen* 22, no. 17). [13 x 9 mm]

Ground line. A woman dancing and playing the flutes: round her shoulders, a swirling wrap: back view, the head turned to the left.

The same design on two sards in the British Museum, one slightly, the other strongly convex (*BM Gems* nos. 2258-9), on a convex plasma in Berlin (Furtwängler, *Berlin* pl. 22, 2424), on a sardonyx in the same collection (*ibid.*, pl. 49, 6829), and on two other stones (King, *Antique Gems and Rings* II, pl. 17, 16; Gravelle, *Recueil de pierres gravées antiques* II, pl. 98 = Reinach, *Pierres gravées* pl. 81). In the second and in the last the head is turned to the left, in the others to the right.

A kindred figure in the wall paintings of the Villa Item at Pompeii (*JRS* 3, pl. 13; Pottier, *RA* 1915, ii, 19) and on the Berlin relief with which Miss Mudie Cooke compares the painting (*JRS* 3, pl. 14, 166). Comparable also, figures on a sarcophagus in Rome (Reinach, *Répertoire de reliefs* III, 326, 5), and in another Pompeian painting (*Zeitschrift für Bildende Kunst* 1901, 289).

The ring no doubt belongs to the third century AD, and that the stone is of the same period may be inferred from the analogous workmanship of the stones in the other rings of the same type, and perhaps from the excellent harmony of stone and setting.

125. [27.782]

Formerly in the possession of Charles Dawson at Lewes.

Plasma, slightly convex, in a bronze ring of the same type as no. 124. [11 x 10 mm]

Ground line. Diomede with the Palladion. Diomede, naked, holding the image in his left and his sword in his right, steps over an altar, the side of which is rounded: in front of him, a pillar with a statue on it.

A small, rough, late version of a design which was extremely popular with gem-engravers in the Greco-Roman period (see Furtwängler, *JdI* 3, 213-14; F. II, 205 and 233), and which also occurs on a sarcophagus and in a painting (see Robert, *Die antiken Sarko-phagenreliefs* II, 150-1). A fragmentary stone, with a Diomede of the usual type, has recently been acquired for the Munich collection (*Münchener Jahrbuch* 5, pl. B, 9).

Third century AD.

Renaissance

126. [27.784]

Formerly in the Arundel, Marlborough (Story-Maskelyne, *The Marlborough Gems* 6, no. 32), and Evans collections; F., pl. 66, 12.

Chalcedony, almost colourless. [21 x 17 mm]

Triton and Nereid. The Triton, who wears, on his head and back, the skin of an animal, perhaps an antelope, with long horns and big ears, clasps the waist of the Nereid, who holds a ship's standard (*stylis*) in her left hand and grasps the Triton's throat with her right: his tail is wound round her legs: one of her feet shows the sole. A little naked boy, with wind-blown hair, sits on the Triton's tail and holds it with both arms.

The type seems to be an antique one: it occurs, reversed, on a sard, formerly in the collection of Lorenzo de' Medici, which is published by Imhoof-Blumer and Keller (*Tier- und Pflanzenbilder* pl. 26, 50; also Raspe, pl. 31, no. 2633 (*Margin*: now in

Naples, number 225), and which seems to be ancient, although the authors express a doubt; on a gem of which there is an imprint in the Impronte dell' Instituto: further, on a fragmentary cameo in Berlin, which Furtwängler counts antique (*Berlin* pl. 66, no. 11082), and on an intaglio figured in the *Dactyliotheca* of Gorlaeus (II, 488).

Furtwängler accepts our stone as antique: against its antiquity, the obscurity of the Triton's torso, his curious costume, the treatment of the water, the athletic form of the Nereid, and the Raphaelesque putto.

Arundel died in 1646. The stone is probably sixteenth-century work.

Story-Maskelyne says (*loc. cit.*) that "the somewhat floriated tail, as well as the material, betrays a Renaissance hand".

A paste after this stone in the Stosch collection (second class, no. 461).

II. Cameos

127. [23.592]

From the Tyszkiewicz collection. Tyszkiewicz said that an Oriental brought it to Sambon of Naples. *Collection Tyszkiewicz* pl. 33, 5; F., pl. 61, 47.

Fragment of a sardonyx cameo: the background is lost: the upper layer is watered grey. [49 x 40 mm]

Head of a Ptolemaic queen, wearing the cap of vulture's feathers and the diadem: formal curls, of corkscrew type, on the brow. The pupil and the outer line of the iris incised. The nose somewhat irregular. Egyptianizing style.

A cameo with the portrait of an Egyptian queen, wearing feather cap and horned disk, was formerly in the Marlborough collection (*Gemmarum Delectus Ducis Marlburiensis* II, pl. 17 = Reinach, *Pierres gravées* pl. 114) and was assigned by Story-Maskelyne (*Marlborough Gems* no. 366) to the Hellenistic period.

Hellenistic.

128. [27.750]

Bought in 1899 from Dr. W. Hayes Ward of New York, who acquired it in or near Bagdad while a missionary in those parts. Mentioned by A.S. Murray, *Handbook of Greek Archaeology* 172, and by Babelon, *Catalogue des camées antiques* xl. F., III, 447, fig. 230, enlarged.

Sardonyx cameo, white on brown, mounted in a Turkish gold ring. [21 x 16 mm]

Ground line. Aphrodite and Eros. The goddess stands with left knee bent and left foot nearly frontal, the head inclined towards her left shoulder, the right arm falling along her side, the left bent up from the elbow. She wears a transparent chiton which has slipped down so as to bare her right shoulder and breast, and a himation the upper line of which repeats the upper line of the chiton. The back of the head is veiled. Eros, a little child, flutters at her left shoulder. Below, the stump of a tree. The artist's signature, in two straight lines, engraved downwards, PROTARCHOS EPOIEI. The letters, which have no end-dots, are not remarkably neat. The iotas are large, the omega and the omicron small: the horizontal strokes of the omega are rather long. In the first pi, the cross-bar overlaps on both sides; in the second, only on the right, while the first

vertical stroke projects beyond the cross-bar. The alpha has a V-shaped cross-bar, in which the left-hand stroke is the stronger.

The drapery of our goddess, the thin chiton leaving breast and shoulder bare, and the himation starting below the hip on the stiff leg and curving up towards the shoulder with a line which repeats the upper line of the chiton, may be compared with that of the Epidaurian Aphrodite (Brunn-Bruckmann, no. 14), the original of which has been dated about 400. Here the position of the legs is much the same as on the stone, but the head is turned in the other direction and the body is supported by the sceptre which was held in the left hand, whereas our goddess seems to lack support on her right side, as if her elbow had been resting on a tree of which only the stump is represented.

Figures which offer a general resemblance to ours are not uncommon on fourth-century vases. A lady on a lekanis in Petrograd (*Compte rendu* 1860, pl. 1; FR, pl. 68 [*ARV* 1476, 3]) stands in the same way and has her clothing similarly disposed: her left elbow rests on a slender sapling. A woman on an Italian vase (Millin, *Peintures de vases grecs* II, pl. 52; *Elite des monuments céramographiques* IV, pl. 23) also rests her elbow on a sapling, and her legs are in the same position. Another lady in the same attitude is to be seen on an Attic vase belonging to the middle of the fourth century, the bell-krater F 68 in the British Museum (Panofka, *Cabinet Pourtalès* pl. 16; phot. Mansell, 3280 [*ARV* 1446, 1]): the upper part of her chiton is differently rendered, but her left elbow, like that of our Aphrodite, seems to rest on space.

Figures which show more or less kinship with ours are found on statues and reliefs belonging to the end of the fifth and the fourth century (Brunn-Bruckmann, pl. 673, pl. 338; Conze, *Attische Grabreliefs* pll. 150, 186, 187, and 418; *Bulletin de correspondance hellénique* 1901, 263), and in later works derived from older models, such as a Roman clay relief (von Rohden and Winnefeld, *Architektonische Reliefs der Kaiserzeit* pl. 17) and even a Byzantine ivory diptych (Reinach, *Répertoire de reliefs* II, 455, 4).

The type used by Protarchos seems to have been developed in the course of the fourth century: one of the fourth-century versions may conceivably have been a painting of Aphrodite resting her elbow on a tree. Protarchos himself lived later: the lettering of his signature points, as Furtwängler notices, to the second century BC.

Another gem with the signature Protarchos is preserved

in Florence, a cameo with Eros, mounted on a lion, playing the lyre (*JdI* 3, pl. 26, 20; F., pl. 57, 1 [Vollenweider, *Steinschneidekunst* pl. 12.1]). The signature on the Florentine Protarchos is in relief, not engraved as in ours, and the spelling is EPOEI: yet the two signatures seem to be by one hand, for the lettering is similar in both; in particular, the first diagonal of the chi is the dominant one in the Florentine cameo as in ours, and the horizontal bar of the tau is no less vigorous.

129. [27.749]

Bought from W.T. Ready in 1897. Formerly in the Montigny collection. This is probably the gem figured by Raspe (*Descriptive Catalogue of a general Collection of Gems cast by James Tassie, Modeller* (1791), pl. 21, no. 1199). *Collection de M. de Montigny, vente a l'hôtel Drouot 23-25 mai* 1887, pl. 5, no. 650.

Cameo in three layers, the upper transparent, the middle one milky white and in part discoloured, the ground translucent with a milky patch at the bottom of the stone. [32 x 14 mm]

Ground line. Leda, her left leg bare, her right knee resting on an altar, submits herself to the embraces of the swan, whose neck encircles hers.

The stone was condemned by A.S. Murray, and considered genuine by Tyszkiewicz and Furtwängler.

130. [21.1220]

From the Saulini collection (*Catalogue des objets antiques recueillis par M. le Chev. Louis Saulini, Rome 24-26 avril 1899* no. 97).

Fragment of a sardonyx cameo, white on pale brown. [22 x 18 mm]

Ground line. A young satyr, seated on a rock, which is covered with a lionskin, draws a boy towards him. The satyr has a skin over his loins. The decenza did not deter Hauser from regarding the stone as antique.

A similar scene on a fragmentary cameo with the signature of Dioskourides (F., pl. 57, 8 [Vollenweider,

Steinschneidekunst pl. 68, 7]). Dioskourides' cameo probably represents a hermaphrodite tempting a young satyr: for the design, as far as it is preserved, is the same as that of a Calene clay relief, a paste cameo in Brunswick, and several marble statues (Paul Herrmann in Roscher's *Lexikon s.v.* Hermaphroditus, 2339-40): the original group probably formed a kind of pendant to the group of a bearded satyr tempting a hermaphrodite which is described by Arndt in *La Glyptothèque Ny-Carlsberg* text to pl. 139.

In our stone, the seated figure is certainly a satyr, though described as a "fauness" in the Saulini catalogue: the other is probably a young boy, though the breast is a trifle full.

For the action, slab 520 of the Phigaleian frieze may also be compared.

Early imperial.

131. [27.755]

Formerly in the Arundel, Marlborough, and Schröder collections (Story-Maskelyne, *The Marlborough Gems* 35, no. 206; *Schröder Sale Catalogue* 1910, no. 63).

Fragment of a sardonyx cameo, white on brown. [20 x 16 mm]

The subject obscure: a young satyr pushes or supports the shoulder of a bearded Silenus who wears a short garment about his loins. This Silenus seems to be pulling something or somebody: another figure is needed to explain the thyrsus which passes behind both figures.

Early imperial.

132. [21.1221]

Bought from Rollin and Feuardent in 1907. The previous history is given by Babelon (*Histoire de la gravure sur gemmes en France* 156-7). According to a tradition which Babelon calls apocryphal, it was found by a peasant from the Roman Campagna, and purchased for a small sum by Cardinal Albani. The Cardinal presented it to Countess Cheroffini, in whose possession it was when Winckelmann published it. The stone soon became famous under the title of 'the Tears of Achilles'. The family of the countess sold it to Monsignor Ferretti, and the King of Naples, Joachim Murat, made unsuccessful attempts to acquire it. About 1820 it was in the possession of a collector named Vincenzo Natti, who sold it to a Frenchman, M. de S., in whose family it remained till lately.

There is a cast in the Impronte dell' Instituto.

Fragmentary sardonyx cameo in two layers, the upper milky white, the lower dark brown and almost opaque. [29 x 23 mm]

Uneven exergual space representing the ground. Orestes and Pylades in Tauri. Orestes seated, resting his bowed head on his right hand, his left arm dropped on his left thigh with the half-closed hand hanging listlessly by his knee. To the left of his legs, part of a stone structure in courses, with faint horizontal striations: possibly an altar. Orestes seems not to be sitting on this, but on something else, perhaps a stone, only a small part of which is visible: between this seat and his thigh, a piece of drapery can be made out. In front of Orestes, Pylades looking down at him, his right hand resting on a high pillar, his head on the hand, his left arm lowered with the hand open. A garment falls in front of his right leg and is held between ham and knee: higher, it is seen in front of his chest and under his armpit. Behind, part of a doorway, with a fillet hanging from the lintel: the architectural fragments above the lintel are hard to interpret. Behind Orestes, and in front of the doorway, a guard, clean-shaven, with Roman helmet and shield; also the hand and bent sleeved arm of a fourth figure, the elbow as if resting on a ledge concealed by the head of Orestes.

The cameo has often been copied. An imprint in the Stosch collection is thus described by Winckelmann (*Description des pierres gravées* pl. 373-4):

> Sard engraved by le Sieur Barnabé Florentin [Felice Bernabé]. Antilochus, son of Nestor, announcing the death of Patroclus to Achilles. This engraving is made after a fragment of a cameo belonging to the Countess Cheroffini in Rome: the missing part of the cameo has been supplied on our stone, including the two maidens, Achilles' companions, who, according to Homer's account, mourned the death of Patroclus.

A sard intaglio in Berlin, of the same type, is attributed by Furtwängler to the Renaissance (*Berlin* pl. 63, no. 8859).

In Winckelmann's *Monumenti antichi inediti* (1767), fig. 129, the missing part of our cameo is supplied, in summary fashion, by completing the figure of Orestes. In most modern versions a fourth figure is added, the owner of the sleeved arm on the left of the fragment: so in the sard intaglio, signed by Marchant, in the British Museum (Dalton, *Catalogue of the Engraved Gems in the British Museum: Post-Classical Period* pl. 31, 817); on the intaglio of red jasper, signed by Louis Siriès, in the Cabinet des Médailles (Babelon, *Histoire de la gravure sur gemmes en France* pl. 12, fig. 8); on the stone attributed to one of the Pichlers (Inghirami, *Galleria omerica* I, pl. 31; Overbeck, *Gallerie heroischer Bildwerke* pl. 30, 5), which is said to have been in the Blacas collection, but which does not appear in the manuscript catalogue of the Blacas gems which is preserved in the British Museum; and on a cameo belonging to Mr. Warren [Boston 34.1436]. A second cameo, also in this collection [Boston 34.1437], adds the fourth figure, but does not complete the Orestes. The paste in Munich published by Furtwängler (F., pl. 67, 24) is a copy, by Tassie according to Dalton, of Marchant's stone in London. Dalton mentions, without particulars, two modern stones in Petrograd: there are many others.

A variant of the design, with the same Orestes and Pylades, but different watchman and background, on a sard, from the Pulsky collection, in the British Museum (no. 1476 [old catalogue]): the stone is counted ancient in the British Museum catalogue, but seems to be poor modern work. There is a figure somewhat resembling our Pylades in the 'Sacrifice to Diana' on a small Italian plaquette, of the sixteenth century, in the British Museum. A similar composition forms part of the Oresteia on three sarcophagus reliefs (Robert, *Die antiken Sarkophagenreliefs* II, pl. 59). On the Berlin sarcophagus, Orestes is seated, head muffled, on a rock: in front of him, Pylades, leaning on a pillar, with his stick in his hand: behind Orestes, a bearded guard, in Roman armour, with spear and sword; in the background, a bearded man wearing chlamys and Phrygian cap and holding a spear. The Weimar sarcophagus presents certain variations: the legs of the friends are differently posed, the person with the cap is youthful, and the fourth figure is characterized as a Scythian by his untrimmed beard and hair, by his shoes, and by the sleeved and trousered garment which he wears with his Roman corslet. The third example is the fragment, described and figured by Winckelmann (*Monumenti antichi inediti* fig. 130), which is embedded in the wall of the Palazzo Mattei at Rome. In general it resembles the Berlin version, but it shares with the Weimar sarcophagus the Scythian costume of the soldier and the youthfulness of the figure in the background: to the right is part of an additional figure, another youth wearing a Phrygian cap. The Berlin sarcophagus was discovered in 1828: the Weimar came from the Palazzo Grimani at Venice and is first mentioned in 1789. The Mattei relief is conjectured to have been attached to the Palazzo Mattei when it was built in 1616.

Robert supposes that the subject of these reliefs is taken from lines 657-724 of Euripides' *Iphigeneia in Tauris*: Pylades has consented to take home the letter from Iphigeneia, while Orestes is to remain and be sacrificed. Other less satisfactory interpretations are mentioned by Höfer in Roscher's *Lexikon s.v. Orestes*.

The original reproduced by the reliefs is naturally much older than they. The figure of Orestes occurs in reliefs on Etruscan cinerary urns of the third or second century BC (Brunn, *I rilievi delle urne etrusche* pl. 84 and pl. 85, 3, and 106-12). The urns represent a different moment in the story, and the place of Pylades is taken by Iphigeneia, resting her head and hands on a pillar. The scene may be a modification of the original from which the Roman reliefs are derived. The motive of the drapery caught between the knees, as in Pylades, does not occur before the very end of the fifth century, but is frequent in the fourth; for the two figures of Pylades and Orestes, compare the first and fourth figures on an Attic bell-krater in Vienna (Laborde, *Vases de Lamberg* I, pl. 16 [*ARV* 1423, 1]), which belongs to the early fourth century.

Babelon (*op. cit.*, 157) considers our cameo to be a renaissance copy of the Mattei relief. The cameo differs from the relief in many points, the head of Orestes unveiled, the left hand of Pylades empty, his right hand placed differently on a higher pillar, the supernumeraries changed. These variations cannot be used as an argument either for or against a modern origin: but at least one detail suggests that the cameo is not an imitation of the Mattei relief. The hand of Orestes lies half open beside his knee: on the relief, it is wrapped in his drapery: but on the Weimar sarcophagus it is placed as on the cameo. The cameo is copied, it may be urged, from the Weimar and not from the Mattei version: that is impossible, for the Weimar Pylades differs from both the Mattei and the cameo. The Berlin sarcophagus is out of the question, as it was not discovered till the nineteenth century. It is unlikely that a modern artist would have contaminated the Mattei and the Weimar versions. Either the cameo is ancient or it is copied from a fourth sarcophagus which has disappeared.

There is nothing, however, in the style of the cameo which would prevent it from being antique: and it is well known that the engravers of gems and the sculptors of sarcophagi often drew their compositions from the same source.

It may be added that Furtwängler saw the cameo and thought it antique.

133. [27.754]

From the Boulton collection (sale catalogue, no. 92).

Fragmentary sardonyx cameo, white on brown. [24 x 22mm]

A concert in the open air. A faun, wreathed with ivy, seated on a lionskin under a tree with a nymph on his lap, and smiling at a bearded satyr of rough appearance who is dancing the oklasma. Herbage: rocky ground to the left.

The scene may be completed with the help of a cameo in the Beverley collection (F., pl. 57, 18), where the nymph is perhaps clapping her hands to accompany the dancer, who is, however, omitted and replaced by an urn, while an aegipan holds his syrinx ready, and the faun conducts. A fragment of another cameo in the same collection, of which there is a cast in the Impronte dell'Instituto, contains the dancer and the head of the faun, and part of the tree with an oscillum dangling from it. A fourth cameo of the same type belonged to the Mantua and Worsley collections (*Museum Worsleianum* II, 37; Visconti, *Museo Worslejano* pl. 30, 16): here the aegipan is replaced by a little boy, who plays the flutes, and the nymph appears to be holding a bowl.

The cut published by Aeneas Vicus (*Ex gemmis et cameis antiquorum aliquot monumenta* pl. 8) represents a cameo of this type; possibly the former of the Beverley stones, with the urn transformed into an aegipan standing on a rock in the distance and playing the double flute. Vicus has added the motto suggested by the cup in the nymph's hand: "Libidinis fomes. / Si vina tollas et Venus statim perit / nec dulce quidquam restat hinc mortalibus."

The figure of the nymph occurs in other compositions: so on another cameo in the Beverley collection (F., pl.

57, 20). For the gesture of the faun, a fragmentary cameo in the British Museum (*BM Gems* no. 3501) may be compared: an old Silenus seated playing the lyre, and a hand with the index and middle fingers extended, the first vertically and the second diagonally, and the rest closed.

III. Supplement: Intaglios

134. [27.706]

Formerly in the Evans collection. Published in a Paris sale catalogue. (*Margin: Coll. d'ant.* 11 mai 1903, 73, no. 290.)

Chalcedony, slightly convex. The lower left-hand part lost. [26 x 19 mm]

Ground line, swelling towards the middle. A woman with a vessel at a fountain. Thin chiton, undergirt; the mantle has slipped back from the shoulders. Coiled hair.

The same design on several Greco-Roman gems (*BM Gems* no. 561; F., pl. 39, 26-7 [Zwierlein-Diehl, *Wien* I, no. 295]; Furtwängler, *Berlin* pl. 7, no. 345 [*AGDS* II, no. 386]) and on a convex sard in New York which is probably Hellenistic like ours. The vessel has been called a hydria, but as no side-handles are indicated in any of the versions it is probably an oinochoe.

The upper part of the chiton is treated in the moist 'Ionian' manner; similarly on the stone F., pl. 39, 6 [*Cambridge* no. 95]; in the other versions the treatment is more severe.

The original may have been a picture, or a marble relief, of the fifth century. The severer versions recall the Persephone on the Triptolemos relief from Eleusis.

Hellenistic.

135. [27.737]

Acquired in Rome, 1919. The stone was found in 1918 by a man working in a vigna at Rome. He sold it to an old Roman dealer, who sold it to another dealer for a trifle ("una sciocchezza"). The inscription was read by a third dealer, a Greek, who seems to have urged the second dealer to buy it.

Sard, fragmentary: the upper half missing, and the lower right-hand portion fractured. [17 x 13 mm]

Thick, irregular ground line. Bellerophon mastering Pegasos. The hero is naked save for a chlamys: his right foot frontal and his right leg bent at the knee; the outer part of the right foot broken away. The horse's body foreshortened. Inscription, in the exergue ...URIDOU, [Diosko]uridou, the signature of the artist Dioskourides. The letters are end-dotted: the lines of

the delta concave inwards. Six letters remain: the dealer who sold the stone to its present owner stated that a seventh, presumably the second omicron of the name, was broken away in mounting the stone. Mr. A.P. Ready observes that the end-dots of the letters are not bored perpendicularly, but slightly undercut, so that the stone is liable to fracture in sealing. The imprint is misleading in one point: by smoothing away the traces of the break the maker of the imprint has produced the semblance of a seventh letter before the first upsilon: there is no such letter in the original.

Mr. John Marshall points out that the sard is of the same colour, kind, and excellence as that used by Dioskourides for his Achilles in Naples (F., III, 356); the quality of the fracturing is the same in both.

The missing part of the design can be restored by comparison with the Bellerophon gem published by Beger in his *Spicilegium Antiquitatis* (1692) 68. The hero's head is turned away from the horse, and appears in three-quarter profile; his right arm is not visible; his left is extended beyond the animal's forehead as if he were grasping its forelock. The position of Pegasus is not quite the same in Beger's gem: the right wing is lower, both forelegs are raised, and the hind quarters seem to be on the ground. Beger notices that the engraver differs from Pausanias, but agrees with Strabo, 379, who says of Pirene, "They say that Pegasos was drinking there when Bellerophon caught him."

(*Margin*: A gem like Beger's and presumably the same is published by Aeneas Vicus, pl. 4, with the caption *Exemplum grave prebet ales / Pegasus terrenum equitem gravatus Bellerophontem.*)

In *Annali* 1874, 9, Engelmann mentions a fragment of a relief in the Villa Carpegna which has the same design as Beger's gem. (*Margin*: Now in Budapest.)

A variant on an ancient paste cameo in Berlin (Furtwängler, *Berlin* 351, no. 11272): here Bellerophon faces to the right and his right arm is bent at the elbow; and Pegasos is almost in profile. Compare also Herakles and the Bull on a sard in the British Museum (F., pl. 35, 29).

On Dioskourides, Augustus' favourite engraver, see F. III, 355-7, and Furtwängler's earlier essay in *Jdl* 3, 211-25. The portrait of Demosthenes in amethyst (F., pl. 49, 7 [Vollenweider, *Steinschneidekunst* pl. 57, 1-3, 5]) is now in the collection of Sir Arthur Evans [now 'Private'].

Abbreviations

The groups of letter and number immediately following the catalogue number refer to the archives: B.B., Black Book; G.P., General Provisional; R., Register; T.L., Temporary List; Bu. with letter and number after it, to the exhibition of ancient Greek art at the Burlington Fine Arts Club in 1904.

[The present inventory number in the Boston Museum of Fine Arts is given immediately after the Lewes House number. We have relegated the Warren archive letters and numbers (above) to the list of added references at the end of the book. The following list has been adjusted and added to, following modern conventions, to include also the works mentioned in the additional bibliographies.]

AA

Archäologischer Anzeiger

ABV

J.D. Beazley, *Attic Black-figure Vase-painters* (1956)

ActaA

Acta Archaeologica

AGDS

Antike Gemmen in Deutschen Sammlungen I Munich (by E. Brandt, E. Schmidt, A. Krug, W. Gercke, 1968, 1970, 1972); II Berlin (by E. Zwierlein-Diehl, 1969); III Braunschweig, Göttingen, Kassel (by P. Zazoff, V. Scherf, P. Gercke, 1970); IV Hamburg, Hannover (by M. Schlüter, G. Platz-Horster and P. Zazoff, 1975)

AJA

American Journal of Archaeology

AntK

Antike Kunst

ArchEph

Archaiologike Ephemeris

ARV

J.D. Beazley, *Attic Red-figure Vase-painters* (ed. 2, 1963)

AthMitt

Athenische Mitteilungen

Babelon, *Traité*

J. Babelon, *Traité des monnaies grecques et romaines* (1901-32)

BABesch

Bulletin van de Vereeniging tot Bevordering der Kennis van de Antieke Beschaving

BCH

Bulletin de correspondance hellénique

Beazley, *EVP*

J.D. Beazley, *Etruscan Vase-Painting* (1947)

Beazley, *VA*

J.D. Beazley, *Attic Red-figured Vases in American Museums* (1918)

Berlin

A. Furtwängler, *Beschreibung der geschnittenen Steine im Antiquarium: Königliche Museen zu Berlin* (1896)

BMFA

Bulletin of the Museum of Fine Arts, Boston

BM *Coins of...*

British Museum: Catalogue of the Greek Coins of...

BM *Finger Rings*

F.H. Marshall, *Catalogue of the Finger Rings, Greek, Etruscan and Roman, in the Departments of Antiquities, British Museum* (1907)

BM *Gems*

H.B. Walters, *Catalogue of the Engraved Gems and Cameos, Greek, Etruscan and Roman in the British Museum* (1926). [Beazley's references to Arthur Smith's Catalogue of 1888 have all been replaced by references to Walters.]

BMQ
> *British Museum Quarterly*

Boardman, *Archaic*
> J. Boardman, *Archaic Greek Gems* (1968)

Boardman, *GGFR*
> J. Boardman, *Greek Gems and Finger Rings* (1970; with additional chapter, 2001)

Boardman, *Ibiza*
> J. Boardman, *Escarabeos de piedra procedentes de Ibiza* (1984)

Boardman, *Ionides*
> J. Boardman, *Engraved Gems: The Ionides Collection* (1968)

Boardman, *Island*
> J. Boardman, *Island Gems* (1963)

Boardman, *Private*
> J. Boardman, *Intaglios and Rings* (1975); these are now in the J. Paul Getty Museum, Malibu

Boardman and La Rocca, *Eros*
> J. Boardman and E. La Rocca, *Eros in Greece* (1978)

Borbein, *Campanareliefs*
> A.H. Borbein, *Campanareliefs* (*RM* Erg. 14, 1968)

Bossert, *Altkreta*
> H.T. Bossert, *Altkreta* (1923)

Bothmer, *Amazons*
> D. von Bothmer, *Amazons in Greek Art* (1957)

Boulter, *Greek Art*
> C.G. Boulter (ed.), *Greek Art: Archaic into Classical* (1985)

Bowra, *Classical Greece*
> C.M. Bowra, *Classical Greece* (1965)

BPW
> *Berliner philologische Wochenschrift*

Brommer, *Denkmälerlisten*
> F. Brommer, *Denmälerlisten zur griechischen Heldensage* I (1971); II (1974); III (1976)

Broustet
> M.A. Broustet (ed.), *La glyptique des mondes classiques: Mélanges en hommage à Marie-Louise Vollenweider* (1997)

Brown, *Lion*
> W.L. Brown, *The Etruscan Lion* (1960)

Brunn-Bruckmann
> *Denkmäler griechischer und römischer Skulptur*

BSA
> *Annual of the British School at Athens*

Buchholz, Jöhrens and Maull, *Jagd*
> H.-G. Buchholz, G. Jöhrens and I. Maull, *Jagd und Fischfang* (*Arch. Homerica* J, 1973)

BurlMag
> *Burlington Magazine*

Burlington Catalogue
> *Burlington Fine Arts Club: Exhibition of Ancient Greek Art, 1904: Illustrated Catalogue*

BWPr
> *Winckelmannsprogramm der Archäologischen Gesellschaft zu Berlin*

Cambridge
> M. Henig, *Classical Gems. Fitzwilliam Museum, Cambridge* (1994)

Chase, *Antiquities*
> G.H. Chase, *Greek and Roman Antiquities: A Guide to the Classical Collection* (1950)

Chase and Vermeule, *Classical Collections*
> G.H. Chase and C.C. Vermeule, *Greek Etruscan and Roman Art* (1972)

Cheney, *Sculpture*
> S. Cheney, *Sculpture of the World: A History* (1968)

Classicism
> M. Henig and D. Plantzos (eds.), *Classicism to Neo-classicism. Essays dedicated to Gertrud Seidmann* (Oxford, BAR International Series 793, 1999)

CMS
> *Corpus der minoischen und mykenischen Siegel*

Cook, *Greek Art*
> R.M. Cook, *Greek Art* (1972)

Cook
> C.H. Smith and C.A. Hutton, *Catalogue of the Antiquities (Greek, Etruscan and Roman) in the Collection of the late Wyndham Francis Cook, Esqre* (the gems by Miss Hutton) (1908)

Curtius, *Antike Kunst*
> L. Curtius, *Die Antike Kunst* II, 1: *Die klassische Kunst Griechenlands* (1938)

Ducati, *Arte Classica*
> P. Ducati, *L'Arte Classica* (1944)

EAA
> *Enciclopedia dell'arte antica, classica e orientale*

Evans, *Minos*
> Sir Arthur Evans, *The Palace of Minos* IV, 2 (1935)

F.
> A. Furtwängler, *Die antiken Gemmen: Geschichte der Steinschneidekunst im klassischen Altertum* (1900)

Festschrift Hausmann
> *Praestant Interna: Festschrift für Ulrich Hausmann* (1982)

Fischer-Graf, *Spiegelwerkstätten*
> U. Fischer-Graf, *Spiegelwerkstätten in Vulci* (1980)

FR
> A. Furtwängler and K. Reichhold, *Griechische Vasenmalerei* (1904-32)

von Freytag Gen. Löringhoff, *Giebelrelief*
> B. von Freytag Gen. Löringhoff, *Das Giebelrelief von Telamon* (*RM* Erg. 27, 1986)

Gardner, *Types*
> P. Gardner, *The Types of Greek Coins* (1883)

GettyMusJ
> *The J. Paul Getty Museum Journal*

Giuliano, *Tesoro*
> A. Giuliano, in N. Dacos *et al.*, *Il Tesoro di Lorenzo Il Magnifico: Le Gemme* (1973)

Guarducci, *Epigrafia Greca* III
> M. Guarducci, *Epigrafia Greca* III: *Epigrafi di Carattere Privato* (1974)

Herrmann, *Shadow*
> J.J. Herrmann, Jr., *In the Shadow of the Acropolis* (1984/1988)

Hoffmann and Davidson, *Greek Gold*
> H. Hoffmann and P.F. Davidson, *Greek Gold* (1965)

Hornbostel, *Norddeutschem Privatbesitz*
> W. Hornbostel *et al.*, *Kunst der Antike: Schätze aus norddeutschem Privatbesitz* (1977)

Horster, *Statuen*
> G. Horster, *Statuen auf Gemmen* (1970)

Houser, *Dionysos*
> C. Houser, *Dionysos and his Circle* (1979)

IstMitt
> *Istanbuler Mitteilungen*

Jahreshefte
> *Jahreshefte des Oesterreichischen Archäologischen Institutes*

JberlMus
> *Jahrbuch der Berliner Museen*

JdI
> *Jahrbuch des Deutschen Archäologischen Instituts*

JHS
> *Journal of Hellenic Studies*

JRS
> *Journal of Roman Studies*

JWalt
> *Journal of the Walters Art Gallery*

Kenna, *Cretan Seals*
> V.E.G. Kenna, *Cretan Seals with a Catalogue of the Minoan Gems in the Ashmolean Museum* (1960)

Krauskopf, *Thebanische*
> I. Krauskopf, *Die thebanische Sagenkreis und andere griechische Sagen in der etruskischen Kunst* (1974)

Kyrieleis, *Bildnisse*
> H. Kyrieleis, *Bildnisse der Ptolemäer* (1975)

LCS
> A.D. Trendall, *The red-figured Vases of Lucania, Campania and Sicily* (1967)

LHG
> J.D. Beazley, *The Lewes House Collection of Ancient Gems* (1920)

LIMC
> *Lexicon Iconographicum Mythologiae Classicae*

Lippold, *Gemmen*
> G. Lippold, *Gemmen und Kameen des Altertums und der Neuzeit* (1922)

Maas and Snyder, *Stringed Instruments*
> M. Maas and J.M. Snyder, *Stringed Instruments of Ancient Greece* (*c.* 1989)

Maaskant-Kleibrink, *The Hague*
> M. Maaskant-Kleibrink, *Catalogue of the Engraved Gems in the Royal Coin Cabinet The Hague* (1978)

Martini, *Ringsteinglyptik*
> W. Martini, *Die etruskische Ringsteinglyptik* (*RM* Erg. 18. 1971)

MFA, *Trojan War*
> *The Trojan War in Greek Art: A Picture Book* (1965)

Moret, *Palladion*
> J.-M. Moret, *Les pierres gravées antiques représentant le rapt du Palladion* (1997)

Mulas, *Antiquity*
> A. Mulas, *Eros in Antiquity* (1978)

MuM
> Münzen und Medaillen, *Vente Publique*

Neverov, *Intaglios*
> O. Neverov, *Antique Intaglios in the Hermitage Collection* (1976)

Neverov, *Cameos*
> O. Neverov, *Antique Cameos in the Hermitage Collection* (1971)

New York
> G.M.A. Richter, *Catalogue of the Engraved Gems in the Metropolitan Museum of Art* (1956)

Nikulina
>N.M. Nikulina, *Iskusstvo Ionii i Achemenidskogo Irana po materialam glyptiki* (1994)

Oxford
>J. Boardman and M.-L. Vollenweider, *Catalogue of the Engraved Gems and Finger Rings in the Ashmolean Museum* I (1978)

Paralipomena
>J.D. Beazley, *Paralipomena* (1971)

PBSR
>*Papers of the British School at Rome*

Periplous
>G.R. Tsetskhladze, A.J.N.W. Prag and A.M. Snodgrass, eds., *Periplous: Papers on Classical Art and Archaeology presented to Sir John Boardman* (London, 2000)

Plantzos
>D. Plantzos, *Hellenistic Engraved Gems* (1999)

Porada, *Seals*
>E. Porada (ed.), *Ancient Art in Seals* (1980)

Poulsen, *Probleme*
>F. Poulsen, *Probleme der römischen Ikonographie* (1937)

RA
>*Revue archéologique*

Richter, *Animals*
>G.M.A. Richter, *Animals in Greek Sculpture: A Survey* (1930)

Richter, *Greeks and Etruscans*
>G.M.A. Richter, *The Engraved Gems of the Greeks and the Etruscans* (1968)

Richter, *Romans*
>G.M.A. Richter, *The Engraved Gems of the Romans* (1971)

Richter, *Sculptors*
>G.M.A. Richter, *The Sculpture and Sculptors of the Greeks* (1950/1970)

RM
>*Römische Mitteilungen*

Robertson, *History*
>M. Robertson, *A History of Greek Art* (1975)

Robertson, *Shorter History*
>M. Robertson, *A Shorter History of Greek Art* (1981)

RVP
>A.D. Trendall, *The red-figured Vases of Paestum* (1987)

Schefold, *Griechen*
>K. Schefold, *Die Griechen und ihre Nachbarn* (1967)

Schefold and Jung, *Urkönige*
>K. Schefold and F. Jung, *Die Urkönige, Perseus, Bellerophon, Herakles und Theseus in der klassischen und hellenistischen Kunst* (1988)

Schoder, *Masterpieces*
>R.V. Schoder, *Masterpieces of Greek Art* (1960)

Schürmann, *Minerva-Kultbilder*
>W. Schürmann, *Untersuchungen zu Typologie und Bedeutung der stadtrömischen Minerva-Kultbilder* (1985)

Sena Chiesa, *Aquileia*
>G. Sena Chiesa, *Gemme del Museo Nazionale di Aquileia* (1966)

Snowden, *Blacks*
>F.M. Snowden, *Blacks in Antiquity* (1970)

Southesk
>*Catalogue of the Collection of Antique Gems formed by James, Ninth Earl of Southesk, K.T., edited by his daughter, Lady Helena Carnegie* (1908)

Spier, *Gems*
>J. Spier, *Ancient Gems and Finger Rings: Catalogue of the Collections, The J. Paul Getty Museum* (1992)

Tharros
>R.D. Barnett and C. Mendleson (eds.), *Tharros* (1987)

Thorvaldsen
>P. Fossing, *Catalogue of the antique engraved gems and cameos, Thorvaldsen Museum* (1929)

Vermeule, *Prehistoric*
>E. Vermeule, *Greece in the Bronze Age: Prehistoric through Perikles* (1964)

Vermeule, *Death*
>E. Vermeule, *Aspects of Death in Early Greek Art and Poetry* (1979)

Vermeule, *Portraits*
>C.C. Vermeule, *Greek and Roman Portraits 470 BC - AD 500* (1959/1972, with M.B. Comstock)

Vermeule, *Art*
>C.C. Vermeule, *The Art of the Greek World* (1982)

Vives
>A. Vives y Escudero, *Estudio de Arqueologia cartaginesa: la Necropoli de Ibiza* (1917)

Vollenweider, *Deliciae*
>M.-L. Vollenweider, *Deliciae Leonis* (1984)

Vollenweider, *Genève*
>M.-L. Vollenweider, *Catalogue raisonné des sceaux, cylindres et intailles* I (1967), II (1976-9), III (1983)

Vollenweider, *Porträtgemmen*

    M.-L. Vollenweider, *Die Porträtgemmen der römischen Republik* (1972, 1974)

Vollenweider, *Steinschneidekunst*

    M.-L. Vollenweider, *Die Steinschneidekunst und ihre Künstler in spätrepublikanischer und augusteischer Zeit* (1966)

Walter-Karydi, *Alt-Ägina*

    E. Walter-Karydi, *Alt-Ägina* II, 2: *Die äginetische Bildhauerschule* (1987)

Weinberg, *Numismatics*

    G.D. and S.S. Weinberg, in *Greek Numismatics and Archaeology* (Essays in honor of Margaret Thompson, eds. O. Mørkholm and N. Waggoner, 1979)

Wohlfeil

    J.B. Wohlfeil, *Die Bildersprache minoischer und mykenischer Siegel* (BAR International Series 685, 1997)

Zagdoun, *Sculpture*

    M.-A. Zagdoun, *La sculpture archäisante dans l'art hellénistique et dans l'art romain du haut-empire* (1989)

Zazoff, *Gemmen*

    P. Zazoff, *Die antiken Gemmen* (1983)

Zazoff

    P. Zazoff, *Die Etruskische Skarabäen* (1968)

Zwierlein-Diehl, *Wien*

    E. Zwierlein-Diehl, *Die antiken Gemmen des Kunsthistorischen Museums in Wien* I (1973), II (1979)

Zwierlein-Diehl, *Würzburg*

    E. Zwierlein-Diehl, *Glaspasten in Martin-von-Wagner-Museum der Universität Würzburg* I (1986)

Indices

These are based on Beazley's Index, rearranged and with some additions.
References are to Catalogue numbers *not* pages.

Ward, 128

Additional Bibliography

1.

27.655 B.B. 37, 7. R. 1304. Bu. O 35.

Bossert, *Altkreta* 36, 235, pl. 326a; Evans, *Minos* IV, 586-587, fig. 579, suppl. pl. 55d; Kenna, *Cretan Seals* 61; Chase and Vermeule, *Classical Collections* 14, 21, fig.7; V.E.G. Kenna, *AJA* 68 (1964), 5-6, 11, pl. 2:30; Vermeule, *Bronze Age* 223, 405, pl. 43B; Vollenweider, *Genève* I, 147, under no. 197; Boardman, *GGFR* 56, 105, 396 (J), pl. 179; Buchholz, Jöhrens, and Maull, *Jagd* J24, no. 82 (with ref. to F. Brein, *Der Hirsch in der griechischen Frühzeit* Diss. Wien, 1964, 94); Kenna and Thomas, *CMS* XIII, 21, no. 20, 4 illus.; J.G. Younger, *AJA* 82 (1978), 290, no. 9, fig. 11; M.A.V. Gill, in *CMS* Beiheft 1, 84; I. Pini, in *L'Iconographie Minoenne* (*BCH* Suppl. XI), 156; *idem*, *AA* 1987, 416, under no. 4; I. Pini, in *CMS* XI, xxii, n. 34; *CMS* V, Suppl. 1A, 8, under no. 4; M. Andreadaki-Vlasakis, *ibid.*, 188, under no. 185; M. Ballintijn in *CMS* Beiheft 5, 25, n. 5; L. Morgan, *ibid.*, 138 (fig. 9), 139.

2.

27.656 G.P. 144, 114. R. 1966. Bu. O 47.

Bossert, *Altkreta* 36, 235, pl. 326c (listed as Lewes, no. 3); Evans, *Minos* IV, 585-586, fig. 575, suppl. pl. 55f (a 'horned sheep'); Kenna, *Cretan Seals* 61; Vermeule, *Bronze Age* 223, 405, pl. 43A; V.E.G. Kenna, *AJA* 68 (1964), 5-6, 11, pl. 2:29; Boardman, *GGFR* 56, 105, 396 (L), pl. 180; Buchholz, Jöhrens, and Maull, *Jagd* J23, nos. 64 and 69; Kenna and Thomas, *CMS* XIII, 26, no. 25, 4 illus.; A. Tamvaki, *BSA* 69 (1974), 266; I. Pini, in *CMS* II,3 LVI (under no. 149), LVIII (under no. 191); I. Pini, in *ibid.*, II, 4, LXII; M.A.V. Gill, in *CMS* Beiheft 1, 84; *CMS* V, Suppl. 1B, XXXV, n. 65; L. Morgan in *CMS* Beiheft 5, 138 (fig. 11), 140; Wohlfeil, 127, 128 (n. 324), 185 (no. 103), fig. 83.

3.

23.576 G.P. 301, 2.

Bossert, *Altkreta* 36, 235, pl. 326b (listed as Lewes,

no. 2); Chase and Vermeule, *Classical Collections* 14, 22, fig. 9; Vermeule, *Bronze Age* 223, 405, pl. 43C; *AGDS* I 1, 23, under nos. 41, 43; *AGDS* II 33, under no. 34; Boardman, *GGFR* 56, 105, pl. 182; Buchholz, Jöhrens, and Maull, *Jagd* J24, no. 90; Kenna and Thomas, *CMS* XIII, 27, no. 26, 4 illus.; J.H. Betts, in *CMS* Beiheft 1, 19, 31; Vermeule, *Prehistoric* 67-68, 105, 216, 360, fig. 119A; I. Pini, in *L'Iconographie Minoenne* (*BCH* suppl. XI), 164, n. 52; J.G. Younger, in *CMS* Beiheft 3 (1989), 344-346, fig. 12, 351; L. Morgan in *CMS* Beiheft 5, 147, n. 71; Wohlfeil, 180-181, no. 95.

4.

27.658 G.P. 341, 2. Bu. L 14.

V.E.G. Kenna, *AJA* 68 (1964), 6, 11-12; Boardman, *GGFR* 56, 58, 105, 395, pl. 181; Kenna and Thomas, *CMS* XIII, 28, no. 27, 4 illus.; J.G. Younger, *JHS* 96 (1976), 255; B. Rutkowski, *Frühgriechische Kultdarstellungen* (*AthMitt* Beiheft 8), 63 (fig. 20, no. 2), 68-69; M. Andreadaki-Vlasakis, in *CMS* V, Suppl. 1A, 200 (under no. 197), 201 (under no. 198); N. Marinatos, *ActaAth* 9 (1986), 15-17.

5.

27.657 G.P. 341, 7.

AGDS II 37, under no. 47; Boardman, *GGFR* 48, 52, 103, pl. 133; Kenna and Thomas, in *CMS* XIII, 29, no. 28, 3 illus.; A. Spetsieris-Choremis, *ArchEph* 1981 (1983), 67, n. 12; A. Tamvaki, in *L'Iconographie Minoenne* (*BCH* Suppl. XI), 279; E. Karantzali, *BCH* 110 (1986), 85, n. 30; Wohlfeil, 79, 81-82, 118, 131 (n. 342), 167 (no. 62), fig. 60.

6-8. *vacant*
(Mesopotamian and Persian)

Phoenician and Greco-Phoenician

9.

27.762 R. 447.

10.

27.763 R. 445.

Boardman, *Archaic* 36, no. 64, pl. 4, no. 64; *AGDS* I 1, 49, under no. 216.

11.

27.659

New York 5, under no. 15; Richter, *Greeks and Etruscans* 36, under no. 34; Boardman, *Ibiza* no. 95.

12.

27.764

Richter, *Greeks and Etruscans* 36, no. 36, 2 illus.; *AGDS* IV 16, under no. 17; Boardman, *Ibiza* no. 100.

13.

27.660

Richter, *Greeks and Etruscans* 37, no. 41, 2 illus.; Boardman, *Ibiza* no. 179.

13 *bis*.

27.765

Boardman, *Ibiza* no. 189; H. Wiegandt, *Charms of the Past: Engraved Gems, Intaglii and Camei* (Marburg, 1998) 37, under no. 49.

Greek: Archaic

14.

27.668 R. 439.

P. Zazoff, *JdI* 81 (1966), 75; *idem, Skarabäen* 23, 159, no. 584; Boardman, *Archaic* 46-49, no. 79, pl. 5, no. 79; Brommer, *Denkmälerlisten* I, 39, no. 1; *Oxford* 50, under no. 211; Zazoff, *Gemmen* 117, n. 99; I. Krauskopf, *LIMC* II, 1, 339, 354, no. 14, pl. 287; S.J. Schwarz, *LIMC* V, 1, 234, no. 357; E. Zwierlein-Diehl, *AntK* 35 (1992), 109, 117, pl. 22, 9.

15.

23.595 G.P. 257, 1. Bu. O 64.

Boardman, *Archaic* 52, no. 88, pl. 6, no. 88: the Plump Satyr Group; *idem, GGFR* 181, pl. 304; Zazoff, *Gemmen* 117, n. 100; Maas and Snyder, *Stringed Instruments* 38, 225 (n. 75), 229 (n. 21); I. Krauskopf and E. Simon, *LIMC* VIII, 787, no. 55, 801.

16.

27.667 G.P. 342, 3.

Boardman, *Archaic* 54, no. 102, pl. 7, no. 102: the Slim Satyr Group; *AGDS* I 1, 47, under no. 207; *AGDS* II 47-48, under nos. 76-78; Boardman, *Private* 101, under no. 114; Zazoff, *Gemmen* 110, n. 69.

17.

23.577 G.P. 188, 479.

Lippold, *Gemmen* 14, 169, pl. 14, 1; Beazley, *EVP* 38; *New York* 8, under no. 29; Boardman, *Archaic* 59-61, no. 110, pl. 8, no. 110; Richter, *Greeks and Etruscans* 47-48, no. 83, 2 illus.; *AGDS* II 47, under no. 76; Boardman *GGFR* 144, 181, pl. 307; *AGDS* IV 362, under no. 18; S. Hurter, *Schweizerische Numismatische Rundschau* 72 (1993), 203, 207, pl. 1, 7; N. Kourou *et al.*, *LIMC* VIII, 1163, no. 231, 1164.

18.

27.669 G.P. 317, 4.

Boardman, *Archaic* 82, no. 211, pl. 13, no. 211; *Oxford* 13, under no. 65; Maas and Snyder, *Stringed Instruments* 238, ns. 1, 3, 21.

19.

27.672

Boardman, *Archaic* 81-83, no. 204, pl. 13, no. 204; *idem*, *GGFR* 146, 183, pl. 335; Vollenweider, *Genève* III, 153, under no. 205, n. 1; H. Sarian, *LIMC* III, 1, 827-828, no. 5, 842.

20.

27.671 G.P. 340, 3. Bu. L 54.

C.T. Seltman, *BSA* 26 (1923-1925), 92, fig. 2a; *New York* 10, under no. 33; Boardman, *Archaic* 73, no. 172, pl. 11, no. 172; *idem*, *GGFR* 146, 183, pl. 333; Vollenweider, *Genève* III, 135, under no. 181, n. 4;

LIMC III, 1, 909, no. 671a; Maas and Snyder, *Stringed Instruments* 117, 230 (n. 39), 237 (n. 84); *7000 Years of Seals* (ed. D. Collon, 1997) pl. 5.9.

21.

27.670 R. 444. Bu. O 15.

Boardman, *Archaic* 97-98, no. 268, pl. 18, no. 268 (as 27.674); Richter, *Greeks and Etruscans* 58-59, no. 135, 2 illus.; Brommer, *Denkmälerlisten* I, 145, no. 4 (as 27.674); M. Moore, *GettyMusJ* 2 (1975), 44, n. 26; Zazoff, *Gemmen* 117, n. 100; F. Brommer, *Heracles: The Twelve Labors of the Hero in Ancient Art and Literature* (translated and enlarged by S.J. Schwarz) (New Rochelle, 1986), 74, n. 44; J. Boardman, *LIMC* V, 1, 68 (no. 2420, as 27.674), 71.

22.

27.674

J. Boardman, *PBSR* 34 (1966), 15; *idem*, *Archaic* 94-96, no. 254, pl. 17, no. 254: by the Semon Master; *idem*, *GGFR* 151, 184, pl. 366; Brommer, *Denkmälerlisten* I, 110, no. 7; O.W. von Vacano, *Gnomon* 45 (1973), 285; Boardman, *Private* 12-13, 80 (no. K, illus.), 113; E. Walter-Karydi, *JBerlMus* 17 (1975), 18 (fig. 21), 20; H. Luschey, in *Festschrift Hausmann* 299, n. 9; Zazoff, *Gemmen* 120, n. 114; Vollenweider, *Deliciae* 20, under no. 30; M.B. Moore, M.Z.P. Philippides, and D. von Bothmer, *The Athenian Agora* vol. 23: *Attic Black-figured Pottery* (Princeton, 1986), 94, n. 176; Walter-Karydi, *Alt-Ägina* 100-103, fig. 149; W. Felten, *LIMC* V, 1, 25 (no. 1886), 33; V. Karageorghis, *Greek Gods and Heroes in Ancient Cyprus* (Athens, 1998), 86 (fig. 41), 303 (no. 41); M.B. Moore, *Attic Red-Figured and White-Ground Pottery* (Princeton, N.J., 1997) 83, n. 17.

23.

27.766 R. 441.

Boardman, *Archaic* 162, no. 590; *AGDS* IV 360, under no. 15.

24.

27.673 T.L. 33,2. Bu. O 70.

New York XXXV; A. Stazio, in *EAA* V (1963), 693; Boardman, *Island* 78-80, no. 337, pl. 12; *idem, Archaic* 116-118, no. 345, pl. 25, no. 345; Richter, *Greeks and Etruscans* 15, 17, 45, 52, no. 103, 2 illus.; Zazoff, 67; Boardman, *GGFR* 142, 147, 184, pl. 351; Robertson, *History* 147-148, pl. 43e; E. Walter-Karydi, *JBerlMus* 17 (1975), 26-27, fig. 29; M. Anderson, in Houser, *Dionysos* 102, MFA 5, illus.; Zazoff, *Gemmen* 83 (n. 49), 125, pl. 19, 2; Maas and Snyder, *Stringed Instruments* 229, n. 21; *7000 Years of Seals* (ed. D. Collon, 1997) pl. 5.5; *Classicism* 220, 224, fig. 9 (J. Boardman).

25.

27.675 B.B. 39, 5. Bu. O 79.

J. Boardman, *AntK* 10 (1967), 26-27, no. N41; *idem, GGFR* 157, 188, pl. 440; *idem, Private* 94, under no. 71; E. Walter-Karydi, *JBerlMus* 17 (1975), 12-13, fig. 8.

26.

27.676 G.P. 340, 1.

L.D. Caskey, *BMFA* 26 (1928), 47-48, fig. 4; Chase, *Antiquities* 40, fig. 48; J. Marcadé, *BCH* 79 (1955), 398, 400, fig. 20; Chase and Vermeule, *Classical Collections* 51, 71, fig. 61; Boardman, *Archaic* 91-92, no. 239, pl. 15, no. 239: Group of the Leningrad Gorgon; Richter, *Greeks and Etruscans* 63-65, no. 163, 2 illus.; Boardman, *GGFR* 152, 185, pl. 381; Vollenweider, *Genève* III, 174, under no. 224; Zazoff, *Gemmen* 111, n. 78; P. Demargne, *LIMC* II, 1, 970, no. 123, pl. 717; J. Boardman, in Boulter, *Greek Art* 93, 95, n. 43, pl. 78d; G.F. Pinney, in J. Christiansen and T. Melander, *Proceedings of the 3rd Symposium on Ancient Greek and Related Pottery, Copenhagen August 31 - September 4, 1987* (Copenhagen, 1988), 469, 476, n. 26; *Cambridge* 27, under no. 45.

27.

21.1194 R. 814. Bu. O 18.

Lippold, *Gemmen* 53, 176, pl. 53, 5; L.D. Caskey, *BMFA* 26 (1928), 47-48, fig. 3; Curtius, *Antike Kunst* II, 1, 243, 313, pl. 24D; Chase, *Antiquities* 40, fig. 48; Chase and Vermeule, *Classical Collections* 51, 71, fig. 61; MFA, *Illustrated Handbook* 1964, 58-59, illus.; *ibid.*, 1976, 90-91, illus.; Schefold, *Griechen* 208, pl. 161a (wrongly as 27.676); Boardman, *Archaic* 93, no. 247, pl. 16, no. 247; Richter, *Greeks and Etruscans* 15, 48, 54, no. 114, 2 illus., pl. B, illus.; *AGDS* II 54, under no. 91; Boardman, *GGFR* 142, 148, 184, pl. 356; *idem, Private* 12-13, 80 (no. C, illus.), 86 (under no. 22), 113; E. Walter-Karydi, *JBerlMus* 17 (1975), 8-9, fig. 3; H. Luschey, in *Festschrift Hausmann* 299, n. 9; Zazoff, *Gemmen* 103, 113, pl. 23, 3; Vollenweider, *Genève* III, 91, under no. 129, n. 2; J. Boardman, in Boulter, *Greek Art* 87, 89, 94, n. 16, pl. 75b; Walter-Karydi, *Alt-Ägina* 85 (no. 64), 101-102, pl. 46; Spier, *Gems* 18-19, under no. 17; *Classicism* 220, 224, fig. 12 (J. Boardman).

28.

27.677 R. 817. Bu. O 14.

L.D. Caskey, *BMFA* 26 (1928), 47-48, fig. 2; Richter, *Animals* 16, 58, pl. 18, fig. 60; Curtius, *Antike Kunst* II, 1, 243, 313, pl. 24,I; Ducati, *Arte Classica* 194, fig. 244; Chase, *Antiquities* 40, fig. 48; *New York* xxxv, 12, under no. 42; Chase and Vermeule, *Classical Collections* 51, 71, fig. 61; Schefold, *Griechen* 208, under no. 161a; Boardman, *Archaic* 92-93, no. 246, pl. 16, no. 246; Richter, *Greeks and Etruscans* 15, 17, 48, 54-55, no. 116, 2 illus., pl. B; *AGDS* II 54, under no. 91; Boardman, *GGFR* 142, 148, 184, pl. 355; Guarducci, *Epigrafia Greca* III, 519, fig. 209; Vollenweider, *Porträtgemmen* 1974, 6, n. 2; Boardman, *Private* 12-13, 80 (no. A, illus.), 86 (under no. 22), 113; E. Walter-Karydi, *JBerlMus* 17 (1975), 8, 10-11, fig. 5; M. Moore, *GettyMusJ* 2 (1975), 40, 44 (n. 26), 46 (fig. 18), 49; Robertson, *History* 148, pl. 43g; E. Langlotz, *Studien zur nordostgriechischen Kunst* (Mainz, 1975) 171, n. 2; Vermeule, *Prehistoric* 125, 223, 433, fig. 185; H. Luschey, in *Festschrift Hausmann* 299, ns. 9, 11; Zazoff, *Gemmen* 101, 103 (n. 19), 113, pl. 23, 2; Vollenweider, *Genève* III, 91, under no. 129, n. 2; J.M. Hemelrijk, *Caeretan Hydriae* (Mainz, 1984) 176, 230, n. 722; J. Boardman, in Boulter, *Greek Art* 87, 94, n. 16, pl. 75d; *GettyMusJ* 14 (1986), 198, under no. 78; Spier, *Gems* 18-19, under no. 17; *Classicism* 220, 224, fig. 10 (J. Boardman).

29.

23.578 B. B. 150, 2. Bu. O 12.

Lippold, *Gemmen* 81, 180, pl. 81, 1; Boardman, *Archaic* 94-95, no. 252, pl. 16, no. 252: the Semon Master; *AGDS* I 1, 43, under no. 170; Richter, *Greeks and Etruscans* 58, 62-63, no. 155, 2 illus.; Boardman, *GGFR* 148, 184, pl. 361; *idem, Private* 12-13, 80 (no. H, illus.), 113; E. Walter-Karydi, *JBerlMus* 17 (1975), 20-21, 23, fig. 24; Vermeule, *Death* 249, n. 42; J. Boardman, in Porada, *Seals* 112, 118, 124, fig. IV-22; H. Luschey, in *Festschrift Hausmann* 299, n. 9; J. Boardman, in Boulter, *Greek Art* 85; Walter-Karydi, *Alt-Ägina* 100-103, fig. 151.

30.

21.1195 R. 820. Bu. O 24.

Boardman, *Archaic* 96-97, no. 261, pl. 18, no. 261; Krauskopf, *Thebanische* 84, n. 280; Boardman, *Private* 12-13, 80 (no. E, illus.), 86 (under no. 19), 113; *Oxford* I, 14, under no. 70; Zazoff, *Gemmen* 102, n. 17; J.R. Mertens, *Metropolitan Museum Journal* 24 (1989), 55-56, fig. 9.

31.

27.682

L.D. Caskey, *BMFA* 26 (1928), 47-48, fig. 6; Bothmer, *Amazons* 123, no. 11, pl. 90, 3; MFA, *Trojan War* fig. 30B; Boardman, *Archaic* 94-95, no. 255, pl. 17, no. 255: the Semon Master; Richter, *Greeks and Etruscans* 58, 62, no. 150, 2 illus.; Zazoff, 39, n. 43; Brommer, *Denkmälerlisten* II, 101, no. 2; E. Walter-Karydi, *JBerlMus* 17 (1975), 20-22, 25, fig. 25; E. La Rocca, *Bullettino della Commissione Archeologica* 87 (1980-81), 62, n. 35; A. Kauffmann-Samaras, *LIMC* I, 615, no. 444, pl. 495; A. Kossatz-Deissmann, *ibid.*, 164-165 (no. 738), 170, 200; H. Luschey, in *Festschrift Hausmann* 299, n. 9; Walter-Karydi, *Alt-Ägina* 100-103, fig. 152; M.I. Davies, in *Images et Société en Grèce Ancienne: L'Iconographie comme Méthode d'Analyse* (Cahiers d'Archéologie Romande, no. 36, Lausanne, 1987) 246, n. 4; V. Karageorghis, *Greek Gods and Heroes in Ancient Cyprus* (Athens, 1998), 92-93 (fig. 51), 304 (no. 51).

32.

27.680 R. 542. Bu. O 28.

C.T. Seltman, *BSA* 26 (1923-1925), 92, fig. 2b; J. Boardman, *AntK* 10 (1967), 25, n. 81; *idem, Archaic* 98-99, no. 274, pl. 19, no. 274; Richter, *Greeks and Etruscans* 55, 57, no. 125, 2 illus.; Vollenweider, *Genève* III, 134 (under no. 180, n. 7), 135 (under no. 181); *idem, Deliciae* 17 (under no. 25), 19 (under no. 29); *LIMC* III, 1, 865, no. 113.

33.

27.767 G.P. 319, 3.

C.T. Seltman, *BSA* 26 (1923-1925), 92, fig. 2c; *New York* 12, under no. 41; J. Boardman, *AntK* 10 (1967), 25, n. 81; *idem, Archaic* 98-99, no. 272, pl. 19, no. 272; *idem, Ionides* 91, under no. 4; *AGDS* I 1, 42, under no. 168; Richter, *Greeks and Etruscans* 55, 57, no. 126, 2 illus.; Boardman, *GGFR* 151, 185, pl. 371; E. Walter-Karydi, *JBerlMus* 17 (1975), 18-19, fig. 20; T. Hackens, Museum of Art, Rhode Island School of Design, *Catalogue of the Classical Collection: Classical Jewelry* (Providence, 1976) 54, under no. 13, n. 3; H. Luschey, in *Festschrift Hausmann* 299-300, pl. 68, 2; Vollenweider, *Genève* III, 134 (under no. 180, n. 7), 135 (under no. 181); *idem, Deliciae* 17 (under no. 25), 19 (under no. 29).

34.

21.1196 R. 562. Bu. O 29.

Boardman, *Archaic* 132-134, no. 428, pl. 31, no. 428: the Aristoteiches Group; *AGDS* I 1, 79, under no. 424; Vollenweider, *Genève* III, 91, under no. 129, n. 2; A. Pekridou, *Das Alketas-Grab in Termessos* (*IstMitt* Beiheft 32), 91, n. 279.

35.

27.681

Boardman, *Archaic* 147, 151, no. 522, pl. 35, no. 522; *AGDS* I 1, 63, under no. 308; *AGDS* II 91, under no. 211; Vollenweider, *Genève* III, 158, under no. 212.

35 bis.

27.689

L.D. Caskey, *BMFA* 26 (1928), 47-48, fig. 5; Richter, *Animals* 27, 71, pl. 45, fig. 138; *New York* 28, under no. 109 (as Lewes, no. 53 *bis*); Bowra, *Classical Greece* 15, illus.; Boardman, *Archaic* 147, 150-151,

153, no. 516, pl. 34, no. 516; *AGDS* I 1, 44, under no. 178; Richter, *Greeks and Etruscans* 73, no. 216, 2 illus. pl. C; *AGDS* II 52 (under no. 88), 88 (under no. 199); Boardman, *GGFR* 152, 186, pl. 394; Guarducci, *Epigrafia Greca* III, 356; Boardman, *Private* 90, under no. 42; Zazoff, *Gemmen* 101, n. 14; Vollenweider, *Genève* III, 158, under no. 212.

Etruscan: Archaic

35 *ter*.

21.1197

P. Ducati, *Storia dell'Arte Etrusca* (Florence, 1927), 303, pl. 129, fig. 336; P. Zazoff, *JdI* 81 (1966), 64, 68-72, 75-78, fig. 4 (as 21197); Vollenweider, *Genève* I, 163, under no. 221; Boardman, *Archaic* 46-48, 162-163, no. 77, pl. 5 (no. 77), pl. 38 (no. 77); Zazoff, 18-19, 21-23, no. 18, pl. 7 (as 21 197); *AGDS* II 49, under no. 80; Boardman, *GGFR* 153, 186, pl. 408; Brommer, *Denkmälerlisten* I, 48, no. 1 (as 21.1117), 120, no. 1; O.W. von Vacano, *Gnomon* 45 (1973) 284; Vollenweider, *Porträtgemmen* 1974, 1 (n. 1), 3, 5, 12; *ibid.*, 1972, 1 (with added references), pl. 1, 1; Brize, *Die Geryoneis des Stesichoros und die frühe griechische Kunst* (*Beiträge zur Archäologie* 12, Würzburg, 1980), 97, 167, NER IV 14; Zazoff, *Gemmen* 107 (n. 40), 215-216, 218-219 (fig. 55a), 228, pl. 55, 3; G. Colonna, *LIMC* II, 1067, no. 200, pl. 783; M. Cristofani, *LIMC* III, 532 (no. 5), 538, pl. 419; Schefold and Jung, *Urkönige* 352, n. 448 (as 21.1117); S.J. Schwarz, *LIMC* V, 1, 229 (no. 305, as 21.197), 250; J. Boardman, *The Diffusion of Classical Art in Antiquity* (Princeton, 1994), 250-251, fig. 7.24a,b; M. Pipili, *LIMC* VI, 828-829, no. 51; M.-C. D'Ercole, *RA* 1995, 286, n. 94; L.M. Michetti, *LIMC* VIII, 168, no. 75; *Classicism* 219, 223, fig. 6 (J. Boardman); J. Spier, in *Periplous* 333, fig. 4 (as 21.197).

36.

21.1198 R. 1916. T.L. 14, 1. Bu. O 80.

Vollenweider, *Genève* I, 164, under no. 222; Zazoff, 36, 150, no. 415; *AGDS* II 49, under no. 80; von

Freytag Gen. Löringhoff, *Giebelrelief* 144; C. Weber-Lehmann, *LIMC* VIII, 179-180, no. 52 (as 21.1199).

37.

21.1199 G.P. 219, 847. Bu. O 68.

F. Poulsen, *Etruscan Tomb Paintings. Their Subjects and Significance* (trans. by I. Andersen) (Oxford, 1922), 55, n. 1; W. Lameere, *BCH* 63 (1939), 47, n. 2; Beazley, *EVP* 138, no. 1; E. Kunze, *Olympische Forschungen* 2 (Berlin, 1950), 156, n. 4; *idem*, in *Studies Presented to David Moore Robinson* I (St. Louis, 1951), 744; MFA, *Trojan War* fig. 35C; Zazoff, 34, 145, no. 333; M.I. Davies, *AntK* 14 (1971), 150, n. 13; *idem*, *AntK* 16 (1973), 63-66, pl. 9, 3 (citing Zancani Montuoro, *Heraion alla foce del Sele* I (1964), 76, 54); B.B. Shefton, *RA* 1973, 205-207 (fig. 2a-b), 209 (n. 3); Brommer, *Denkmälerlisten* III, 15, no. 1; O. Touchefeu, *LIMC* I, 1, 332, no. 141; I, 2, pl. 251, illus.; M. True, in B.D. Wescoat, *Poets & Heroes: Scenes of the Trojan War* (Atlanta, 1986), 54, under no. 14.

38.

21.1200 R. 816. Bu. O 17.

Chase, *Antiquities* 139, fig. 179; Chase and Vermeule, *Classical Collections* 196, 215, fig. 208a; MFA, *Trojan War* fig. 21B; Richter, *Greeks and Etruscans* 200, no. 810, 2 illus.; Zazoff, 35, no. 36, pl. 12, 36; Brommer, *Denkmälerlisten* III, 246 (no. 1), 435 (no. 2); E. Simon, *AA* 1992, 238, n. 25a; D. von Bothmer,

LIMC VII, 700.

39.

27.720 R. 566. Bu. O 22.

Zazoff, 145, no. 328; G. Camporeale, *LIMC* I, 1, 207, no. 113, 212.

40.

21.1201 B.B. 84,2. R. 1261. Bu. O 4.

L.D. Caskey, *BMFA* 26 (1928), 47-48, fig. 8; Richter, *Greeks and Etruscans* 183, no. 726, 2 illus.; Zazoff, 212, no. 1571; *AGDS* II 106, under no. 238; Krauskopf, *Thebanische* 85, n. 287; E. Walter-Karydi, *JBerlMus* 17 (1975), 7-9 (fig. 2a-b), 12; Brommer, *Denkmälerlisten* III, 462, no. 4.

41.

27.717 G.P. 342, 2.

L.D. Caskey, *BMFA* 26 (1928), 47-48, fig. 9; Beazley, *EVP* 138, no. 2; Chase, *Antiquities* 139, fig. 179; *New York* 46, under no. 172; Chase and Vermeule, *Classical Collections* 196, 215, fig. 208c; MFA, *Trojan War* fig. 35A; Vollenweider, *Genève* I, 173, under no. 237; Richter, *Greeks and Etruscans* 195, 201, no. 812, 2 illus.; Zazoff, 146, no. 335; M.I. Davies, *AntK* 14 (1971), 150, n. 10, pl. 46, 2; B.B. Shefton, *RA* 1973, 209 (n. 3), 210 (n. 2); Brommer, *Denkmälerlisten* III, 15, no. 2; O. Touchefeu, *LIMC* I, 329, no. 112, pl. 246; J. Pinsent, *Greek Mythology* (New York, 1990) 126-7, illus.; Moret, *Palladion* 267, n. 3.

42.

21.1202 G.P. 348, 2.

R. Stiglitz, *Jahreshefte* 44 (1959), 115 (no. 12), 117, fig. 72, 12; Vollenweider, in MuM *Vente Publique* 28, 69, under no. 634; Richter, *Greeks and Etruscans* 181, 195, 198-199, no. 800, 2 illus.; Zazoff, 160, no. 589; *AGDS* I 2, 15, under no. 642; Brommer, *Denkmälerlisten* I, 46, no. 3; S.J. Schwarz, *LIMC* V, 1, 232 (no. 339a), 244.

43.

27.718 G.P. 351, 5.

L.D. Caskey, *BMFA* 26 (1928), 47-48, fig. 7; Richter, *Greeks and Etruscans* 195, 197-198, no. 796, 2 illus.; Zazoff, 158, no. 554; *AGDS* II 115, under no. 263; Brommer, *Denkmälerlisten* I, 35, no. 3; S.J. Schwarz, *LIMC* V, 1, 207 (no. 84), 242; G. Tamma, *Le gemme del Museo archeologico di Bari* (1991), 23, under no. 3.

44.

27.719 G.P. 225, 1.

Boardman, *Archaic* 164, no. 602; Zazoff, 180, no. 961.

45.

23.579 G.P. 341, 4. Bu. L 52.

Zazoff, 150, no. 407.

46.

21.1203 R. 446.

Lippold, *Gemmen* 48, 175, pl. 48, 8; Chase, *Antiquities* 138-139, fig. 179; Chase and Vermeule, *Classical Collections* 196, 215, fig. 208b; Richter, *Greeks and Etruscans* 195, 207-208, no. 846, 2 illus.; Zazoff, 169, no. 760; Brommer, *Denkmälerlisten* III, 170, no. 2; Vermeule, *Death* 195, fig. 18; H. Meyer, *Medeia und die Peliaden* (Rome, 1980), 89, 130; M. Vojatzi, *Frühe Argonautenbilder* (Würzburg, 1982), 87, 118, no. 62; A.J.N.W. Prag, *The Oresteia: Iconographic and Narrative Tradition* (Warminster and Chicago, 1985), 117, n. 27; J. Neils, *LIMC* V, 632 (no. 33), 637, pl. 428; J. Neils, in R.D. de Puma *et al.* (eds.), *Murlo and the Etruscans* (Madison, 1994), 194, n. 9.

47.

27.691 B. B. 66, 286. R. 1235. Bu. O 32.

Lippold, *Gemmen* 8, 168-169, pl. 8, no. 4; Chase, *Antiquities* 76, fig. 85; P.E. Corbett and D.E. Strong, *BMQ* 23 (1961), 85, n. 19; Chase and Vermeule, *Classical Collections* 95, 117, fig. 101; Richter, *Greeks and Etruscans* 48, 52, no. 102, 2 illus.; *AGDS* II 73, under no. 153; Boardman, *GGFR* 194, 211, 236, 287, 407, no. 20, pl. 455; E. Walter-Karydi, *JBerlMus* 17 (1975), 33-35, fig. 40; E. Paribeni, *Antike Plastik* 17 (Berlin, 1978), 103, fig. 2; Zazoff, *Gemmen* 146 (n. 104), 153 (n. 144), 159 (n. 173), pl. 34, 9; W. Lambrinudakis, *LIMC* II, 221, 317, no. 309, pl. 208; P.N. Boulter, *AJA* 80 (1984), 386; J. Dörig, *The Olympia Master and His Collaborators* (Leiden, 1984), 13, 21, no. 6, pl. 12b-c; *Scritti di Enrico Paribeni* (Rome, 1985), 184-185, pl. 104, fig. 288.

48.

23.593 R. 819. Bu. O 16.

Chase, *Antiquities* 91, fig. 106; Chase and Vermeule, *Classical Collections* 123-124, 136, fig. 122; Richter, *Greeks and Etruscans* 77-78, no. 220, 2 illus. (as 28.598); Boardman, *GGFR* 216, 296, 417, no. 479, pl. 663: the Waterton Group; Horster, *Statuen* 17, pl. 4, 4; E. Walter-Karydi, *JBerlMus* 17 (1975), 32-33, 35, fig. 39; *Oxford* 51, under no. 217; G. Siebert, *LIMC* V, 353-354 (no. 805), pl. 265; I. Jucker, *Quaderni ticinesi* 11 (1982), 126, n. 31; M. Henig, in *Periplous* 131.

49.

27.686 G.P. 323, 1.

Boardman, *GGFR* 194, 236, 287, 407, no. 17, pl. 452; W. Lambrinudakis, in *LIMC* II, 233, 316, no. 384, pl. 214.

49 *bis*.

27.697

Bothmer, *Amazons* 222-223, no. 82; MFA, *Trojan War* fig. 29B; Boardman, *GGFR* 196, 288, 408, no. 57, pl. 474; *idem*, in D. Kurtz and B. Sparkes, eds., *The Eye of Greece: Studies in the Art of Athens* (Cambridge, 1982), 10, n. 32; A. Kauffmann-Samaras, *LIMC* I, 631, no. 726, pl. 518; Zazoff, *Gemmen* 130 (n. 12), 135-136 (n. 42), pl. 32, 1.

50.

23.580 B. B. 150, 1. Bu. O 13.

A. Hekler, *Greek & Roman Portraits* (New York, 1912), IX, ill. 1; R. Delbrück, *Antike Porträts* (Bonn, 1912), lviii-lix, pl. 58, 1; L.D. Caskey, *BMFA* 26 (1928), 46, 48, 50, fig. 10; P. Jacobsthal, *Die Melischen Reliefs* (Berlin-Wilmersdorf, 1931), 157, fig. 37; Curtius, *Antike Kunst* II, 1, 243, 325, 421, pl. 24F; C. Picard, *Manuel d'archéologie grecque, II: La Sculpture: Période Classique - Ve Siècle* (Paris, 1939), 676-677, 681, n. 4; *ibid.*, III (Paris, 1948), 39, 131, 192-193, fig. 59; L. Laurenzi, *Ritratti greci* (Florence, 1941), 90, no. 12, pl. 3; Ducati, *Arte Classica* 320-321, fig. 408; B. Segall, *JWalt* 9 (1946), 59; Chase, *Antiquities* 89-90, fig. 104; Richter, *Sculptors* 1950, 83, 423, fig. 226; 1970 edition, 55, fig. 235; V. Poulsen, *Les portraits grecs* (Copenhagen, 1954), 13-14; G.M.A. Richter, *Collection Latomus* 20 (1955), 25; *ibid.*, 48 (1960), 14; *New York* xxxii, xxxv; V. Poulsen, *Oldtidsmennesker Blade af den antikke Portraetkunsts Historie* (Copenhagen, 1959), 39, illus.; G.M.A. Richter, *A Handbook of Greek Art* (London, 1959), 236-237, fig. 348; Vermeule, *Portraits* no. 3, illus.; 1972 edition, no. 3, illus.; M.-L. Vollenweider, *Connaissance des Arts* Feb. 1959, 54, 59, F, illus.; L. Vlad Borrelli, in *EAA* III, 81-82, fig. 108; Schoder, *Masterpieces* 9, no. 49b, color illus. and under no. 64; G.M.A. Richter, *Rendiconti della Pontificia Accademia Romana di Archeologia* 34 (1961-1962), 54, 56, fig. 23; A. Hekler and H. von Heintze, *Bildnisse Berühmter Griechen* (Berlin and Mainz, 1962), 53; Chase and Vermeule, *Classical Collections* 123, 135, fig. 120; MFA, *Illustrated Handbook* 1964, 68-69, illus.; 1976 edition, 100-101, illus.; G.M.A. Richter, *The Portraits of the Greeks* (London, 1965), 102; *ibid.*, 1984 edition, 40-41, fig. 6; G.M.A. Hanfmann, *Classical Sculpture* (Greenwich, Conn., 1967), 319, fig. 150; G. Becatti, *The Art of Ancient Greece and Rome: From the Rise of Greece to the Fall of Rome* (Englewood Cliffs, n.d.), 187 (fig. 165), 190; E. Diehl, *Berliner Museen* NF 17 (1967), 45-46, no. II, fig. 2; J.D. Breckenridge, *Likeness: A Conceptual History of Ancient Portraiture* (Evanston, 1968), 95-96, fig. 45; Richter, *Greeks and Etruscans* 15, 17, 76, 89 (under no. 277), 95, 97, no. 326, 2 illus., pl. A; P. Zazoff, *Antike Gemmen, Staatliche Kunstsammlungen Kassel* (Kassel, 1969), 4; J. Boardman, *BurlMag* 1969, 591ff., fig. 21; *AGDS* II 74, under no. 158; C. Vermeule, in *Museum of Fine Arts, Boston: Western Art* (Japan, Kodansha, 1969), 155, pls. 24-25; 1971 ed. (Greenwich, Conn.), 166, pls. 24-25; Boardman, *GGFR* 195-196, 236, 287, 408, no. 49, pl. 466; Horster, *Statuen* 14, n. 4 (as 27.580); Cook, *Greek Art* 138, 168-169, pl. 69g; A. Burford, *Craftsmen in Greek and Roman Society* (London, 1972), 216, pl. 44; T. Dohrn, *RM* 80 (1973), 13, n. 65; Guarducci, *Epigrafia Greca* III, 520, n. 2; H.A. Cahn, *Schweizer Münzblätter* 25 (1975), 86; A. Greifenhagen, *Schmuckarbeiten in Edelmetall* II (Berlin, 1975), 72, under nos. 11, 17; Robertson, *History* 344, 362, pl. 120a; O. Mørkholm and J. Zahle, *ActaA* 47 (1976), 85; *Oxford* 30, under no. 131; M. Vickers, *Scythian Treasures in Oxford* (Oxford, 1979), 46; J. Boardman, in Porada, *Seals* 105, 117, 122, fig. IV-8; E. Zwierlein-Diehl, *Gnomon* 52 (1980), 485, n. 11; C. Vermeule, *Greek Art: Socrates to Sulla* (Boston, 1980), 3, 116, 149, fig. 9; J. Dörig, in *Eikones: Studien zum griechischen und römischen Bildnis* (*AntK* Beiheft 20, Bern, 1980), 91; Robertson, *Shorter History* 129-130, fig. 177 (as 27.580); Vermeule, *Prehistoric* 186-187, 229, 514, fig. 241; Zazoff, *Gemmen* 132-133 (fig. 40c), 136-137, 157 (n. 162), pl. 31, 3; Herrmann, *Shadow* 79; J. Boardman, *Greek Sculpture: The Classical Period: A Handbook* (New York, 1985), 239-240, 247, fig. 244; H.A. Cahn, *AA* 1985, 592; W. Fuchs, in J. Boardman and C.E. Vaphopoulou-Richardson, eds., *Chios: A Conference at the Homereion in Chios 1984* (Oxford, 1986), 276-278, 280, fig. 3; E. Pfuhl, in K. Fittschen, ed., *Griechische Porträts* (Darmstadt, 1988), 230, 232, 242, pl. 27, 1; F. Studniczka, in *ibid.*, 257; W. Schwabacher, in *ibid.*, 281; *Cambridge Ancient History: Plates to Volumes V and VI* (Cambridge, 1994), 50-51, no. 57b, illus.; N. Himmelmann, *Realistische Themen in der griechischen Kunst der archaischen und klassischen Zeit* (*JdI* Erg. 28), 82, fig. 32; *7000 Years of Seals* (ed. D. Collon, 1997) pl. 5.15; *Cambridge* 24, 34 (under no. 53), 35 (under no. 55); R. Osborne, *Archaic and Classical Greek Art* (Oxford/New York, 1998) 222-223, ill.135; *Classicism* 219, 222, fig. 3 (J. Boardman).

51.

23.596 G.P. 342, 4.

Boardman, *GGFR* 410, no. 150.

52.

23.581 G.P. 244, 2. R. 2609. Bu. O 23.

Lippold, *Gemmen* 65, 178, pl. 65, 2; G. Becatti, *EAA* V (1963), 398; Snowden, *Blacks* 26, 52, fig. 23; Richter, *Greeks and Etruscans* 95, 97, no. 323, 2 illus.; Boardman, *GGFR* 201, 290, 410, no. 147, pl. 530; F.M. Snowden, Jr., in *The Image of the Black in Western Art* I: *From the Pharaohs to the Fall of the Roman Empire* (New York, 1976), 167-168, fig. 201; Zazoff, *Gemmen* 139, n. 58; T. Melander, in T. Fischer-Hansen *et al.* (eds.), *Ancient Portraiture: Image and Message* (*Acta Hyperborea* 4, 1992), 78.

53.

23.594 G.P. 272, 5.

Chase, *Antiquities* 91, fig. 106; Chase and Vermeule, *Classical Collections* 123-124, 136, fig. 122; Boardman, *GGFR* 216, 296, 417, no. 484, pl. 666: the Waterton Group; *idem*, *Private* 96, under no. 79; A. Delivorrias, *et al.*, *LIMC* II, 25, no. 156 (as 23.593), pl. 18; A. Hermary, *LIMC* III, 883, no. 397 (as 23.593); Spier, *Gems* 34, under no. 51; D. Salzmann, in Ü. Serdaroğlu and R. Stupperich (eds.), *Ausgrabungen in Assos 1991* (Asia Minor Studien 10, Bonn, 1993) 181, n. 20,2.

54.

21.1204 G.P. 297, 1.

L. Curtius, *RM* 45 (1930) 36, fig. 4; Hoffmann and Davidson, *Greek Gold* 251-252, no. 109, figs. 109a-b; A. Greifenhagen, *Gnomon* 40 (1968), 697; Boardman, *GGFR* 219, 297, 418, no. 515, pl. 680; I. Roeper-Ter Borg, *BABesch* 50 (1975), 45; A. Kauffmann-Samaras, *LIMC* I, 624, no. 585, pl. 506; V. Paul-Zinserling, *Der Jena-Maler und sein Kreis* (1994) 152, n. 1052.

55.

23.582 Bu. O 7.

Lippold, *Gemmen* 54, 176, pl. 54, 5; L.D. Caskey, *BMFA* 26 (1928), 48, 50, fig. 19; Richter, *Animals* 17, 60, pl. 24, fig. 74; Chase, *Antiquities* 89-90, fig. 103; C.C. Vermeule, *JHS* 75 (1955), 112-113, fig. 16; Chase and Vermeule, *Classical Collections* 123, 135, fig. 119; Vollenweider, in MuM *Vente Publique* 28, 68, under no. 631; M.K. Donaldson, *Hesperia* 34 (1965), 81; J.P. Guépin, *BABesch* 41 (1966), 53, fig. 7; E. Diehl, *Berliner Museen* NF 17 (1967), 47, n. 14; *AGDS* I 1, 64, under no. 314; Richter, *Greeks and Etruscans* 98, 100, no. 338, 2 illus., pl. C, illus.; H.A. Harris, *Sport in Greece and Rome* (London, 1972), 160, 171, pl. 63; Boardman, *GGFR* 202, 292, 411, no. 200, pl. 561; *AGDS* III 31, under no. 85; Maaskant-Kleibrink, *The Hague* 79, under no. 18; C. Houser, *Greek Monumental Bronze Sculpture of the Fifth and Fourth Centuries B.C.* (New York, 1987), 116, n. 35; Nikulina, pls. 57, 221.

56.

27.700 B. B. 87, 3. R. 1262. Bu. O 1.

Lippold, *Gemmen* 28, 171, pl. 28, no. 11; Richter, *Greeks and Etruscans* 91, 94, no. 307, 2 illus.; Boardman, *GGFR* 208, 294, 413, no. 285, pl. 604; K. Schauenburg, *JdI* 87 (1972), 294; *Oxford* 85, under no. 299; Zazoff, *Gemmen* 141, n. 70 (as Lewes, pl. 4, 57); E. Zwierlein-Diehl, *AntK* 35 (1992), 107; Spier, *Gems* 36, under no. 58; M.-L. Vollenweider, in N. Bonacasa and A. di Vita (eds.), *Alessandria e il Mondo ellenistico-romano: Studi in onore di Achille Adriani* (repr. Rome, 1992) 364, n. 1.

57.

23.583 T. L. 11, 1. R. 1914. Bu. O 77.

J.D. Beazley, *JHS* 59 (1939), 44; *New York* 22, under no. 80; M.-L. Vollenweider, *Connaissance des Arts* Feb. 1959, 58 (fig. 5), 59, J, illus.; Boardman, *GGFR* 206-207, 236, 293, 412, no. 279, pl. 599; *idem*, *Private* 15, 89 (under no. 35), 90 (under no. 39), fig. 9; *Oxford* I, 87, under no. 301; P. Demargne, *LIMC* II, 966, no. 75, pl. 712; Schürmann, *Minerva-Kultbilder* 122, n. 605; Zagdoun, *Sculpture* 19 (n. 168), 42 (n. 6), 162, 231, no. 112.

58.

27.703 B. B. 86, 2. R. 1302. Bu. O 38.

Chase, *Antiquities* 105, fig. 123; M.-L. Vollenweider, *Connaissance des Arts* Feb. 1959, 59, L, illus.; Chase and Vermeule, *Classical Collections* 144, 158, fig. 142; MFA, *Trojan War* fig. 36B; Richter, *Greeks and Etruscans* 23, 25, 77, 80, no. 234, 2 illus., pl. B; *idem*, *Romans* 57, n. 1; *AGDS* II 155, under no. 403; Boardman, *GGFR* 207, 293, 365, 412, no. 275, pl. 596; B. Andreae, *Antike Plastik* 14 (1974), 100, n. 93; Brommer, *Denkmälerlisten* III, 78, no. 54; Schürmann, *Minerva-Kultbilder* 25, 29, 107 (n. 337), 112 (n. 425); B. Neutsch, *JdI* 101 (1986), 314, n. 17; J. Boardman and C.E. Vafopoulou-Richardson, *LIMC* III, 402 (no. 34), 408, pl. 287; J. Pinsent, *Greek Mythology* (New York, 1990) 126-127, illus.; M. Menninger, *Untersuchungen zu den Gläsern und Gipsabgüssen aus dem Fund von Begram (Afghanistan)* (Würzburg, 1996) 167; Moret, *Palladion* 6-7, no. 3, pl. 1; D. Hatzi-Vallianou, in M.-F. Boussac and A. Invernizzi, eds., *Archives et Sceaux du Monde Hellénistique* (*BCH* Suppl. 29) 212; *Classicism* 39, 44, fig. 1 (D. Plantzos).

59.

23.601 G.P. 313, 5.

Boardman, *GGFR* 232, 302, 427, no. 995, pl. 812; Comstock and Vermeule, *Bronze* 212-213, no. 287, illus.; Vermeule, *Death* 173-174 (fig. 25), 249 (n. 43); A. Hermary, *LIMC* III, 929, no. 963; Vermeule and Comstock, *Stone and Bronze* 122.

60.

23.597 R. 70.

A. Rumpf, *AJA* 55 (1951), 11, n. 77; Boardman, *GGFR* 202, 291, 411, no. 185, pl. 552; *idem* and La Rocca, *Eros* 140, color (as LHG 63); Mulas, *Antiquity* 65, illus. (as LHG 63); R.F. Sutton, Jr., in B. Cohen, ed., *Not the Classical Ideal: Athens and the Construction of the Other in Greek Art* (Leiden, 2000), 188, n. 27 (incorrectly as LHG no. 63).

61.

21.1205 R. 815. Bu. O 30.

Boardman, *GGFR* 201, 291, 316, 410, no. 160, pl. 539; Brommer, *Denkmälerlisten* II, 24; Zazoff, *Gemmen*, 153, n. 144; E. Zwierlein-Diehl, *AntK* 35 (1992), 108, 117, pl. 22, 3; J. Neils, *LIMC* VII, 931, no. 95. Exhibited: Brockton, Brockton Art Museum, 1984-1987; Herrmann, *Shadow* 80-81 (no. 147), 83 (illus.); Salt Lake City, Utah Museum of Fine Arts, 1988-1991.

62.

27.704 B. B. 36, 105. R. 1303. Bu. O 33.

Lippold, *Gemmen* 43, 174, pl. 43, no. 7; L.D. Caskey, *BMFA* 26 (1928), 49-50, fig. 20; *New York* 22, under no. 80; MFA, *Trojan War* fig. 40B; J. Davreux, *La légende de la prophétesse Cassandre* (Liège, 1942) 180, no. 132, fig. 83; Richter, *Greeks and Etruscans* 91-92, no. 293, 2 illus.; *AGDS* II 71, under no. 150; Boardman, *GGFR* 206, 293, 361, 412, no. 265, pl. 591; Brommer, *Denkmälerlisten* III, 196, no. 9; P. Demargne, *LIMC* II, 1, 968, no. 99; Zazoff, *Gemmen* 139, n. 55; Schürmann, *Minerva-Kultbilder* 23, 32, 105 (n. 304), 113 (n. 441), 122 (n. 599); C. Aellen, A. Cambitoglou, and J. Chamay, *Le Peintre de Darius et son Milieu: Vases grecs d'Italie méridionale* (Geneva, 1986) 262, n. 19; M. Maaskant-Kleibrink, *The Engraved Gems: Roman and Non-Roman* (*Description of the Collection in the Rijksmuseum G.M. Kam at Nijmegen* Nijmegen, 1986) 102, under no. 229; Zagdoun, *Sculpture* 46, 231, no. 111; O. Paoletti, *LIMC* VII, 957, no. 5, pl. 670; M. Maaskant-Kleibrink, in Broustet, 26-27, fig. 6.

63.

23.598 G.P. 338, 2.

Richter, *Animals* 37, 80, pl. 59, fig. 191; Boardman, *GGFR* 311, 352, 432, no. 69, pl. 862, 359, 371, pl. 996; *idem* and La Rocca, *Eros* 138-139, colour (as LHG 60); Mulas, *Antiquity* 62-63, colour (as LHG 60); Zazoff, *Gemmen* 394, n. 39; M.-A. Zagdoun, in *L'Antre Corycien* II (*BCH* Suppl. IX), 251, n. 348; V. Paul-Zinserling, *Der Jena-Maler und sein Kreis* (1994) 144, n. 689; Plantzos, 98, 134 (no. 636, pl. 79); M. Henig, in *Periplous* 132.

64.

23.584 Bu. O 44.

Lippold, *Gemmen* 90, 181, pl. 90, 6; Richter, *Animals* 23, 66, pl. 34, fig. 106; *AGDS* I 1, 62, under no. 302; *AGDS* II, 86, under no. 193; J. Boardman, *Iran* 8 (1970), 39, 45, no. 192; *idem*, *GGFR* 312, 352, 433, no. 91, pl. 871; P. Gercke, in *AGDS* III, 150, under no. 538; Zazoff, *Gemmen* 173, n. 64; Nikulina, pl. 28.

65.

27.694 B. B. 86. R. 1301. Bu. O 45.

Lippold, *Gemmen* 84, 180, pl. 84, 13; L.D. Caskey, *BMFA* 26 (1928), 48, 50, fig. 16; Richter, *Animals* 7, 50-51, pl. 7, fig. 23; *idem*, *Catalogue of Greek Sculptures in the Metropolitan Museum of Art* (Cambridge, Mass., 1954), 46, under no. 72; *New York* 15, under no. 54; Richter, *Greeks and Etruscans* 107-108, no. 375, 2 illus., pl. C; Boardman, *GGFR* 200, 290, 410, no. 133, pl. 520; O.W. von Vacano, *Gnomon* 45 (1973), 285; Boardman, *Private* 15, 88 (under no. 33), 91 (under no. 49), fig. 7; I. Caruso, *RM* 88 (1981), 96; Zazoff, *Gemmen* 129 (n. 8), 154 (n. 150).

66.

21.1206 B. B. 163, 30. Bu. O 76.

Lippold, *Gemmen* 95, 182, pl. 95, 6; F. Weege, *Dionysischer Reigen: Lied und Bild in der Antike* (Halle, 1926), 126, illus.; L.D. Caskey, *BMFA* 26 (1928), 46, 50, fig. 12; Richter, *Animals* 37, n. 1; L.D. Caskey, *AJA* 35 (1931), 362; Chase, *Antiquities* 90-91, fig. 105; Richter, *Sculptors* 1950, 116, 468, fig. 371; 1970 edition, 79, fig. 396; E. Lissi, in *EAA* II, 145; M.-L. Vollenweider, *Connaissance des Arts* Feb. 1959, 54, 59, D, illus.; Chase and Vermeule, *Classical Collections* 123, 135, fig. 121; Bowra, *Classical Greece* 14, illus.; E. Diehl, *Berliner Museen* N.F. 17 (1967), 47, no. 3; Cheney, *Sculpture* 109, illus.; Richter, *Greeks and Etruscans* 15, 121, no. 466, 2 illus., pl. A; *AGDS* II 81, under no. 181; Boardman, *GGFR* 198, 289, 409, no. 83, pl. 490; Robertson, *History* 344, 362, pl. 120c; P. Zazoff, in Hornbostel, *Norddeutschem Privatbesitz* 502, under no. 452; Robertson, *Shorter History* 116, 129-130, fig. 176; Zazoff, *Gemmen* 134 (n. 35), 136, pl. 31, 9; Vollenweider, *Deliciae* 24, under no. 34; G. Sena

Chiesa, *ArchCl* 38-40 (1986-88), 269; Nikulina, pl. 79.

67.

27.698 R. 215. Bu. O 26.

Lippold, *Gemmen* 89, 181, pl. 89, 3; L.D. Caskey, *BMFA* 26 (1928), 46, 50, fig. 11; Richter, *Animals* 17, 60, pl. 24, fig. 71; Chase, *Antiquities* 90-91, fig. 105; M.-L. Vollenweider, *Connaissance des Arts* Feb. 1959, 54, 56 (fig. 3), 59, A, illus.; Schoder, *Masterpieces* 9, no. 49a, 2 colour; Chase and Vermeule, *Classical Collections* 123, 135, fig. 121; M.-L. Vollenweider, MuM *Vente Publique* 28, 68, under no. 631; Bowra, *Classical Greece* 15, illus.; E. Diehl, *Berliner Museen* NF 17 (1967), 47, no. 6; Vollenweider, *Genève* I, 159-160, under no. 216; Richter, *Greeks and Etruscans* 15, 107, 114-115, no. 421, 2 illus., pl. A; Boardman, *GGFR* 196, 236, 288, 408, no. 56, pl. 473; Neverov, *Intaglios* 14; Zazoff, *Gemmen* 134 (n. 35), 158 (n. 172), 159, pl. 31, 6; G. Sena Chiesa, *ArchCl* 38-40 (1986-88), 269; Nikulina, pl. 58.

68.

27.693 G.P. 217, 832. Bu. O 72.

L.D. Caskey, *BMFA* 26 (1928), 48, 50, fig. 18; Richter, *Greeks and Etruscans* 123-124, no. 483, 2 illus.; Boardman, *GGFR* 199, 289, 409, no. 121, pl. 514; M. Henig, in Broustet, p. 46; *Classicism* 219, 222, fig. 2 (J. Boardman).

69.

27.768

Richter, *Greeks and Etruscans* 115, no. 424, 2 illus.; Boardman, *GGFR* 236, 287, 408, no. 38, pl. 463; Weinberg, *Numismatics* 286; Vollenweider, *Genève* III, 159-160, under no. 213; M. Henig in *Periplous* 133.

70.

27.692 G.P. 338, 1.

Richter, *Animals* 24, 67, pl. 36, fig. 113; Boardman, *Archaic* 149, 152, no. 554, pl. 36, no. 554; *AGDS* I 1, 58, under no. 267; Richter, *Greeks and Etruscans* 24, 107, 112, no. 405, 2 illus.; P. Gercke, in *AGDS* III, 152, under no. 551; C. Vermeule, *BMFA* 68 (1970), 213, fig. 23a; Vollenweider, *Genève* III, 27 (under no. 36), 156 (under no. 210).

71.

27.696 G.P. 349, 5.

New York 16, under no. 59; Boardman, *GGFR* 317-318, 354, 435, no. 197, pl. 914; Zazoff, *Gemmen* 192, n. 150.

72.

21.1207 B. B. 156, 4. Bu. O 75.

AGDS I 1, 59, under no. 277; Boardman, *GGFR* 408, no. 39; O. Mørkholm and J. Zahle, *ActaA* 43 (1972), 92; Vollenweider, *Genève* III, 159, under no. 212, n. 5; *idem*, *Deliciae* 25, under no. 36.

73.

21.1208 G.P. 347, 5.

Richter, *Animals* 26, 70, pl. 42, fig. 129; *AGDS* I 1, 59, under no. 277; Boardman, *GGFR* 409, no. 104; N.M. Nikoulina, *AntK* 14 (1971), 91-92, no. 1, pl. 33, 1; O. Mørkholm and J. Zahle, *ActaA* 43 (1972), 92; A. Leibundgut, *Die römischen Bronzen der Schweiz* III: *Westschweiz, Bern und Wallis* (Mainz, 1980), 73-74, under no. 62; Vollenweider, *Genève* III, 159, under no. 212, n. 5; Nikulina, pl. 2.

74.

21.1209

L.D. Caskey, *BMFA* 26 (1928), 49-50, fig. 15; Richter, *Animals* 73, pl. 48, fig. 148; *New York* 28, under nos. 107-108; M.-L. Vollenweider, *Connaissance des Arts* Feb. 1959, 57 (fig. 4), 59; *AGDS* I 1, 59 (under no. 280), 60 (under no. 282); Richter, *Greeks and*

Etruscans 107, 116, no. 435, 2 illus.; *AGDS* II, 79, under no. 172; Boardman, *GGFR* 202, 292, 411, no. 209, pl. 566; *AGDS* IV 363, under no. 20; Neverov, *Intaglios* 56, under no. 28; J. Boardman, in Porada, *Seals* 104, 117, 122, fig. IV-7; Vollenweider, *Deliciae* 25, under no. 36; Nikulina, pl. 17.

75.

21.1210 G.P. 336, 2.

L.D. Caskey, *BMFA* 26 (1928), 49-50, fig. 13; *New York* 28, under no. 107; *AGDS* II 79, under no. 172; incorrectly cited 133, under no. 329; Boardman, *GGFR* 202, 292, 411, no. 210, pl. 564; *AGDS* IV 363, under no. 20; Vollenweider, *Deliciae* 25, under no. 36.

76.

21.1211 B. B. 65, 269. R. 1231. Bu. O 43.

Richter, *Animals* 22, 65, pl. 33, fig. 99; *AGDS* I 1, 63, under no. 303; Richter, *Greeks and Etruscans* 111, no. 398, 2 illus., pl. C; *AGDS* II, 78, under no. 170; Boardman, *GGFR* 289, 409, no. 102, pl. 504; N.M. Nikulina, *AntK* 14 (1971), 92, no. 2, pl. 33, 4.

77.

27.699 G.P. 265, 10. Bu. O 71.

M. Wallace, *AJA* 44 (1940), 217, n. 29; *AGDS* II, 54 (under no. 93), 81 (under no. 181); Boardman, *GGFR* 200, 290, 410, no. 139, pl. 524; *Oxford* I, 15, under no. 71; Zazoff, *Gemmen* 154, n. 150.

78.

27.702 G.P. 328, 7.

Richter, *Animals* 36, 78, pl. 57, fig. 182; Boardman, *GGFR* 198, 289, 409, no. 108, pl. 503; Vollenweider, *Genève* III, 176, under no. 226.

79.

23.585 B. B. 131, 6. Bu. O 3.

Richter, *Animals* 22, 65, pl. 32, fig. 97; Chase, *Antiquities* 89, fig. 102; *New York* 27 (under nos. 102 and 103), 35 (under no. 138); Bowra, *Classical Greece* 14, illus.; Chase and Vermeule, *Classical Collections* 123, 134, fig. 118; *AGDS* I 1, 91, under no. 509; Richter, *Greeks and Etruscans* 23-24, 107, 110, no. 389, 2 illus.; *AGDS* II, 78, under no. 171; G.M.A. Richter, *Perspective in Greek and Roman Art* (London, n.d.), 31, fig. 133; Boardman, *GGFR* 198, 289, 409, no. 98, pl. 498; *AGDS* I 3, 194, under no. 3390; *AGDS* IV 385, under no. 69; C. Weiss, *Griechische Flussgottheiten in vorhellenistischer Zeit* (Würzburg, 1984), 203, n. 496c; Nikulina, pl. 38.

80.

21.1212 B. B. 64, 263. R. 1232. Bu. O 46.

Lippold, *Gemmen* 87, 181, pl. 87, 1; Richter, *Animals* 9-10, 52, pl. 9, fig. 31; Boardman, *GGFR* 206, 293, 412, no. 257, pl. 586; M.-A. Zagdoun, in *L'Antre Corycien* II (*BCH* Suppl. IX), 205, under no. 56.

81.

23.586 B. B. 66, 284. R. 911. Bu. L 59.

Lippold, *Gemmen* 94, 182, pl. 94, 10; L.D. Caskey, *BMFA* 26 (1928), 48, 50, fig. 17; Richter, *Animals* 38, 82, pl. 61, fig. 203; *AGDS* I 1, 62, under no. 300; Richter, *Greeks and Etruscans* 24, 119, no. 455, 2 illus.; Boardman, *GGFR* 409, no. 88; *idem, Private* 16, 90, under no. 40; A. Greifenhagen, *AA* 1981, 287, n. 9; Vollenweider, *Deliciae* 27, under no. 39; Spier, *Gems* 60, under no. 117.

82.

27.770

Boardman, *GGFR* 220, 297, 418, no. 536, pl. 692.

83.

27.701 T. L. 57, 1. Bu. O 74.

Richter, *Animals* 19, 62, pl. 27, fig. 83; Chase, *Antiquities* 106, fig. 127; *idem* and Vermeule, *Classical Collections* 144, 160, fig. 148; Hoffmann and Davidson, *Greek Gold* 251-252, no. 110, fig. 110 a-b; A. Greifenhagen, *Gnomon* 40 (1968), 697; Richter, *Greeks and Etruscans* 107, 115, no. 423, 2 illus., pl. C; Boardman, *GGFR* 216, 296, 417, no. 488, pl. 669: The Waterton Group; I. Roeper-Ter Borg, *BABesch* 50 (1975), 45; Weinberg, *Numismatics* 286; *Classicism* 219, 222, fig. 1 (J. Boardman).

84.

27.769 G.P. 326, 5.

Boardman, *GGFR* 208-209 (fig. 215), 284, 413, no. 306.
Exhibited: Brockton Art Museum, 1984-1987; Herrmann, *Shadow* 80, 83-84, no. 158, illus.; Salt Lake City, Utah Museum of Fine Arts, 1988-1991.

85.

27.771 G.P. 340, 5. Bu. L 62.

AGDS I 1, 41 (under no. 157), 62 (under no. 297); Boardman, *GGFR* 202, 292, 412, no. 242, pl. 583; Vermeule and Comstock, *Stone and Bronze* 122. Exhibited: Brockton Art Museum, 1984-1987: Herrmann, *Shadow* 81, 83, no. 151, illus.; Salt Lake City, Utah Museum of Fine Arts, 1988-1991.

Etruscan: Free Style, and Italiote

86.

27.722 B. B. 64, 256. R. 1228. Bu. O 20.

Lippold, *Gemmen* 37, 173, pl. 37, no. 2; Brown, *Lion* 143, n. 3; Richter, *Greeks and Etruscans* 102-103, no. 350, 2 illus.; Zazoff, 164, no. 666; *AGDS* II 2, 112, under no. 1251; Brommer, *Denkmälerlisten* I, 110, no. 6; *AGDS* III 79, under no. 40; S.J. Schwarz, *LIMC* V, 219 (no. 176), 246.

87.

23.587 R. 440. Bu. O 20.

Richter, *Greeks and Etruscans* 193-194, no. 781, 2 illus.; Zazoff, 201, no. 1331; Martini, *Ringsteinglyptik* 13-14, 39, 42, 45, 77 (n. 223), 100; I. Jucker, *et al.*, *Italy of the Etruscans* (Mainz, 1991), 285, under no. 380.

88.

27.724 G.P. 338, 3.

Richter, *Greeks and Etruscans* 195, 197, no. 792, 2 illus.; Zazoff, 159, no. 569; *AGDS* II, 91, under no. 212; Brommer, *Denkmälerlisten* I, 29 (no. 2), 61 (no. 4); Fischer-Graf, *Spiegelwerkstätten* 28, n. 291; B. de Griño and R. Olmos, *LIMC* III, 1, 7, under no. 17; S.J. Schwarz, *LIMC* V, 225 (no. 259), 248.

89.

27.723 R. 843. Bu. O 37.

Lippold, *Gemmen* 36, 172, pl. 36, no. 5; Brown, *Lion* 143, n. 3; Zazoff, 164, no. 669; *AGDS* III 79, under no. 40; Brommer, *Denkmälerlisten* I, 110, no. 5; Fischer-Graf, *Spiegelwerkstätten* 28, n. 288; S.J. Schwarz, *LIMC* V, 219 (no. 176a, with bibliography), 246.

90.

23.599 G.P. 362, 3.

Zazoff, 188, no. 1112; Martini, *Ringsteinglyptik* 31, 66, 77 (n. 219), 92 (n. 297), 94, 127, 134 (no. 25), 161, pl. 7, 4; Krauskopf, *Thebanische* 111; Spier, *Gems* 69, under no. 140; Moret, *Palladion* 62, n. 8.

91.

27.725 G.P. 343, 3.

Richter, *Greeks and Etruscans* 103-104, no. 357, 2 illus.; *AGDS* II, 128 (under no. 306), 132 (under no. 322); I. Touratsoglou, *LIMC* VIII, 678, no. 65.

92.

27.726 B. B. 66, 291. R. 1054. Bu. O 5.

J. Boardman, *PBSR* 34 (1966), 14; Richter, *Greeks and Etruscans* 189-190, no. 761, 2 illus.; *AGDS* IV 26, under no. 39; von Freytag Gen. Löringhoff, *Giebelrelief* 40, n. 100.

93.

27.713 G.P. 322, 5.

L.D. Caskey, *BMFA* 26 (1928), 49-50, fig. 21; Chase, *Antiquities* 123, fig. 155; E. Paribeni, in *EAA* V (1963), 894; Chase and Vermeule, *Classical Collections* 172, 187, fig. 177; Cheney, *Sculpture* 109, illus.; J. Davreux, *La Légende de la prophétesse Cassandre* (1942) 180, no. 133, fig. 82; Richter, *Greeks and Etruscans* 136, 144, no. 558, 2 illus.; Borbein, *Campanareliefs* 76, n. 346; Boardman, *GGFR* 361, 371, pl. 1004; Cook, *Greek Art* 169, pl. 69h; Brommer, *Denkmälerlisten* III, 196, no. 10; H. Froning, *Marmor-Schmuckreliefs mit griechischen Mythen im 1. Jh. v. Chr.: Untersuchungen zu Chronologie und Funktion* (Mainz, 1981), 76, 151, pl. 60, 1-2; Schürmann, *Minerva-Kultbilder* 23, 105 (n. 306), 113-114 (n. 450); O. Paoletti, *LIMC* VII, 957 (no. 4a), pl. 670; Spier, *Gems* 95, under no. 222; M. Maaskant-Kleibrink, in Broustet, 27, fig. 7; Plantzos, 95-96, 133 (no. 626), pl. 77; Moret, *Palladion* 154, n. 9, 173, n. 13.

94.

27.707 G.P. 359,2.

L.D. Caskey, *BMFA* 26 (1928), 49-50, fig. 22; J. Davreux, *La Légende de la prophétesse Cassandre* (1942) 180, no. 134; J. Boardman, *Greek Art* (London, 1964), 245, fig. 230; Vollenweider, *Steinschneidekunst* 42, 105, pl. 35, 2-3; Richter, *Greeks and Etruscans* 144, under no. 558; Borbein, *Campanareliefs* 76, n. 346; G. Bühler, *AA* 1972, 120-121, no. 1a; O. Paoletti, *LIMC* VII, 957, no. 4b (as 27.713); K. Schefold, *Die Sagen von den Argonauten...* (Munich, 1989), 398, n. 655; Spier, *Gems* 95, under no. 222; Plantzos, 95-96, 133 (no. 627), pl. 77; Moret, *loc. cit.*

95.

27.711 B. B. 67, 292. R. 1240. Bu. O 41.

J. Sieveking, in G. Wissowa, *et al.*, *Paulys Real-Encyclopädie der classischen Altertumswissenschaft* XIII, part 2 (Stuttgart, 1927), col. 2300, no. 15; G.H. Macurdy, *Hellenistic Queens: A Study of Woman-Power in Macedonia, Seleucid Syria, and Ptolemaic Egypt* (Baltimore, 1932), 104, fig. 4c; A. Adriani, *Testimonianze e Momenti di Scultura Alessandrina* (Documenti e Richerche d'arte alessandrina, II (Rome, 1948), 18, 41, n. 56 (with additional bibliography), pl. 15, 4; M. Bieber, *The Sculpture of the Hellenistic Age* (New York, 1961), 90; *New York* xxxvi; A. Stazio, *EAA* IV, 748, fig. 907; *AGDS* I, 1, 72, under no. 367; Richter, *Greeks and Etruscans* 18, 160, no. 635, 2 illus.; Kyrieleis, *Bildnisse* 117, 120, pl. 100, 2; *Oxford* 70 (as Lewes, no. 93), 73, 79 (under no. 282), 82 (under no. 290); Vollenweider, *Genève* II, 41 (under no. 39), 43 (under no. 40), 66 (under no. 62), 67-68 (under no. 63); C.M. Havelock, *Hesperia* 51 (1982), 274; Zazoff, *Gemmen* 196 (n. 17), 197, 206 (n. 77), pl. 53, 4; Vollenweider, *Deliciae* 148, under no. 257; P.A. Pantos, *BCH* 111 (1987), 348 (with ref to E. La Rocca, *L'Eta d'oro di Cleopatra indagine sulla Tazza Farnese* 1984, 28, n. 67); E.D. Reeder, *Hellenistic Art in the Walters Art Gallery* (Baltimore, 1988), 246; R.R.R. Smith, *Hellenistic Royal Portraits* (Oxford, 1988), 76; J. Spier, *JWalt* 47 (1989), 21, 31, 36, n. 8; *idem*, *AntK* 34 (1991), 91, n. 5; Plantzos, 42, 52-54, 63, 102, 115 (no. 48), pl. 9; S. Adamo Muscettola, in N. Bonacasa and A. di Vita (eds.), *Alessandria e il Mondo ellenistico-romano: Studi in onore di Achille Adriani* (repr. Rome 1992) 124; H.P. Laubscher, *AM* 110 (1995), 403, pl. 89, 3.

96.

27.709 B. B. 66, 285. R. 1234. Bu. O 34.

Lippold, *Gemmen* 67, 178, pl. 67, 1; J. Spier, *JWalt* 47 (1989), 23 (no. 1), 25 (fig. 5), 30, 35; Plantzos, 49-51, 61, 78, 92, 98 (n. 1), 100 (n. 1), 114 (no. 35), pl. 7.

97.

27.710 B. B. 66, 289. R. 1238.

Lippold, *Gemmen* 70, 178, pl. 70, 7; L.D. Caskey, *BMFA* 26 (1928), 49-50, fig. 24; Richter, *Greeks and Etruscans* 166, no. 665, 2 illus., pl. D; *AGDS* II, 98, under no. 226; Boardman, *GGFR* 360, 371, pl. 1000; Cook, *Greek Art* 169, pl. 69i; P. Zazoff, in Hornbostel, *Norddeutschem Privatbesitz* 508, under no. 462; J. Spier, *JWalt* 47 (1989), 22, 29 (no. E), 35; Plantzos, 60, 92, 117 (no. 137), pl. 24; D. Plantzos in *Greek Offerings* (ed. O. Palagia, 1997) 197-9, fig. 2.

98.

27.716 B. B. 110, 3. R. 1612. Bu. O 8.

Lippold, *Gemmen* 70, 178, pl. 70, 8; Richter, *Greeks and Etruscans* 165, no. 662, 2 illus.; D. Plantzos in *Greek Offerings* (ed. O. Palagia, 1997) 199-200, fig. 5; *Classicism* 220, 223, fig. 7 (J. Boardman); Plantzos, 60, 92, 118 (no. 139), pl. 25.

99.

27.735 G.P. 349, 4.

L.D. Caskey, *BMFA* 26 (1928), 49-50, fig. 23; Vermeule, *Portraits* no. 26, illus.; 1972 edition, no. 28, illus.; D. Plantzos in *Greek Offerings* (ed. O. Palagia, 1997) 206, n. 12 - as modern.

100.

27.714 B. B. 67, 296. Bu. O 2.

Lippold, *Gemmen* 67, 178, pl. 67, 10; Poulsen, *Probleme* 17-18, pl. 29, fig. 35; Vollenweider,

Steinschneidekunst 78, n. 72; Richter, *Greeks and Etruscans* 170-171, no. 687, 2 illus.; Vollenweider, *Porträtgemmen* 1974, 80-81, 88 (n. 21); *ibid.*, 1972, 37, pl. 51, 4, pl. 52, 1, 5.

101.

27.715 B. B. 66, 288. R. 1237.

Lippold, *Gemmen* 69, 178, pl. 69, 2; L.D. Caskey, *BMFA* 26 (1928), 49-50, fig. 25; Poulsen, *Probleme* 17-18, pl. 29, fig. 34; Chase, *Antiquities* 123, fig. 154; Vermeule, *Portraits* no. 27, illus.; 1972 edition, no. 29, illus.; Chase and Vermeule, *Classical Collections* 172, 187, fig. 176; Richter, *Greeks and Etruscans* 170, no. 684, 2 illus., pl. D; Vollenweider, *Porträtgemmen* 81-83, 85, 88 (n. 21), 90 (n. 30), 91-92; *ibid.*, 1972, 37, pl. 52, 4, 6-7; R.R.R. Smith, *JRS* 71 (1981), 33, pl. 2, no. 3; *idem*, *JRS* 87 (1997), 192, n. 129.

102.

21.1213 G.P. 340, 4. Bu. L 90.

K.G. Vollmoeller, *AthMitt* 26 (1901), 355-356; *New York* xxxvi, 39, under no. 153; Hoffmann and Davidson, *Greek Gold* 61-62; B. Segall, *BWPr* 119/120 (1966), 29, fig. 10; *AGDS* I 1, 93, under no. 529; Sena Chiesa, *Aquileia* 159, n. 4; Richter, *Greeks and Etruscans* 16, 18, 124, 136, 143, no. 552, 2 illus.; Vollenweider, *Porträtgemmen* 1974, 185, n. 51; Guarducci, *Epigrafia Greca* III, 527, n. 4; N. Himmelmann, *Drei hellenistische Bronzen in Bonn* (Mainz, 1975), 15, n. 37d; *AGDS* IV 22, under no. 33; A. Herrmann, in *The Search for Alexander: An Exhibition* (Boston, 1980), 153, no. 99, illus.; W.A. Daszewski, *Report of the Department of Antiquities Cyprus 1982*, 197, pl. 44, 4; Zazoff, *Gemmen* 205, pl. 53, 1; A. Delivorrias, *et al.*, in *LIMC* II, 75, no. 658, pl. 65; A. Alessio, in E.M. De Juliis, *et al.*, *Gli Ori di Taranto in Età Ellenistica* (Milan, 1984), 263, 274, n. 87; M. Pfrommer, *Untersuchungen zur Chronologie früh- und hochhellenistischen Goldschmucks* (1990) 210 (n. 1351), 211 (n. 1361), 239; J. Flemberg, *Venus Armata* (Stockholm, 1991), 58; W. Neumer-Pfau, *Gnomon* 66 (1994), 708-9; M.-L. Vollenweider, in N. Bonacasa and A. di Vita (eds.), *Alessandria e il Mondo ellenistico-romano: Studi in onore di Achille Adriani* (repr. Rome 1992) 365; P. Chini, in *Rivista di studi pompeiani* 8 (1997), 138-139, fig. 14; Plantzos, 68-69, 76, 119 (no. 165), pl. 29.

103.

21.1214 R. 595. Bu. O 27.

Lippold, *Gemmen* 83, 180, pl. 83, 1; E. Vermeule and S. Chapman, *AJA* 75 (1971), 289, n. 10; Vermeule, *Death* 186-187 (fig. 8), 250 (n. 9).

104.

23.600 G.P. 322, 4.

AGDS III 35, under no. 100; *AGDS* IV 77, under no. 294; P.B. Rawson, *The Myth of Marsyas in the Roman Visual Arts* (Oxford, 1987), 68, 106 (n. 5), 224, no. A91.

Greco-Roman

105.

27.733 B. B. 66, 290. R. 1239. Bu. O 36.

Lippold, *Gemmen* 4, 168, pl. 4, 7; L.D. Caskey, *BMFA* 26 (1928), 50, fig. 26; Poinssot, *Revue Tunisienne* 1938, 33-36; Vermeule, *Portraits* no. 38, illus.; 1972 edition, no. 40, illus.; Vollenweider, *Steinschneidekunst* 51-52, 61 (n. 75), 109, pl. 49, 2; Cheney, *Sculpture* 109, illus.; K. Schefold, *Museum Helveticum* 25 (1968), 188; P. Zazoff, *Gnomon* 41 (1969), 200; Richter, *Romans* 92, 101, no. 483, 2 illus.; G. Hafner, *Aachener Kunstblätter* 43 (1972), 120, n. 38; Zwierlein-Diehl, *Wien* II, 127, under no. 1089; Giuliano, *Tesoro* 49, under no. 14; H.P. Laubscher, *JdI* 89 (1974), 248-250 (fig. 9), 253; Vollenweider, *Porträtgemmen* 1974, 213 (n. 124), 214; K. Schefold, *Wort und Bild: Studien zur Gegenwart der Antike* (Basel, 1975), 142; *AGDS* IV 68, under no. 244; *Oxford* 85, under no. 297; K. Vierneisel and P. Zanker, *Die Bildnisse des Augustus* (Munich, 1979), 17, illus.; W.H. Gross, in *Aufstieg und Niedergang der römischen Welt* II, 12, 2 (Berlin, 1981), 601; T. Hölscher, *JdI* 99 (1984), 213; Vollenweider, *Deliciae* 113, under no. 189; S. Stucchi, *Archeologia Classica* 36 (1984), 207; T. Hölscher, *Klio* 67 (1985) 97-8, fig. 10; E.S. Brettman, *Vaults of Memory: Jewish and Christian Imagery in the Catacombs of Rome: An Exhibition* (Boston, 1985), 27, no. 123; P. Zanker, *Augustus und die Macht der Bilder* (Munich, 1987) 102-3 (fig. 82), 360 (as fig. 81); C. Maderna, *Iuppiter Diomedes und Merkur als Vorbilder für römische Bildnisstatuen: Untersuchungen zum römischen statuarischen Idealporträt* (Heidelberg, 1988), 68; P. Zanker, *The Power of Images in the Age of Augustus* (Ann Arbor, 1988), 97-98 (fig. 82), 374 (listed as fig. 81); C.

Maderna-Lauter, in *Kaiser Augustus und die verlorene Republik* (Mainz, 1988), 448-451, 454, 467, no. 247, illus. (with additional bibliography); W.-R. Megow, *AA* 1989, 448; A. Wallace-Hadrill, *JRS* 79 (1989), 157, 159; C.C. Vermeule, *AJA* 93 (1989), 618; E. Zwierlein-Diehl, in H.-U. Cain, H. Gabelmann, and D. Salzmann, eds., *Festschrift für Nikolaus Himmelmann* (Mainz, 1989), 425, pl. 67, 5; T. Gesztelyi, *Wiss. Z. WPU Rostock* 37 (1988), 2, 53; E. Zwierlein-Diehl, *AA* 1990, 545, nn. 22, 24; E. Walter-Karydi, *JdI* 106 (1991), 257; A. Wallace-Hadrill, *Augustan Rome* (London, 1993), 86-7, fig. 30; O. Dräger, *Religionem Significare* (*RM* Erg. 33), 120, n. 625; J.J. Herrmann, Jr. in J.B. Carter and S.P. Morris, eds., *The Ages of Homer* (Austin, 1995), 521, n. 60; E. Simon, *LIMC* VII, 489 (no. 69), 496-7, pl. 384; B. Kellum, *Journal of Roman Archaeology* 11 (1998) 518, = 'cameo' with Octavian as Neptune; Plantzos, 98, 101, 134 (no. 633), pl. 78.

106.

23.588 R. 823. Bu. O 25.

Richter, *Romans* 26, 46, no. 187, 2 illus.; Zwierlein-Diehl, *Wien* I, 97 (under no. 246), 149 (under no. 476); *AGDS* III 123, under no. 332; Spier, *Gems* 96, under no. 226; Moret, *Palladion* 182, n. 2; *Cambridge* 101, under no. 184.

107.

27.731 B. B. 67. R. 1244. Bu. O 431.

Lippold, *Gemmen* 48, 175, pl. 48, 3; Sena Chiesa, *Aquileia* 271, under no. 719, n. 3; Vollenweider, *Steinschneidekunst* 52, n. 27; *AGDS* II, 96, under no. 222; Richter, *Romans* 57, 69, no. 322, 2 illus.; *AGDS* I 3, 93, under no. 2710; *AGDS* III 36, under no. 103; Brommer, *Denkmälerlisten* II, 24, no. 10; *AGDS* IV 82, under no. 316; Maaskant-Kleibrink, *The Hague* 265, under no. 712; Vollenweider, *Deliciae* 268, under no. 463; Schefold and Jung, *Urkönige* 236 (fig. 285), 373; J. Neils, *LIMC* VII, 924 (no. 10), pl. 622; Spier, *Gems* 115, under no. 294; Moret, *Palladion* 153, n. 18; *Cambridge* 160, under no. 336.

108.

27.738 G.P. 348, 4.

T.B.L. Webster, *Monuments Illustrating New Comedy* (2nd ed., University of London, Institute of Classical Studies, Bulletin Supplement no. 24, 1969), 230, under no. UJ 8; Richter, *Romans* 72, 75, no. 361, 2 illus.; *AGDS* IV 109, under no. 453; Vollenweider, *Genève* II, 305-306, under no. 327; *Cambridge* 113, under no. 210.

109.

21.1215 G.P. 348, 1.

Richter, *Romans* 24, 32, no. 80, 2 illus.; E. Simon, *LIMC* II, 1, 395, 2 illus., no. 159.

110.

27.740 G.P. 256, 7. Bu. O 73.

MFA, *Trojan War* fig. 20B; Richter, *Romans* 65, no. 299, 2 illus.; Zwierlein-Diehl, *Wien* I, 87, under no. 205; *AGDS* IV 41, under no. 97; Brommer, *Denkmälerlisten* III, 102, no. 6; F. Lissarrague, *RA* 1980, 5, n. 14; D. Williams, *LIMC* III, 662 (no. 20), 664, pl. 528; Moret, *Palladion* 126, nn. 3, 5.

111.

27.736 G.P. 343, 5.

112.

27.780 G.P. 322.

AGDS III 118, under no. 296; Richter, *Romans* 158, no. 738, 2 illus.

113.

21.1216 B. B. 66, 287. R. 1236. Bu. O 9.

Vollenweider, *Steinschneidekunst* 64, pl. 68, 4; Richter, *Romans* 71, no. 336, 2 illus.; *AGDS* IV 118, under no. 511; Brommer, *Denkmälerlisten* III, 178, nos. 3-4; F. de Ruyt, *Alba Fucens* III: *Sculptures d'Alba Fucens (pierre, marbre, bronze)* (Brussels, 1982), 29-30, under no. 9 (as a cameo); N. Yalouris, *LIMC* V, 672 (no. 102).

114.

27.734 B. B. 105, 9. R. 1561. Bu. O 11.

H. Brunn, *Geschichte der griechischen Künstler* II (Stuttgart, 1859), 558-560; Lippold, *Gemmen* 163, 187, pl. 163, 4; L.D. Caskey, *BMFA* 26 (1928), 46-47, fig. 1; Richter, *Animals* 33, 77, pl. 55, fig. 172; Chase, *Antiquities* 159-160, fig. 213; *New York* xxxix, 90, under no. 405; Chase and Vermeule, *Classical Collections* 229, 268, fig. 256; Hoffmann and Davidson, *Greek Gold* 62; Cheney, *Sculpture* 109, illus.; Richter, *Romans* 132, 139-140, no. 655, 3 illus.; Zwierlein-Diehl, *Wien* I, 129, under no. 386, and *Würzburg* I, no. 147; *AGDS* IV 145, under no. 693; Zazoff, *Gemmen* 320, 338, pl. 94, 3; J.-M. Moret, in Broustet, 16-17, fig. 5; Plantzos, 99, 136 (no. 709), pl. 85; *Cambridge* xvi (D. Scarisbrick).

115.

23.589 B. B. 15. R. 845. Bu. O 40.

Lippold, *Gemmen* 86, 181, pl. 86, 7; *New York* xxxix; A. Stazio, *EAA* IV (1961), 62; Vollenweider, *Steinschneidekunst* 80, n. 83; Richter, *Romans* 135, 153, no. 719, 3 illus. (ref. to Greifenhagen, *Berliner Museen* 1960, Sonderheft, 18, with n. 14); *AGDS* II, 192, under no. 540; Zazoff, *Gemmen* 322-323, pl. 96, 5; Vollenweider, *Deliciae* 276, under no. 480.

116.

27.741 G.P. 341, 1. Bu. L 148.

Vermeule, *Portraits* no. 28, illus.; 1972 edition, no. 30, illus.; C. Weiss, *AA* 1995, 558.

117.

27.739

Chase, *Antiquities* 159-160, fig. 214; Vermeule, *Portraits* no. 34, illus.; 1972 edition, no. 36, illus.; Chase and Vermeule, *Classical Collections* 229, 268, fig. 257; Richter, *Romans* 162, no. 760, 2 illus.; Zwierlein-Diehl, *Wien* I, 167, under no. 546.

118.

21.1217 G.P. 363, 1.

Richter, *Romans* 125, 127, no. 621, 2 illus.

119.

21.1218 G.P. 347, 4.

Richter, *Romans* 125, 128, no. 628, 2 illus.

120.

23.590 G.P. 359, 7.

Richter, *Romans* 125-126, no. 619, 2 illus.

121.

23.591 B. B. 125, 2. R. 1053. Bu. O 10.

Richter, *Romans* 125-127, no. 620, 3 illus.

122.

21.1219

Chase, *Antiquities* 159-160, fig. 215; *idem* and Vermeule, *Classical Collections* 229, 268, fig. 258; Richter, *Romans* 94, 114, no. 558, 2 illus.; L. Teposu-Marinescu, *Dacia* 38-39 (1994-1995), 113, n. 48.

123.

27.781 B. B. 49. R. 1264.

Sena Chiesa, *Aquileia* 271, under no. 719 (n. 4), under no. 720 (n. 1); *AGDS* III 36, under no. 103; Richter, *Romans* 57, 69, no. 324, 2 illus.; *AGDS* I 3, 93, under no. 2710; Brommer, *Denkmälerlisten* II, 24, no. 9; *AGDS* IV 82, under no. 316; Vollenweider, *Deliciae* 268, under no. 463; Spier, *Gems*, 115, under no. 294.

124.

27.783

Sena Chiesa, *Aquileia* 201, under no. 449, n. 1; *AGDS* III 30, under no. 79; Richter, *Romans* 73, no. 344, 2 illus.

125.

27.782

Vollenweider, *Steinschneidekunst* 51, n. 24; Richter, *Romans* 67, no. 310 *bis*, 2 illus.; *AGDS* III 113, under no. 258; *AGDS* I 3, 93 (under no. 2711), 170 (under no. 3219); *AGDS* IV 196, under no. 968; Brommer, *Denkmälerlisten* III, 78, no. 55; Schürmann, *Minerva-Kultbilder* 109, n. 372; J. Boardman and C.E. Vafopoulou-Richardson, *LIMC* III, 1, 403, under no. 52; Moret, *Palladion* 197, no. 305, pl. 60.

Renaissance

126.

27.784 G.P. 341, 6. Bu. L 120.

Giuliano, *Tesoro* 50, under no. 15.

Cameos

127.

23.592 R. 813. Bu. O 21.

Vermeule, *Portraits* no. 19, illus.; 1972 edition, no. 21, illus.; H. Jucker, *AntK* 8 (1965), 52, n. 93 (as F., pl. 56, 47); Kyrieleis, *Bildnisse* 117, n. 458 (ref. to I. Noshy, *The Arts in Ptolemaic Egypt* 1937, 139, pl. 17, 1); J.J. Pollitt, *Art in the Hellenistic Age* (Cambridge, 1986), 263, illus. 285; D. Plantzos, *OJA* 15 (1996) 54-55 (no. B5, fig. 21), 57.

128.

27.750 B. B. 150, 4. R. 1663. Bu. M 6.

Chase, *Antiquities* 122, fig. 153; *New York* xxxvi; Chase and Vermeule, *Classical Collections* 171, 187, fig. 175; A. Stazio, in *EAA* VI, 494; Vollenweider, *Steinschneidekunst* 24, 96, pl. 13, 1, 3; Richter, *Greeks and Etruscans* 16, 19, 137, 150, no. 592, illus.; Giuliano, *Tesoro* 41, under no. 4; Vollenweider, *Genève* II, 426, under no. 481, n. 15; Zazoff, *Gemmen* 207, pl. 54, 5; A. Delivorrias, *et al.*, in *LIMC* II, 26 (no. 165), 119 (no. 1230), pl. 19; Vollenweider, *Deliciae* 255, under no. 435; W.-R. Megow, *JdI* 100 (1985), 487.

129.

27.749 R. 514. Bu. O 19.

130.

21.1220 G.P. 317, 7.

Giuliano, *Tesoro* 47, under no. 10; M. Anderson, in Houser, *Dionysos* 105, MFA 17, illus.

131.

27.755 G.P. 327, 1.

132.

21.1221 G.P. 320, 1.

C.C. Vermeule, *Cameo and Intaglio: Engraved Gems from the Sommerville Collection* (The University Museum, Philadelphia, 1956), under no. 475; A. Giuliano, *Archeologia Classica* 25-26 (1973-1974), 304, n. 2; Brommer, *Denkmälerlisten* III, 330, no. 9; V. Machaira, *LIMC* VII, 602-603, no. 6, pl. 487.

133.

27.754 G.P. 344, 11.

Giuliano, *Tesoro* 47, under no. 11; *Classicism* 209, n. 22 (J. Spier).

Supplement: Intaglios

134.

27.706 G.P. 341, 3.

AGDS II, 150, under no. 386.

135.

27.737

F. Brommer, *Marburger Winkelmann-Programm* 1952/1954, 15, no. 17; T. Gericke, *AthMitt* 71 (1956), 197, Beil. 109, 2; *New York* xxxix; Vollenweider, MuM *Vente Publique* 28, 70, under no. 639; *idem, Steinschneidekunst* 61-63, 115, pl. 68, 6; H. Kähler, *Alberti Rubeni Dissertatio de Gemma Augustea* (Berlin, 1968), 40, n. 100, no. 8; *AGDS* II, 167, under no. 445; Richter, *Romans* 133, 143, no. 669, 3 illus.; Zwierlein-Diehl, *Wien* I, 108, under no. 291; Brommer, *Denkmälerlisten* II, 45, no. 3 (ref. to Hiller, 111, no. 1); Zazoff, *Gemmen* 317, pl. 91, 8; C. Lochin, *LIMC* VII, 222 (no. 128), 230, pl. 156; Moret, *Palladion* 148, n. 6; M Pugliara, *RdA* 20 (1996) 97, n. 49; Plantzos, 96, n. 238.

Mary B. Comstock

Concordance

A - Museum of Fine Arts, Boston, Accession number

B - *LHG* Catalogue number

A	B	A	B	A	B
21.1194	27	23.579	45	27.669	18
21.1195	30	23.580	50	27.670	21
21.1196	34	23.581	52	27.671	20
21.1197	35 *ter*	23.582	55	27.672	19
21.1198	36	23.583	57	27.673	24
21.1199	37	23.584	64	27.674	22
21.1200	38	23.585	79	27.675	25
21.1201	40	23.586	81	27.676	26
21.1202	42	23.587	87	27.677	28
21.1203	46	23.588	106	27.680	32
21.1204	54	23.589	115	27.681	35
21.1205	61	23.590	120	27.682	31
21.1206	66	23.591	121	27.686	49
21.1207	72	23.592	127	27.689	35 *bis*
21.1208	73	23.593	48	27.691	47
21.1209	74	23.594	53	27.692	70
21.1210	75	23.595	15	27.693	68
21.1211	76	23.596	51	27.694	65
21.1212	80	23.597	60	27.696	71
21.1213	102	23.598	63	27.697	49 *bis*
21.1214	103	23.599	90	27.698	67
21.1215	109	23.600	104	27.699	77
21.1216	113	23.601	59	27.700	56
21.1217	118	27.655	1	27.701	83
21.1218	119	27.656	2	27.702	78
21.1219	122	27.657	5	27.703	58
21.1220	130	27.658	4	27.704	62
21.1221	132	27.659	11	27.706	134
23.576	3	27.660	13	27.707	94
23.577	17	27.667	16	27.709	96
23.578	29	27.668	14	27.710	97

A	B	A	B	A	B
27.711	95	27.731	107	27.762	9
27.713	93	27.733	105	27.763	10
27.714	100	27.734	114	27.764	12
27.715	101	27.735	99	27.765	13 *bis*
27.716	98	27.736	111	27.766	23
27.717	41	27.737	135	27.767	33
27.718	43	27.738	108	27.768	69
27.719	44	27.739	117	27.769	84
27.720	39	27.740	110	27.770	82
27.722	86	27.741	116	27.771	85
27.723	89	27.749	129	27.780	112
27.724	88	27.750	128	27.781	123
27.725	91	27.754	133	27.782	125
27.726	92	27.755	131	27.783	124
				27.784	126

PLATES

Plates copyright

© R.L. Wilkins – Plates 1 – 30 above
© Plate 30 below, 2002 Museum of Fine Arts, Boston

Plate 1

1

2

Plate 2

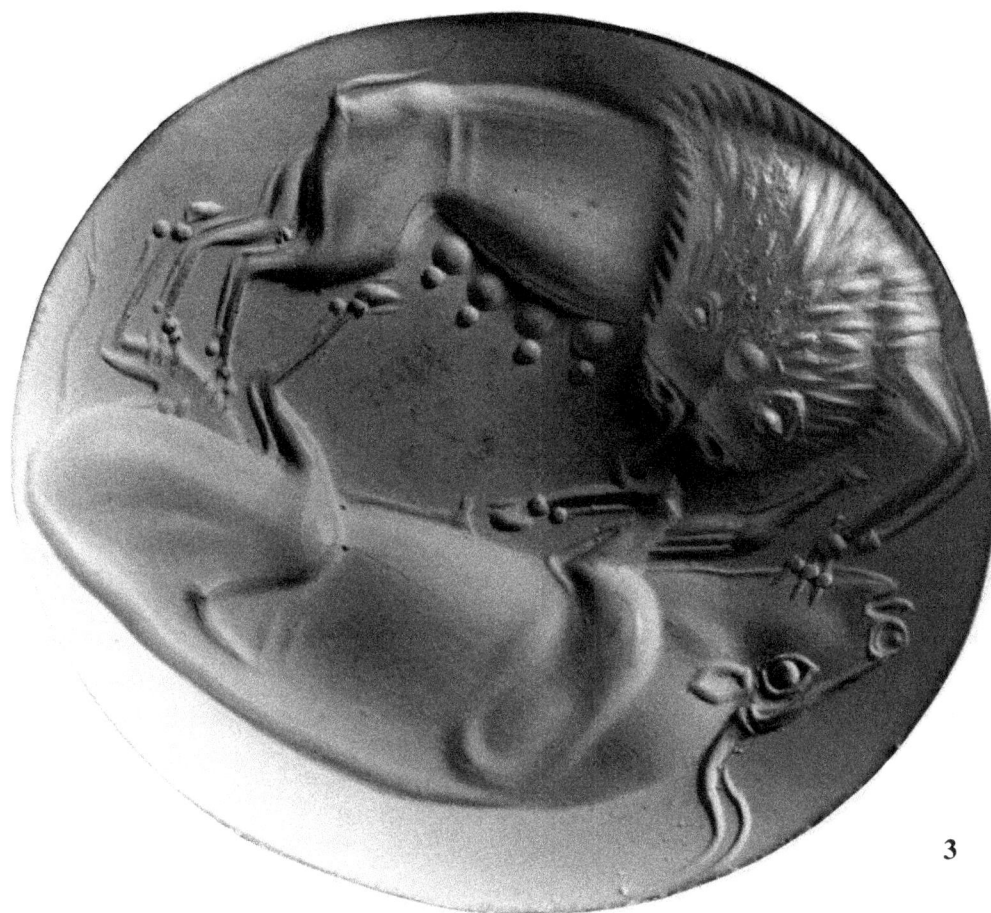

3

4

Plate 3

5

9

10

11

12

13

13bis

Plate 4

14

15

16

17

18

19

20

21

22

23

24

25

26

27

28

Plate 5

Plate 6

29

30

31

32

34

33

35

35bis

Plate 7

35ter

36

37

38

39

40

41

42

43

44

Plate 8

45

46

48

47

49

49bis

Plate 9

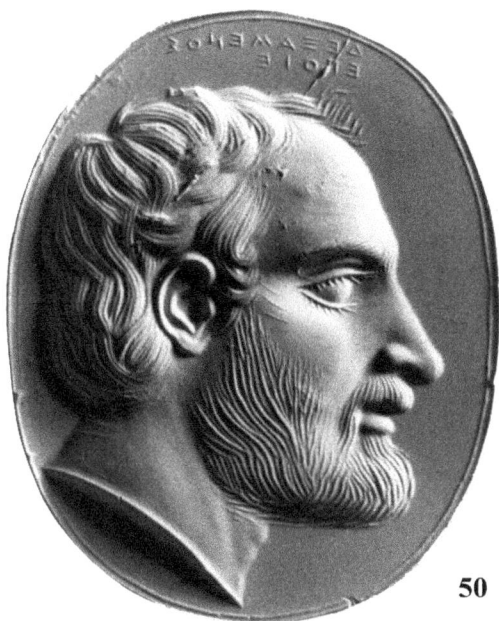

50

52

51

53

54

Plate 10

55

56

57

Plate 11

59

58

60

Plate 12

62

61

63

Plate 13

64

65

66

67

Plate 14

68

69

70

71

72

73

Plate 15

74

75

76

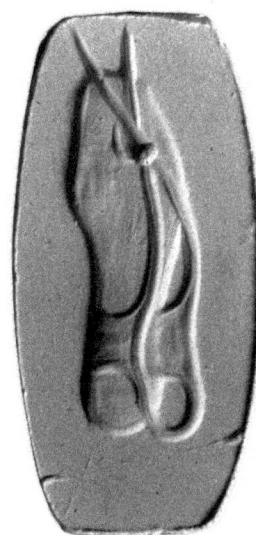

77

Plate 16

78

79

80

Plate 17

81

82

83

84

85

Plate 18

86

87

88

89

90

91

92

Plate 19

93   94

95   96

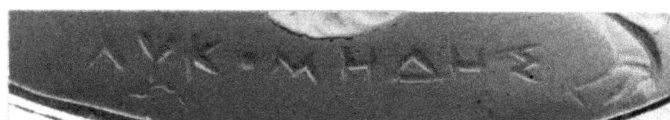

Plate 20

97

98

99

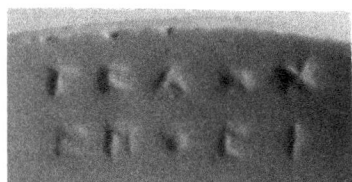

Plate 21

100

101

103

104

102

Plate 22

105

106

108

107

109

Plate 23

110

111

112

114

113

Plate 24

115

116

117

118

119

Plate 25

120

121

122

123

124

125

Plate 26

126

127

128

Plate 27

129

130

131

132

Plate 28

133

134

135

Plate 29

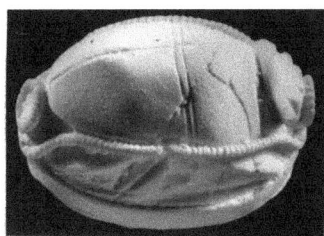
9

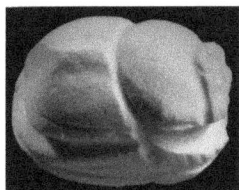
10

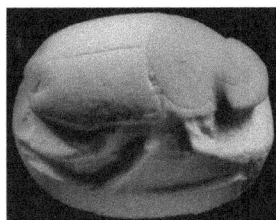
11

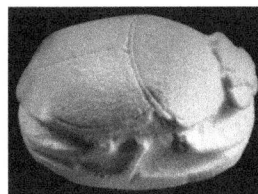
12

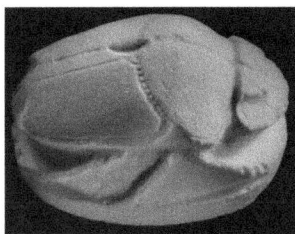
13

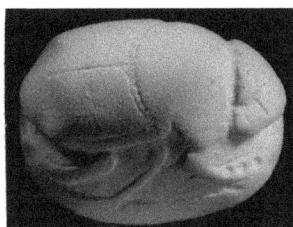
13bis

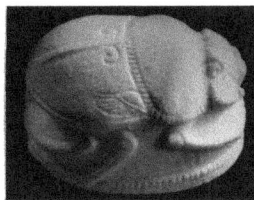
14

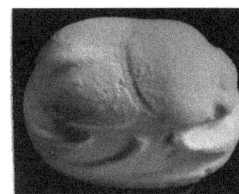
15

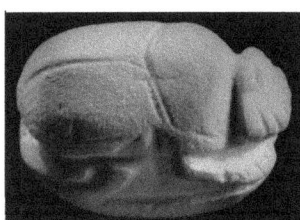
16

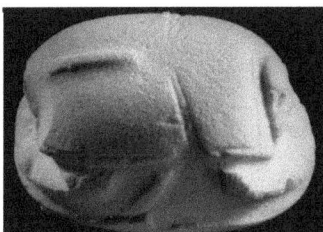
17

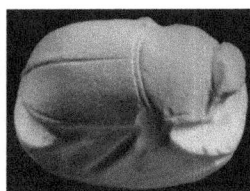
18

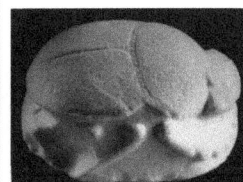
21

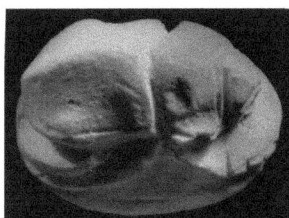
24

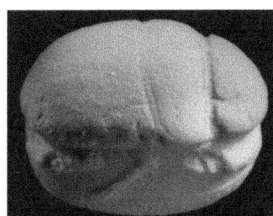
36

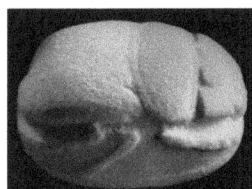
37

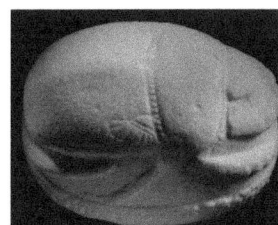
38

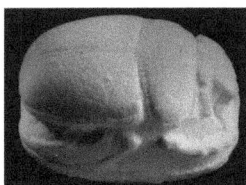
39

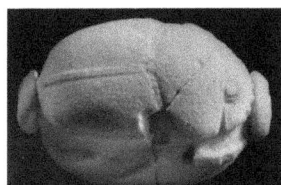
40

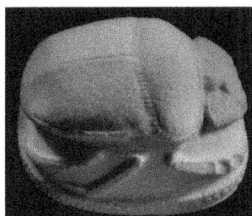
41

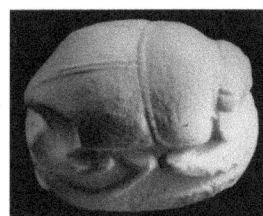
42

Plate 30

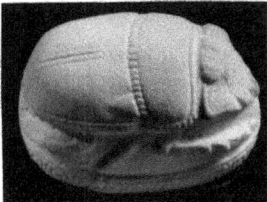

43

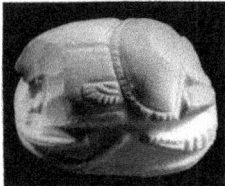

45

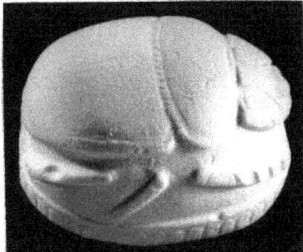

46

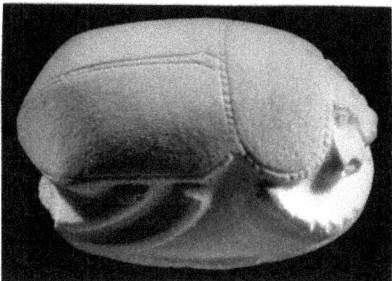

52

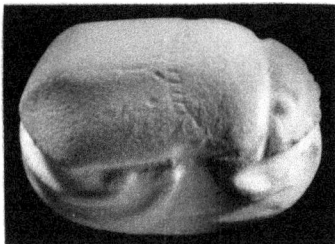

86

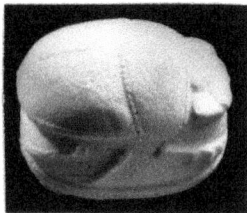

87

35ter

23

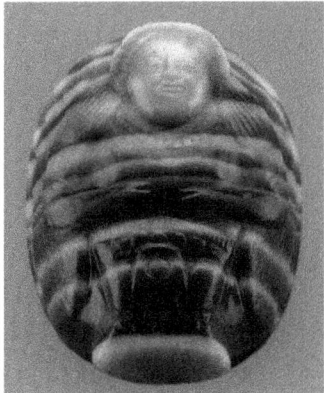

44

www.ingramcontent.com/pod-product-compliance
Lightning Source LLC
Chambersburg PA
CBHW060959030426
42334CB00033B/3290

9 781841 714530